The Afrikaner's Emancipation

To Augusta, whose love and assistance is a part of this book.
And to our sons Gert and Hendrik.

The Afrikaner's Emancipation

✦

Freeing South Africans from their Apartheid Mindset

Barry Botha

iUniverse, Inc.
New York   Bloomington

The Afrikaner's Emancipation

Freeing South Africans from their Apartheid Mindset

iUniverse books may be ordered through booksellers or by contacting:

iUniverse
1663 Liberty Drive
Bloomington, IN 47403
www.iuniverse.com
1-800-Authors (1-800-288-4677)

ISBN: 978-0-595-52415-0 (pbk)
ISBN: 978-0-595-62469-0 (ebk)

Printed in the United States of America

iUniverse rev. date: 11/07/2008

Contents

PREFACE

The subject of the author's doctoral thesis was the issue of land and voting rights for blacks in the Cape colonial and the South African parliaments in a hundred-year period that ended in 1976 with the so-called independence of Transkei, which was rejected by the UN.

Whereas the thesis focused on blacks, the author wrote a new contemporary history, specifically focused on finding an explanation for the Afrikaners' apartheid mindset which was, at its core, a mentality of superiority.

The author relocated from the Eastern Cape in 1980 to Linden, Johannesburg, where he served in the divisional council of the National Party in the constituency of the former national government minister of foreign affairs, Mr Pik Botha. He is not related to the former minister or to former President P W Botha.

Whereas the former president failed to cross the Rubicon in 1985 by accepting a new policy of negotiations for voting rights for blacks, the former minister of foreign affairs and the author both supported this proposed policy of universal suffrage, albeit with reservations, which later fell away.

INTRODUCTION

The idea of emancipation and of a change in Afrikaner Nationalist mentality dates back many decades. These two aspects of political transition were first identified by J. H. Hofmeyr, cabinet minister and leading liberal thinker, and by the renowned author, Alan Paton.

In a 1931 *New York Times* book review on Hofmeyr's book, *South Africa* the comment on South Africa's tragedy was that it was too late to apply a policy of differentiated development. The word "tragedy" illustrated how difficult it was for the Cape Dutch to emancipate themselves from the slaveholding sentiment of the past. The fact that the black person had ceased to be a serf and refused to be a segregated captive of the past, insisting on the position of co-worker in the building up of South Africa's economic life, was not seen as a tragedy but an opportunity.

To this comment Alan Paton added in his biography of Hofmeyr that almost every white South African found it difficult to emancipate themselves. He wrote that it was fear speaking: the fear of the white South African whose mind could not encompass and whose soul could not rejoice in the idea of the liberation of his non-white fellow citizens from every restriction to true liberty.

Addressing students at the University of the Witwatersrand on the idea of freedom from prejudice in 1946, Hofmeyr said South Africans as a nation were to a large extent the slaves of prejudice. He identified the dominant mentality in white South Africa as that of a Herrenvolk, a group regarding itself as naturally superior. He believed that the true solution to these problems were to be found in the changing of this mentality.

More and more South Africa was suffering because its policies and dominant attitudes of mind did not measure up to international standards of values, he said. The nation's chief loss was a moral loss. As long as South Africans continued to apply a dual standard in South Africa, to determine their attitudes towards and their relationships with Europeans and non-Europeans on different ethical bases, to assign to Christian doctrine a significance based on the colour of men's skins, South Africans would suffer, Hofmeyr said.

The Afrikaner nation is unique in the history of the world; a nation in Africa of European descent with its own language and culture, believing in the Bible. The nation's uniqueness has been based on a singular world and life view, namely that the Afrikaner is a chosen people of God, and that apartheid has been God's will. This world and life view was reinforced by the doctrinal documents of the Synod of the Dutch Reformed Church, particularly in the period 1943 to 1974. However, this conviction was finally overturned, after two hundred years of delusion, by a resolution of the Dutch Reformed Church Synod in 1986 rejecting racial discrimination and apartheid.

Since the formation of the Union of South Africa in 1910, politics had been dominated by formulating, implementing, and maintaining apartheid by legislation and through force. This led to growing resistance by blacks and unanimity of world opinion against the South African government and support for sanctions to bring an end to apartheid.

The way was prepared under H.F. Verwoerd with the appointment of John Vorster as minister of justice to use more force against blacks resisting apartheid through violent action with the introduction of new legislation, particularly the ninety-day clause, and the reorganization of the security force under General Hendrik van den Berg.

A process was already underway within the Afrikaner electorate before 1986 that led to support for a policy that accommodated blacks as voters in a new constitutional dispensation, although qualified by protective reservations. In the eighties, President P. W. Botha lifted many apartheid restrictions and attempted to reorganize the tricameral parliament to accommodate blacks through a proposed scheme of power sharing. However, he kept the cornerstone legislation that upheld apartheid in place and refused black majority rule.

The problem was how to bring about real change to accommodate the majority black voters in such a way that it would be supported by the majority of Afrikaner Nationalists in the National Party (NP), in spite of their fear of the idea. This was successfully accomplished by F. W. de Klerk through clever political tactics directed towards negotiations with the African National Congress (ANC). He relied on the idea that some form of group rights and protection of minority rights could be resolved between the two parties, the NP and the ANC.

The possibility that this concept could be realised, together with the promise of a referendum afterwards to approve the negotiated constitution, persuaded the National Party majority to support negotiations to end apartheid. This was accomplished by persuading the Afrikaner Nationalists to accept a plan the leadership in their heart of hearts knew would not succeed: to negotiate a settlement that would include the concepts of group rights, consensus, and minority rights. The die was cast when Roelf Meyer reported to de Klerk after negotiations with Cyril Ramaphosa of the ANC that a black majority government had been agreed upon without qualification in a constitution of universal democratic voting rights. De Klerk reacted with the exclamation, "You have given away our country!" However, Meyer could not have done this without de Klerk's blessing regardless of the consequences.

The Afrikaner Nationalist accepted the inevitable and abdicated his hold on power peacefully. The long struggle to implement the unjustifiable system of apartheid came to an end when the Afrikaner Nationalist was outmanoeuvred by his own leaders to accept transfer of power to a black majority in the same way he had been led in the past by his leaders to accept apartheid as righteous. Although the majority of Afrikaners subconsciously refused to admit to the dawning knowledge that an unjust system could not continue, they nevertheless capitulated to the inevitable reality.

Another hurdle was the reconciliation process between the two opposing groups, black and white; and two opposing parties, the ANC and the NP. They met peacefully and had to confront the truth about their past; victims and perpetrators on both sides. A huge responsibility still rests with a large number of Afrikaners who need to admit to and apologise for the wrongs of apartheid.

It is incomprehensible that the NP leadership refrained from their responsibility to lead their followers to do what is right. Instead they opposed and ridiculed the Truth and Reconciliation Commission (TRC). The majority of Afrikaners who refrained from responding to the Truth and Reconciliation Commission still need to respond individually with contrition. Collectively, that acknowledgement could contribute to an improvement in relations with the ANC and the black South Africans.

The development of the apartheid policy and its demise is examined in an attempt to explain the Afrikaner mindset, his abdication from power, and reluctant participation in the reconciliation process. A review of politics, the negotiation process, and the work of the Truth and Reconciliation Commission provide explanations for the Afrikaner's peaceful abdication from power and also for their reluctance to apologise for the wrongs of apartheid. A complete change in mindset had not taken place.

Nevertheless, a columnist in the newspaper, *Sondag*, Vincent Hendricks, believed that the old paradigm based on racism would never again be the inheritance of the new white child to be born in the new South Africa (26 August 2007).

A crucial issue is the unanswered question of black families: where are their relatives who disappeared? Were they murdered? In what circumstances did they die? This issue became a cloud hanging over the head of the reconciliation process and has become an impediment in relations between black and white, ANC and Afrikaners. It also has economic connotations.

The debate surrounding the criminal court case against former Justice Minister Adriaan Vlok and Police Commissioner Johan van der Merwe which started in July 2007 highlights the critical issues of political responsibility and of accountability by perpetrators of attacks on ANC members by security officers not dealt with by the Truth and Reconciliation Commission.

The final implication of reconciliation is the condition set by some ANC leaders that transformation precede reconciliation. This idea has economic connotations since it refers to affirmative action and black economic empowerment and to dwindling opportunity for participation in the economy and the state by whites.

CHAPTER 1

BEGINNING OF AN EXPLANATION

The unresolved issue of reconciliation in the new South Africa era is the dissatisfaction and unhappiness caused by the lack of information about black people who died during the security force operations of the national government.

What happened to the people who disappeared or died because of security actions? Who was responsible for these actions?

Responsibility lay with the apartheid cabinet and with everybody directly and indirectly connected to the consequences of the government's decision to meet force with force. It started under Prime Minister Verwoerd and his minister of justice, B. J. Vorster. The persecutions reached a high under the total onslaught strategy of President P. W. Botha, as was proven by the Vlakplaas operations and others.

Instead of admitting the impossibility of maintaining apartheid and acknowledging the injustice it caused in a common society, the national government's answer was fiercer oppression of the black resistance with its armed struggle. The opposition turned into resistance, armed struggle, and a mass movement of the affected people, which led to the total black population striving for equal rights and majority rule.

Who were those in addition to the Nationalist Party cabinet who were directly and indirectly involved in the cover up and suppression of evidence? Who were the people who failed to disclose facts and information on atrocities? They were the individuals and organisations who supported the national government: The state president and his cabinet, the NP caucus in parliament, the government departments of police, defence, justice, finance; the National Party members and its supporters; the churches, Broederbond, cultural organisations such as the Federasie van Afrikaanse Kultuurvereenigings (FAK), Rapportryers. Afrikaners retained their obstinate belief that apartheid was scripturally justified, although this view was rejected by the DRC General Synod in 1986.

The cause for this sorry state of affairs, that there was no real reconciliation, lay with the leadership of the national government, the president and his cabinet. Already under Verwoerd with the report by the Cottesloe consultation of delegates from the World Council of Churches and South African Churches in 1960, the choice became clear. Apartheid was not scriptural and instead of maintaining it, negotiations for settlement of equal rights for black and white was the way to become a just society. But the Afrikaans Churches and the NP rejected it. The NP, DRC, and the Broederbond ostracized Rev. Beyers Naude, who supported the Cottesloe report, resulting in Vorster's banning orders and restricting his freedom, without any Afrikaner objection to unfairness, injustice, and intolerance! He was even jailed for obstruction of justice.

At every stage thereafter the option of negotiations was rejected by the national government leading to the farcical, shameful, and scandalous "Rubicon speech" by P. W. Botha in 1985 rejecting his special cabinet's resolution on the possibility of accommodating the black majority in the constitution through negotiations.

A real moral challenge to the Afrikaner apartheid mindset was posed in 1986 by the Dutch Reformed Church (DRC) document, *Church and Society*, a confession that racial discrimination was a sin and thus apartheid also. Instead of confronting the issue, the P. W. Botha government continued with its total onslaught. This was a moment of collective and individual responsibility, to stop the suppression and negotiate a settlement, or to live with the consequences and everyone with his conscience if reconciliation was not reached.

The Afrikaner Christian alternated between claiming that, on the one hand, he supported apartheid because he believed it to be biblical, while on the other hand, he would accept black majority rule, while still believing in the same Bible. In 2004, the Afrikaner gave up his apartheid ideology, supremacy, and everything it entailed without protest nearly 160 years after the Great Trek, when the Afrikaners had set out to establish their own domain in Africa. The ideal of apartheid could not be realised or justified.

The ideology of apartheid started forming the Afrikaner's mindset in the Cape Colony more than two centuries ago. They considered themselves a nation chosen by God to be separate, white, and the supreme ruler of their own destiny, and this excluded any thought of voting rights for black people.

A study of the periods of government in South Africa since 1910 provide a good description of the formulation of the apartheid ideology, the start of which pre-dates 1910, and also a clear indication of the misguided, unfounded, and unchristian motivations for the various elements of the policy of apartheid.

The phase of enactment of all the measures to implement the various aspects of apartheid came to an end with the assassination of Verwoerd in 1966. The only exception was legislation for the granting of independence to Transkei under the Vorster government in 1976, which was immediately rejected by the United Nations.

The period after 1978 formed the phase of transition as described by President de Klerk, until he finally ended apartheid in 1990 by unbanning the ANC and Communist Party and starting the process of negotiations to include blacks in a new constitution.

The dismantling of apartheid proved the falsehoods underlying the original measures and their motivations, the injustice of the system, and how the adherents and proponents of apartheid deluded themselves and misled others. They tried to justify the unjustifiable and rejected black majority rule.

The establishment of the Republic of South Africa in 1961 set the stage for a power struggle between two opposing forces of nationalism. White nationalism that was bent on retaining their independence and hegemony and black nationalism that resisted oppression and fought for equal rights and black majority rule.

Reverend Beyers Naude, minister of the Aasvoëlkop congregation of the DRC in Johannesburg, stood alone against the doctrinal documents of the Synod of the Dutch Reformed Church in the period 1943–74 which justified apartheid in terms of scripture. Rev. Naude, a leading theologian in the DRC, was ostracised by the Broederbond, Afrikaans churches, and society. His belief in the unrighteousness of apartheid was strengthened by the killing of black protestors by police at Sharpeville in 1960, by the Cottesloe consultation of delegates of the World Council of Churches and South African Churches in December 1960, which criticised apartheid restrictions as unchristian, and an earlier conference of Afrikaans Churches in Potchefstroom that confirmed apartheid as scripturally justified. He became an important opponent of apartheid and was banned and restricted by government orders from 1977 to

1984, first for five years by Vorster, the minister of justice, then for a further two years under P. W. Botha.

A major aspect of this struggle was the white government's use of force to suppress black resistance led by the ANC. It became an ever increasing conflict with both sides developing new tactics. Of great concern to the Truth and Reconciliation Commission and many other parties were the occurrence of violent deaths on both sides and the identification of responsibility, accountability, and remorse. An unforeseen stumbling block for the TRC was the enormous void created by the unresponsiveness of the previous white government and its supporters. Many on the NP side ignored the TRC, but if they participated, they reported ignorance of the activities perpetrated by the security forces, those responsible and those who were directly or indirectly involved. A final question to be discussed was the absence of the principle of collective responsibility.

The lack of information left an unhappy and dissatisfied black population and the ANC government who wanted to know the truth about what happened to their relatives and comrades. It certainly was the cause of a hardening of attitude in the ANC leadership and a souring of relationships between black and white with economic consequences.

According to President de Klerk the process of transition that ended in the decision to negotiate a new dispensation that included a black majority took twelve years, from 1978 to 1990. Four years of negotiations from 1990 led the NP to reject the apartheid system, and the whites settled for black majority rule.

Alan Paton, a highly respected author and a wise South African liberal, on a visit to the USA in May, 1974, told Mr Cyrus Vance, then US secretary of state, that "the Nationalist – not only through stubbornness, but also through psychological inability – would be totally unable to accept the demand for immediate majority rule in a unitary state."[1] Paton had made his observation four years before the period of transition within the National Party leadership, which started in 1978. This description fit the Afrikaner with his apartheid mindset.

Paton's observation of the Afrikaner's characteristics of stubbornness and psychological inability is true. These characteristics of the Afrikaner contributed to the decision resulting in the Great Trek, the First and Second War of Independence (Anglo Boer War 1899–1902) his strong opposition to the enforcement of the English language by the British government in the Cape Colony after 1820 and by Lord Milner in the defeated Boer Republics after 1902. The Afrikaans language did become an official language in South

---

1   John D'Oliviera, *Vorster – the Man*, 1977. p. 290, from an article in the journal *Reality*, printed in part in the *Star*, 2 September 1977.

Africa in 1925 under the pact government (NP and Labour Party) of General Hertzog. During the Second World War years between 1940 and 1945 the Afrikaners also faced an increasing preference for the English language in government and schools which caused a stronger Afrikaans Nationalist sentiment and feelings for the Afrikaans language to develop.

The Afrikaner's "psychological inability" is based on a deep-rooted set of political and Christian (albeit misguided) values. These include his belief in apartheid as a value system and that it is God's will for him to be a separate nation. An explanation for this mindset of the Afrikaner Nationalist is given in this study in order to understand why he eventually discarded his ideals of white supremacy.

The miracle of the peaceful transition

President Mandela told the General Synod of the DRC in October 1994 that its readiness to caution some of its own members against racism and reckless war talk made an important contribution to the miracle of South Africa's peaceful transition to democracy.

Lawrence Schlemmer, former director of the Helen Suzman Foundation in Johannesburg, reported in January 2004 on his participation in a UNESCO conference in Germany where South Africa was the last item on the agenda, partly because of its "miracle" of peaceful transition from extended domination.[2]. The conference dealt with countries that were deeply and brutally divided by religion and language.

The conference organisers acknowledged that very few societies could provide examples of a highly mobilised racial and ethnic group, like the white Afrikaners, who voluntarily relinquished power and abandoned language based political parties. South Africa showed no organised rejection of the new state authority, the most common feature in the other countries examined at the conference.

Many delegates were genuinely mystified that white Afrikaners, whose bitter struggle for language rights was centuries old, were accepting resignedly the more or less complete exclusion of Afrikaans from official communication in South Africa and its steady erosion as a language of public education. They could not explain this in a world in which people were slaughtering each other en masse in the name of religion, language, tribe, tradition, and race.

Some obvious reasons were suggested, namely gifted leadership by Nelson Mandela, F. W. de Klerk, and outstanding religious figures; economic sanctions that exerted compelling pressure but which were not sufficiently effective to lead to the reactionary politics of despair; a long history of liberal

2   *This Day*, 7 January 2004.

values in South African politics; and a sincere commitment to peaceful accommodation by most churches, including the Dutch Reformed Church, since 1986.

Among reasons debated at the conference was that, the grand dreams of apartheid notwithstanding, South Africans had never lived in closed and economically self-sufficient racially mixed communities. Compared with the unmitigated hostility and sense of completely separate nationhood among, say, Serbs, Croats, and Bosnians, or Singhalese and Tamils in Sri Lanka, South Africans had for long tolerated and benefited from each other in the workplace and in commerce.

Another factor was that most ethnic groups elsewhere were not in the least apologetic about their claims. In the other countries mentioned, the sectarian or ethnic groups had an unyielding sense of justification. In South Africa, on the other hand, from the early eighteenth century onwards the morality of segregation was widely debated, with the result that even the proponents of apartheid had a sense of guilt or unease about the morality of the system. This factor made whites particularly vulnerable to international moral pressures against apartheid.

A factor not normally recognised was the fact that whites, by virtue of becoming predominantly middle class with typical middle-class individualism, supported by the emphasis on individual witness and responsibility to God, relied less and less on group support. In the latter years of apartheid, therefore, whites lost their fear of group survival, and as the high emigration rates testified, white middle-class careers and interests had become "portable".

Hence, all appearances notwithstanding, in the midst of late apartheid, race and ethnicity became less and less relevant in the personal, political, and economic commitments of the dominant group. This did not mean that whites were losing their preferences for the company of people with similar language and lifestyles. But informal lifestyle segregation was universal and relatively harmless compared with the brutal, indeed lethal, group loyalties encountered in many ethnically divided countries, as reported by Laurence Schlemmer.

A detailed analysis of these and other reasons for peaceful change is given at the end of this study, particularly President de Klerk's tactics to lead the NP supporters into negotiations with the idea of group rights to protect minorities. He knew the ANC would reject these tactics, which they did.

The "miracle" of a peaceful transition of power in 1994 was foreshadowed in a poem written in 1911 by the well loved Afrikaner poet, Prof. J. D. du Toit, under his pen name, Totius: with a prophetic suggestion that the racial tables might one day be turned (translated into English):

Black man's song
The black man first comes; the white man he comes later
The white man seizes the land; the black man seizes later...
The white man he lives now, the black man he lives later
The white man he laughs now, the black man he laughs later.
(Totius, *Versamelde gedigte*, Tafelberg, Cape Town, 1941)

A description of apartheid and its fallacies

The ideology of apartheid is a multifaceted and multidimensional system of values, ideas and beliefs. It includes the culture of the Afrikaner as a nation characterised by its distinctively shared customs, outlook, history, language, and way of life; a sense of belonging to a particular white group with a race consciousness that is an awareness of racial differences between people and ethnic groups; convictions of supremacy related to a religious belief in the Christian faith that is closely connected to the Afrikaner's adherence to apartheid; and a way of thinking as a group which forms the basis of an economic and political system regarded as justification for actions to be maintained irrespective of events.

Prof. J. A. Heyns, former moderator of the Dutch Reformed Church, said, "Apartheid is a legally regulated political and social pattern of thought and action which, in forcibly separating groups of people, actually envisaged the well-being of all those involved, but could not, in the process of its implementation, bring about the full realization of its initial objectives; on the contrary, it not only advantaged one population group at the expense of the other, but also wronged individuals."[3]

The TRC stated, "It can never be forgotten that the system itself was evil, inhumane and degrading for the many millions who became its second and third class citizens. Amongst its many crimes, perhaps the greatest was its power to humiliate, to denigrate and to remove the self-confidence, self-esteem and dignity of its millions of victims"[4]

At a press conference at the WCC's sixth assembly (Vancouver 1983), Desmond Tutu was asked, "How can we help you in the struggle against apartheid?" He responded, to the journalists' surprise, "Have you tried prayer?" Tutu saw no dichotomy between prayer and the struggle for social justice in South Africa because he saw the latter as a profoundly spiritual and theological matter.[5]

---

3   JA Heyns: Teologiese Etiek, p. 50   (In *Journey with Apartheid*, p. 4).
4   Final Report of the TRC, October 1998
5   Peter Lodbert, Apartheid as a church-dividing ethical issue. *The Ecumenical Review*, Vol. 48, Issue 2, World Council of Churches, 1996.

Apartheid is often described and analysed in political, economic, sociological, or cultural terms. Tutu would not deny the importance of this broad interpretation of apartheid, but his answer to the journalists pointed to the fact that apartheid is first and foremost an ethical challenge to Christian theology, because it touches upon the dignity of every human being as created in the image of God, the understanding of salvation in Christ, and the unity of the church. [6]

In other parts of the Protestant tradition, such terms as confessing church and status confessionis served as key words in formulating the churches' theological response to the apartheid system. Apartheid was understood as a system that destroys the very being and unity of the church, and therefore had to be rejected as such in church and society. [7]

In the historical process of the transition of power from a white minority to the black majority in South Africa in the period 1910 to 1994, the Afrikaner ideologist demonstrated intellectual dishonesty in his interpretation of history and motivation for the apartheid policy. The justification of apartheid was untruthful and delusional, unchristian and sinful. These assertions are substantiated by analyses and comparisons of statements by statesmen in the course of the history of the white South African governments in the eighty years since formation of the Union of South Africa in 1910, outlined in the following chapters.

Concepts and forces of history

How is the history of apartheid and its demise to be reported, analysed and interpreted, being so complex a set of interrelated factors, including Christian beliefs?

In history, useful concepts are found such as causation, historical change, and methods of making comparisons by comparing facts in relation to each other. The great questions of historical causation, however, admit no simple and perhaps no single explanation. Historical change is indivisible, and its processes cannot be studied usefully in isolation from each other. The facts in relation to each other are, however, studied, keeping a sense of proportion by making comparisons along the way and in chronological order except where other occurrences interrupt the sequence of events.

Universal history enables us to keep this sense of proportion and to make these comparisons, both in time and in space. The portrait of Nationalism in nineteenth century Europe looks very different in twentieth century Asia or Africa. A well presented "universal history" enables us to see these differences,

6   Ibid
7   Ibid.

to trace these influences, and to make these comparisons. The doctrinal beliefs of the Dutch Reformed Church supporting apartheid as if it were scripturally justified and then rejecting it in 1986 exercised great influence. Universal history also enables us to see behind the differences, to see the resemblances and deduce the constant forces. It will not, off course, replace national history; but it will put it in a new perspective, a perspective which more detailed national history may test and at times correct.[8]

This study is a dialogue between universal and national history and between philosophy and history. Examples are the liberal thoughts that were opposed to apartheid expressed by cabinet minister J H Hofmeyr and Mandela. One of the great changes in universal history was brought about by historical movements, of which one example is the series of bourgeois revolutions which began in 1789 in France. This great movement rolled through the following centuries of world history like a wave, affecting many nations throughout the world, including Africa. In South Africa two opposing forces of nationalism, one white, one black, fuelled it. Eventually, nationalism of the black South Africans represented by the ANC won.

It is interesting that Verwoerd negated the idea of the profound influences of the forces of universal history. In a speech at the start of the academic year at the University of Stellenbosch on 25 February 1959, he referred to the effects of change in society and a nation's ability to deal with it. Explaining change to be brought about by the explosion in knowledge and variations in nations he referred to the example of the French Revolution (revolutionary change from totalitarianism to democracy) as the beginning of radical change in various areas in the history of Europe,[9] as if it was an event restricted to that part of the world.

He believed African Nationalism could be channelled into separate homelands for black nations in South Africa and that he could resist the growing expression of African nationalism in South Africa that demanded democratic rights in a unitary state.

The ideological creed of the ANC is, and always has been, the creed of African nationalism, Mandela read in his address to the Supreme Court in April 1964 at the Rivonia trial. He explained that it was not the concept of African nationalism expressed in the cry, 'Drive the white man into the sea'. The African nationalism which the ANC stood for, he said, was the concept of freedom and fulfilment for the African people in their own land. He continued "We want equal political rights. I know this sounds revolutionary to the whites in this country, because the majority of voters will be Africans. This makes the white man fear democracy. This is what the ANC is fighting

8   Foreword by Hugh Trevor Roper to Larousse Encyclopedia of *Modern History from 1500 to the present day*, Marcel Dunan (ed.), Hamlyn, London, revised ed. 1981, Second impression 1984

9   A. N. Pelzer, *Verwoerd aan die Woord*, p. 233.

for. The struggle is a truly national one. It is a struggle of the African people, inspired by their own suffering and their own experience. It is a struggle for the right to live."[10]

The whites relinquished their system of apartheid and the white electorate accepted the new negotiated democratic constitution in 1994. They voluntarily abdicated their position of power. Why?

All the white governments of South Africa, 1910–90, opposed the pressure from the blacks to gain universal political rights. Verwoerd thought he could resist the pressure with a policy that would create independent black states neighbouring the separate white state. He tried to persuade the European nations, the black people in South Africa, and the African states that it was the best and only solution for maintaining rights for the white group and the same rights for its black neighbours .His counter to resistance to apartheid by blacks after the establishment of the Republic of South Africa in 1961 was stricter security measures under his new minister of justice, B. J. Vorster.

Although Verwoerd's arguments were logical they were divorced from reality and abstract in terms of the facts on the ground. He was trying to swim upstream against world opinion and against two great movements of history. One such movement was the democratic revolution started in France at the end of the eighteenth century. The other started many centuries earlier with the beginning of nationalism in Europe after the fall of the Roman Empire. In South Africa, the whites decided that the black majority was not to gain democratic rights in white areas even if they fought for it as the ANC did. They believed apartheid was fair to all groups and that it was God's will to maintain a white nation. This idea was, of course, misguided and could not be sustained. They clung to white supremacy and opposed black majority rule until president de Klerk persuaded the NP that a constitution recognising group rights should be negotiated, although he knew it would not be accepted by the ANC in place of their demand for equal democratic rights.

Main Role Players

The main role players in the development, enforcement, and justification of apartheid as an ideology and a system were organisations and individuals. The most important organisations were the National Party government and the security forces, the Afrikaans churches, the Afrikaner Broederbond, and the Afrikaans Press. The individuals who played an important role were the National Party prime ministers, presidents, and ministers of justice (police).

10   Nelson Mandela, *Long Walk to Freedom*, p. 354.

On the opposition side rejecting apartheid were J. H. Hofmeyr, minister in Hetzog's cabinet in the thirties, and Smuts as prime minister in the forties. Church leaders in the Dutch Reformed Church opposing apartheid were many, but most significant were two moderators, Rev. Beyers Naude and Prof. Johan Heyns.

The Dutch Reformed Church was a very influential organisation because of its size and the dominant role it played in the Afrikaans society. It played a major role in the formulation and justification of apartheid as a policy based on their interpretation of scripture. But it was this church which in the end sounded the death knell of apartheid with the publication of the document *Church and Society* in 1986. This confession, as accepted by the General Synod of the DRC under the chairmanship of the moderator, Prof. Johan Heyns, rejected apartheid. Prof. Heyns was tragically murdered a few years later in his home in Pretoria. The main sections of the document dealt with apartheid, justification, and church and state. In many aspects, the DRC document did corresponded with the Cottesloe Declaration of 1960, which the DRC rejected.

Acceptance of the DRC document did not go as smoothly as would appear. Not everybody was in agreement with it. Many church members had objections and were opposed to the change in interpretation concerning the sin of apartheid. Heyns now had friends and enemies within his own rank. The discord did not die down easily nor immediately. In any event, it took the church until 1990 to finally ratify and formally approve the document, albeit with minor changes. Heyns stood out as a leader of conviction about the true interpretation of scripture and apartheid as sin, despite opposition from his own church.

President de Klerk referred to 1986 as the end of an eight-year period of transition in which he had come to the conclusion that apartheid was wrong. It does seem that he could (among other factors) also have been persuaded by the document *Church and Society*. He acknowledged that he was greatly assisted by Prof. Johan Heyns because of the role he played in persuading all parties in the protest march in Cape Town in 1989 to act responsibly.[11] De Klerk also followed up a suggestion by Prof. Heyns and initiated an invitation to South African Churches to express their views on racial discrimination in December 1989.

In the early eighties the Broederbond disseminated circulars to all its cell groups, in which responses were sought about the acceptability by the public and members of the Broederbond to changes in the apartheid policy (according to the recollections of a member of the Broederbond). This exercise pointed to the forthcoming meeting of the General Synod of the DRC in

11   F W de Klerk, *The Last Trek – A New Beginning*, p. 160.

1986. Here the broeders were the leading members. Many of the church ministers and elders in the churches, were broeders as well as influential people in society. They laid the groundwork in preparing the delegates at the synod to be receptive to change and the confession by the church that apartheid was wrong. The time was now ripe for such a mind shift. The old view that apartheid was justified had become outmoded, outdated, out of sync with world opinion, and was, they came to believe, sinful. Circumstances as well as their mindset had changed. The Afrikaners in small but growing numbers were now ready to come to terms with reality and with their new conviction of justice for all. They prepared themselves to think about change and to accommodate the movements of resistance to apartheid, namely the ANC and the Communist Party.

The Afrikaner Broederbond was a very influential organisation but a difficult one to describe as it was a secret organisation. Membership remained a secret. In the beginning the organisation canvassed teachers and church ministers as members; later businessmen, farmers, professional people, and university lecturers; thereafter also members of the security forces and the defence force (officers and senior officers) and people from any other organisation, such as banks and insurance companies. They had to be Afrikaner Nationalists supporting the National Party and its apartheid policy and be members of one of the three Afrikaans Protestant churches. Later the Apostoliese Geloofsending (Afrikaans branch of the Apostolic Faith Mission) was also approved as a source for membership.

It was in the parsonage in Roodepoort of Rev. Jozua Francois Naude, father of the apartheid opponent Dr. C. F. Beyers Naude, that a meeting of fourteen men was held on 24 May 1918, to plan the launch of the secret Afrikaner Broederbond. The meeting took place shortly afterwards, on 6 June 1918, at the house of Danie du Plessis in Johannesburg, later to become manager of the South African Railways. The Broederbond was formed to promote Afrikaner political and economic interests and to resist British influence. Regarded as the spiritual father of the Broederbond, Naude (senior) was elected the first president.

In the Second War of Independence (Anglo Boer War), Jozua Naude left his theological studies at the University of Stellenbosch to joint the force of General Christiaan Frederick Beyers to fight against the British in Transvaal. He was one of four Boer delegates who refused to sign the Peace Treaty of Vereeniging in 1902. He started the first Afrikaans school in Transvaal at Roodepoort.

By 1963, at least 50 percent of the DRC ministers were members of the Broederbond. Together with teachers they constituted more than 40 percent of the membership of this Afrikaner Nationalist organisation. The membership then totalled only 2000, organised in small cells across the country. The cells met once a month in absolute secrecy. Membership grew steadily to more than 10,000 in 1990.

The Broederbond had great influence by the very nature of its secret operations, for example, the decisions to appoint people to positions of leadership in parastatals, as heads of departments, and principals in schools. In many cases a person's promotion was reliant on one's demonstration of support for apartheid and the National Party policies which were identical to those of the Broederbond. The role of the broeders over the decades can be characterised as that of practitioners of the most serious form of discrimination. Discrimination even extended to such idiosyncrasies as an Afrikaner with an English surname or an Afrikaner with a wife of English origin. The secrecy took on a sinister nature. Everybody was mistrusted if they were not closely aligned to or identified with the Broederbond's goals of Afrikaner nationalism and apartheid.

After Rev. C. F. Beyers Naude, former DRC minister, had resigned from the organisation in March 1963, he said that he had learned what magical and mythical power the Broederbond held on the thoughts of the Afrikaner. The Broederbond nurtured and demanded loyalty towards the idea of Afrikaner nationalism that was stronger than obedience to the command of the gospel. He decided to resign after being elected as moderator of the Southern Transvaal Synod of the DRC on 25 March 1963.

After twenty-two years of Broederbond membership, Beyers Naude had reached the stage where he realised that the Broederbond had an ideological stranglehold on the DRC. No change would come from within the Church until the Broederbond influence was broken.

As a Christian and a church minister he was by now convinced that his conscience could not be bound by a secret oath, as his highest allegiance was to God, which superseded his Broederbond oath.

Vorster, in the late sixties and seventies, easily manipulated the unholy alliance of the NP, Broederbond, the DRC and the security forces because of cross membership, as will be explained in a following chapter.

In the sphere of ideas and policies a very important role player is the media. With apartheid it was the Afrikaans press which served as an ideological institution and an instrument of apartheid propaganda. In fairness, though, it must be noted that particularly the editorial comments of Schalk Pienaar in the Nasionale Pers newspapers in the '70s contributed to awakening the conscience of some Afrikaners to question the apartheid norms that were then accepted as truths. Only after 1990 when president de Klerk announced his policy of democratic rights for all citizens did the Afrikaans press finally start to disengage themselves structurally and philosophically from the National Party.

The influence of the Afrikaans press was not only limited to statements in leading or main articles and columns for opinions but just as apartheid itself also embraced various other aspects. It supported apartheid as a political system that denied blacks basic human rights, such as the franchise. It supported an oligarchy to remain in power within an economic system in which the Afrikaans press (Nasionale Pers) became a business giant through exploiting benefits and advantages. The Afrikaans press also supported apartheid as an inhumane system that degraded blacks to become second class citizens. Blacks were not people but "unpeople" in the way the Afrikaans press reported about them or ignored them, according to Herman Wasserman, a former journalist at *Die Burger* and one of the Naspers journalists who signed the TRC declaration.[12]

The Afrikaans press supported or ignored the cruel apartheid legislation and the government's enforcement of it. Those journalists who supported the idea of majority rule were driven out of the Afrikaans press establishment. (Ibid)

Wasserman said that journalists in the Afrikaans press had to learn how to edit their stories to be accepted by the Afrikaans papers. Journalists were reprimanded if they dared refer to the concept of "collective guilt". Even for reviews, journalists were told what issues should not receive prominent coverage, for example, the death of Joe Slovo, the white Communist. Finally, the 130 journalists who signed the TRC declaration were denounced as traitors by the Afrikaans press. (Ibid)

The last mentioned role players were external organizations, namely, communism, foreign countries, and institutions both in the United States and international, such as the United Nations. Another important role player was Great Britain. Great Britain had been closely involved and connected to South Africa and its history. Part of its role is described in the chapters leading up to the winds of change speech by the British prime minister, Mr Harold Macmillan, before the joint session of the Union Parliament on 3 February 1960 in Cape Town. This was a year prior to Verwoerd's application to the Commonwealth of Nations that South Africa remain a member after becoming a Republic.

In his speech, Macmillan said, "Ever since the break-up of the Roman Empire, one of the constant facts of political life in Europe had been the emergence of independent nations. They came into existence over the centuries in different forms with different kinds of government. But all have been inspired by a deep, keen feeling of nationalism, which had grown as the

---

12   Article in *By*, a supplement of *Beeld*, 9 February 2008

nations have grown. In the twentieth century, and especially since the end of the war, the processes which gave birth to the nation-states of Europe have been repeated all over the world. The awakening of national consciousness has been seen in people who have, for centuries, lived in dependence on some other power. Fifteen years ago, this movement spread through Asia. Many countries there, of different races and civilizations, pressed their claim to an independent national life. The same thing is happening in Africa," he said.[13]

The most striking of all the impressions Macmillan formed of his month long Africa tour was the strength of the African national consciousness. In different places it took different forms. But it was happening everywhere. A wind of change was blowing through the continent. Whether liked or not, this growth of national consciousness was a political fact. Britain's policies had to take account of it. South Africans understood this better than anyone. He said, "South Africans are sprung from Europe, the home of nationalism and, here in Africa, South Africans have created a free nation, a new nation. In the history of recent times, South Africans will be recorded as the first of the African nationalisms," Macmillan said. "This tide of national consciousness which has emerged in Africa is a fact for which South Africa, Britain and other nations of the Western World are ultimately responsible. The growth of national consciousness in Africa is a political fact and must be accepted. This meant everyone must come to terms with it, otherwise we may imperil the precarious balance between East and West, on which the peace of the world depend," he concluded.[14]

Macmillan's reference to the beginning of nationalism in Europe since the break-up of the Roman Empire and the establishment of nation states that spread all over the world from its birthplace in Europe was significant. He was referring to nationalism as a constant fact of political life in Europe. It is identified as one of the forces of universal history. He described it as the awakening of national consciousness in people who had, for centuries, been dependent on another power. It had spread through Asia, and he was impressed by the strength of the African national consciousness he observed on his tour.

Verwoerd's policy was to resist this force of black nationalism with his approach of separate freedoms for blacks in their traditional areas that totally excluded any common rights in South Africa for both black and white. By his appointment of B. J. Vorster as minister of justice in 1962 after South Africa became a republic, Verwoerd signalled that he was prepared to use security measures and force to deal with resistance to apartheid.

---

13   John D'Oliviera, *Vorster The Man*, 1977, p119
14   Ibid

The other main external influence putting pressure on South Africa to change its apartheid ways, apart from communism, came from the United States. The earlier reference to the article by Alan Paton actually dealt with the pressure from abroad on South Africa. According to D'Oliveira, the line between pressure that encouraged change and that which inhibited change was narrow. There was a real danger that the West – and the United States in particular – was pushing too hard. Under the guise of concern for all the peoples of South Africa, they were, in fact, trying to serve their perception of their own interests. Tragically, they appeared to be more concerned with what is in their interests than what is in the interest of the people of South Africa as a whole. Or, according to D'Oliveira, it is perhaps just that the US lacks the knowledge and the skill to apply pressure positively in South Africa.[15]

On a visit to America in May 1974 Alan Paton met with Cyrus Vance, secretary of state, and urged him to exercise American pressure with skill and wisdom. "This is no time to go easy (on the Nationalists), but I reject utterly a future that can be secured only by devastation," he said.[16]

The initial foreign policy involvement of the United States in South Africa ten years earlier during the late sixties was limited to the exchange of students, academics, and leaders in society, mainly to sponsor South Africans to visit the United States. Already at that early stage the drastic recommendation was violent assault on white resistance if nothing was achieved in changing apartheid and attaining voting rights for blacks.[17]

Two books published by the Council on Foreign Relations in 1967 give an outline of American policy objectives "Exchange of persons and cultural programs are especially likely to be designed to promote general understanding and goodwill. One of the purposes of bringing young political leaders to the United States, for instance, is to let them see this country before their attitudes become set in traditional patterns.[18]

Waldemar A. Nielsen, president of the African-American Institute, was not satisfied with the progress made with these programmes. In the second book Nielsen wrote that an area in which American thinking and practice could be sharpened is that of cultural and educational exchange, a growing altogether minor aspect of United States foreign policy and programs. In Southern Africa such activities rank very high among those available and useful to the United States government.[19]

15   John D'Oliveira, p. 290.

16   Ibid.

17   B Botha, The Aims and Motives of American Liberal organisations in South Africa, Nasionale Jeugbond Jaarblad, Voortrekkerpers, Johannesburg, 1967.

18   W Phillips Davidson, International Political Communication, P, 281, in NJB Jaarblad, 1967, p. 2.

19   W A Nielsen, African American Battleline – American policy choices in Southern Africa. Quoted in NJB Jaarblad, 1967, p. 142.

According to Nielsen, the fundamental commitment (of American diplomacy in Southern Africa) should have been to assist and encourage political change in the direction of majority rule and self government.[20] In Southern Africa, American diplomacy is confronted with the task to develop contact and communication with those groups presently not in control of government but likely to assume control in the future.[21]

In Southern Africa the Unites States could (failing other means) take a line paralleling that of China or Russia in violent and revolutionary assault on white resistance.[22]

Eventually in 1986 the US congress passed the comprehensive Anti-Apartheid Act which was designed to establish a nonracial democracy in South Africa.

A year before Nielsen's recommendation that American policy should promote attack on the apartheid government in South Africa, members of the ANC were charged in the treason trials with conspiring to prepare for invasion by forces from outside the country.

When the Rivonia group was brought to trial nearly four months after their arrest in July 1960, it was alleged that they had conspired with others to commit a number of acts of sabotage in South Africa in preparation for guerrilla warfare and invasion by forces from outside the country. The ANC as a role player demanded equal voting rights, resisted apartheid governments, and broadened the struggle as the organisation representing the black masses. The ANC represented the black South African population in their attempt to overthrow the government and its apartheid system by violent means and later by negotiating a democratic constitution with universal rights for all citizens.

During the treason trial in 1960, Nelson Mandela said in court that the ANC was willing to negotiate for change in government over a period of time towards black majority rule. In his first meeting in 1990 with de Klerk after his release from prison, Mandela told de Klerk that the ANC was prepared to negotiate for a new constitution with voting rights for a black majority.

The question addressed later in the study is how de Klerk succeeded in persuading the Afrikaner Nationalists to abdicate their powers as a minority group peacefully in the process of negotiations for his proposed group rights which he knew the ANC would reject.

The Great Trek 1836 and Independence for the Voortrekkers

---

20   Ibid., p. 135.
21   Ibid., p. 139.
22   Ibid., p. 138.

The Voortrekkers who participated in the Great Trek in 1836 were mostly Afrikaner farmers from the eastern and northeastern borders of the Cape Colony who despaired of the unsympathetic British government. Their dissatisfaction changed to distrust in the government who allowed Xhosa raiders to retain cattle stolen from the farmers, distrust in the government's tolerant and unrealistic attitude towards the border tribes, distrust in the government's willingness and ability to protect them and guarantee their possessions, who did not provide enough soldiers for their protection, who limited their stock of ammunition in dangerous times, and who seemed indifferent towards the ruination and obliteration of the white border pioneers. They distrusted the government who undermined their domestic discipline over workers and delegated such matters to magistrates who were difficult to reach; whose border administration fell into chaos; and who left them in a condition of uncertainty, unsafety, unrest and fear, and defenceless against their enemies.[23]

The summary of reasons for the Afrikaners to trek out of the Cape Colony makes for interesting comparisons with the reasons that the Afrikaners give after thirteen years of government in the new democratic republic of South Africa to emigrate.

When the Voortrekkers moved out, they relinquished their British citizenship for the ideal of a new beginning outside the borders of British rule with a government of their own in a new state under their own laws. Piet Retief, one of the Trekker leaders, wrote in his well known manifesto, "We quit this Colony under the full assurance that the English government has nothing more to require of us, and will allow us to govern ourselves without its interference in future." (Ibid.)

On 17 April 1837 at a gathering the Trekkers constituted their own government. Their next goal was a state of their own. But before this in 1836 the Colonial government passed the Cape of Good Hope Punishment Act which gave British magistrates authority over British subjects in uninhabited areas up to the twenty-fifth degree of latitude.

The trekkers moved between the two strongest African tribes in Southern Africa and defeated the Matabeles under Mzilikazi. On 16 December 1838 the mighty Zulu army under Dingaan was defeated at the battle of Blood River by a small group of Voortrekkers under General Pretorius. When a number of Trekkers settled in Natal, the British government annexed the territory in 1842. On 3 February 1848 Sir Henry Smith, the new Cape Governor, annexed the Orange River sovereignty. In response, the Voortrekkers within two months resolved to take up arms against the British troops in the Orange

23   Duvenage, G.D.J. 1981, *Van Tarka na die Transgarieb*, p.19, en J.M.G. Storm, *Die Konvensie van Sandrivier* as afsluiting van die Groot Trek, Hervormde Teologiese Studies, Jaargang 45, September 1989, p681

River Colony under leadership of Commandant General A. W. J. Pretorius and regain possession of the land between the Orange River, Drakensberg, and the Vaal River. North of the Vaal River up to the Limpopo River the Trekkers lived under their own government in Transvaal.

In London, the British government deemed Smith's actions as unwise, and in July 1850 a commission recommended that, "all officers who represent, or may hereafter represent Your Majesty in Southern Africa, should be interdicted, in terms as explicit as can be employed, and under sanctions as grave as can be devised, from making any additions, whether permanent or provisional, of any territory, however small, to the existing dominions of Your Majesty in the African Continent"[24]

In 1851 in the Eastern Cape the government was engaged in the Eighth Border War and lost a battle in June against the Basutu across the Orange River. The Cape government accepted a written offer for negotiations dated 9 September 1851 from Pretorius. The British commissioner Major W. S. Hogg and C. M. Owen met a deputation under Pretorius on 16 January 1852 at the farm Zandrivier of P. A. Venter, halfway between Bloemfontein and the Vaal River. On 17 January 1852 the two parties signed the Sand River Convention, sixteen years after the Voortrekkers left the Cape Colony, which recognised the sovereign independence of the Voortrekkers north of the Vaal River. From September 1853 the new state was known as *De Zuid-Afrikaan*sche Republiek.

The Sand River Convention of 1852 and the Bloemfontein Convention of 1854

The Zuid Afrikaansche Republiek and the Republic of the Orange Free State gained the right through treaties with Great Britain in 1852 and 1854 to govern themselves as independent states on the land and areas that the Voortrekkers had settled. The trekkers could settle border disputes with African tribes and employ Africans as labour, but slavery was prohibited. The trekkers could also establish commercial ties with Britain and purchase weapons.[25]

The settlement and establishment of jurisdiction and sovereignty by the Voortrekkers in the territories of Transvaal and the Orange Free State through treaties with Great Britain after defeating the two main black power structures could be called a type or form of colonialism and imperialism.

---

24   C W de Kiewiet: British Colonial Policy and the South African Republics [Londen 1929] p. 35 in G. D. Scholtz, Die Ondertekening van die Sandrivier-Konvensie Herdenk [1852–1952] FAK, Johannesburg, 1951, p. 25

25   See Minutes of treaty in G D Scholtz

Within the boundaries of each of the two states African tribes lived in their own settlement areas. These areas formed an arch around the western, northern, and eastern boundaries of the Transvaal and along the Eastern border of the Orange Free State. These African tribes were not party to the conventions that recognised the new states. Their traditional areas were included in the area of jurisdiction of the new states. They became subjects of the Voortrekker governments but without voting rights in the new republics. In the constitution of the Zuid Afrikaansche Republiek of 1858, voting rights were expressly confined to burgers of European descent and excluded voting rights for blacks. The constitution of the Republic of the Orange Free State had a similar clause. The ZAR constitution declared that the people, the burgers, were not prepared to allow any equality of non-whites with the white burgers in the church or the state.

A historical mistake was made to declare white superiority in Church which is not founded in God's Word. This line of thought has been resonating in the minds of many members of the Afrikaans Protestant Churches in the Northern Provinces till today: DRC and Nederduitsch Hervormde Kerk.

This is the origin of the concept of traditional areas for blacks and trusteeship of the white government over the land of the black people.

Actually, the question should be asked why these black areas were included in the boundaries of the new states in the first place. They could have been excluded. This would have given meaning to the argument that black workers from traditional black areas did not have voting rights in white areas where they worked. They could have been considered foreigners in the correct sense of the word.

The myth of territorial separation – land and voting rights

The claim was repeatedly made by proponents of apartheid that whites settled on vacant land in South Africa, called white areas. History does not support this impression altogether. There are many exceptions. The following two cases give insight into the issue of ownership and prior ownership. The first concerns the Voortrekkers in Natal.

Retief, favouring a negotiated treaty with Dingaan for land to settle in Natal, met the Zulu king in October 1837. Dingaan promised the extensive area between the Mzimvubu and Tugela rivers, on condition that Retief recover his cattle stolen by Sekonyela, the Tlokwa chief, which Retief did. On 6 February 1838, just before the signing ceremony, Dingaan persuaded Retief to instruct his men to leave their arms outside the chief's village, whereupon the Zulu king's men seized all the un-armed trekkers and their servants and clubbed them to death.

Two months later, in November 1838, Andries Pretorius arrived with a party of sixty and a bronze cannon. Pretorius' self-confidence bordered on arrogance, but he was, as Stockenstrom observed, 'no fool' and a brilliant military and political strategist. He was appointed commandant-general and led his men out on a carefully planned showdown with the Zulu army. He encouraged the idea of a covenant, and on 9 December and over the following few days the commando, led by Sarel Cilliers, made a vow that if God granted them victory, they and their descendants would commemorate the day of the battle and would build a church.[26]

A few days later, Pretorius had them draw up a laager at a branch of the Buffalo River (later named Blood River). On 16 December 1838, 468 trekkers, 3 Englishmen, and 60 blacks faced ten thousand to twelve thousand Zulu warriors. The battle lasted two hours. Three trekkers were slightly wounded, none were killed, but three thousand Zulu lay dead. The defeat dealt a crippling blow to Dingaan's power. The Zulu nation split.

In 1839, a Voortrekker republic was established in Natal with Pietermaritzburg as the capital of two new towns: Congella near Port Natal and Weenen. The constitution of the fledgling republic provided for a Volksraad.[27]

The second area to be mentioned as illustration of earlier settlement is Johannesburg. In her article, "Joburg's Earliest Settlers", Lucille Davie gives a history of the earlier African Settlements in Johannesburg.[28]

In a wave of migration Bantu peoples again settled in Limpopo, about 1000 years ago. The Venda were the first South Africans. Another group reached the Soutpansberg in the Northern Province about AD 1300 and spread further into the Magaliesberg about AD 1400. These settlements grew southwards to the Witwatersrand. It was only in the 1700s that these groups re-established themselves in the Melville Koppies and Klipriviersberg areas in Johannesburg.[29]

These Johannesburg settlements that stretched from Northcliff and Lonehill in the north through Melville in the west, Bruma in the east, to Klipriviersberg in the south, lived and traded peacefully with one another. That is, until 1823, when the Matabele warrior and leader, Mzilikazi, settled in the area. He was ousted from Zululand by the powerful Zulu king Shaka. Later he was also defeated by the Voortrekkers in the Orange Free State. Mzilikazi consolidated his army from defeated tribes, mainly Ndebele, at his

26   Gilliomee, p.166
27   Gilliomee, p.166
28   City of Johannesburg, 13 March 2003
29   Lucille Davie, Joburg's earliest settlers

capital near Heidelberg, 80 kilometres south of Johannesburg. His control stretched from Heidelberg westwards, and by 1827, he had established a new capital in the Magaliesberg, 80 kilometres north west of Johannesburg. By 1829, his army was between 6000 and 8000 strong.

But then a combination of factors led to the dispersal of the people. Possibly a drought hit the area, wiping out the settlements. At that time the Voortrekkers moved into the area, and as a result, in 1837 Mzilikazi was forced to move further north into Zimbabwe, after having earlier been defeated by the Voortrekkers.

The Voortrekkers took large tracts of land as their farms, farming peacefully alongside the sparse remnants of Mzilikazi's subjects, the Ndebele. Many members of the local tribes who fled from the Zulu armies and from Mzilikazi returned to the area after he and his tribe moved away from the Voortrekkers to Zimbabwe.

The Melville Koppies were part of the farm Braamfontein that originally stretched from Commissioner Street in the centre of Johannesburg to Oxford Road in the east, Road number 3 in Victory Park, and the police flats on the border between Westdene and Triomf. The Geldenhuys family bought part of it in 1885. They prospected unsuccessfully for gold, and then became farmers.

Everything changed in 1886, when gold was discovered on the Witwatersrand. Europeans, Boers, and blacks moved into the area in great numbers.[30]

Very little is written about the Difaquane or Mfecane where thousands of blacks died, as mentioned in the report of the TRC.[31] Before Mzilikazi and his impis were ousted from Zululand by King Shaka of the Zulus in 1823 the Zulu impis had attacked, murdered, and scattered the African tribes living in Transvaal. Many were Ndebeles. For this reason the Voortrekkers found uninhabited areas of land where they settled in 1836. In 1837 they drove Mzilikazi away from the Magaliesburg area, north of Johannesburg. He fled to Zimbabwe.

The Voortrekkers had defeated the two main black powers in the interior North of the Orange River: Dingaan, king of the Zulus, in Natal; and Mzilikazi, the Matabele and tribal leader North of the Vaal River.

The Voortrekkers were accompanied by non-white labourers on the Great Trek. Some of the Voortrekkers used emancipated slaves who preferred to stay on with their masters. Some of them were converted to Christianity. In their new republican constitutions the Voortrekkers excluded these non-white labourers as voters.

---

30   Fact File on Melville Koppies, City of Johannesburg, pp4-5
31   Volume 1, Chapter 2, par.7

The labour issue from early times

Labour relations between black and white started in the Cape Colony after annexation of Xhosa territory in the Eastern Cape by Great Britain and later by the Cape Colony. The policy goals of both governments stated that these territories and the Xhosa tribes were to be administered in such a way, that labourers could be recruited for service in the colony and elsewhere in Southern Africa.

A great demand for labour existed, mainly for unskilled labourers, in the Cape Colony. The economy was dominated by agriculture and consisted mainly of white owners, employees, tradesmen, and farmers who needed unskilled labourers. The organisation of labour after annexation was based on the economic principle of supply and demand and was voluntary.

The reports of the Cape Colonial Administration mentioned that transactions were voluntary, and particularly that the Xhosas were unwilling to accept work as labourers. If they were not satisfied with the conditions or wages or circumstances they then elected to stay at home.[32]

The Voortrekkers were well aware their critics suspected that they intended to embark on a campaign of African dispossession. They saw Africans as people with whom they had to reach a working relationship. They coveted them as labourers and wanted them as allies against other African tribes, and their commandos always included Africans, usually as *agterryers,* people entrusted with tending the horses and preparing the food. The first large commando of armed burghers on horseback, headed by Potgieter and Maritz, had 103 trekkers and 40 coloured men, with 60 Africans to assist them.[33]

A myth was created by the NP policy ideologists from 1948 that the implementation of the policy of development of the traditional black areas would cause blacks living in the white industrial areas to return to their homelands. When the number of blacks further increased in the white areas Verwoerd said that it would dwindle in time, and a reverse flow would be created by blacks returning to their traditional areas. He indicated the year 1978 as the date that the reverse flow would start. The Afrikaners were the only people to believe this propaganda to be true.

Even if Verwoerd had implemented the recommendation in the Tomlinson Commission report (1954) of investment of 208 million rand, nothing would have changed. But he rejected the recommendations and proposed R20 million per year instead for development of black areas. A few years later he stated in parliament that according to statistical projections by

32   W A Botha Thesis p.77
33   Gilliomee, p.163

the year 2000 the blacks in white industrial areas would number 6 million. He observed that a number of up to 7 million blacks could be accommodated within his perception of separate areas for black and white. By the year 2000 the number of blacks in urban areas exceeded 20 million!

Theological foundations of apartheid

The Afrikaner's apartheid mindset has a theological foundation. Many factors influenced and shaped the Afrikaners' apartheid ideology, the most profound being the belief, albeit misguided, that apartheid was God's will. Another concept was the Afrikaner Christians' association with Israel of the Old Testament as God's chosen people. Likewise the Christian Afrikaners considered themselves as a chosen people, superior to others. They also believed, and some still believe, that by God scattering the people of Babel over the face of the earth, it was God's will for different nations to exist apart from each other (Genesis 11:8).

One of the principles for a racial policy which was well received by the Volkskongres of the FAK (Peoples' Congress of the Federation of Afrikaans Cultural Organisations) in 1944, attended by members of the reformed churches and Nationalist organisations, was the argument expounded by Prof. J. D. du Toit of Potchefstroom that God had intervened to disperse the builders of the tower of Babel. They wished to create a single nation, but God caused them to speak different languages. It thus meant that those whom God joined together should remain united and those who God separated should remain apart.[34]

A gospel of an omnipotent God who intervened directly in the lives of individuals and communities was preached in the days of the early Cape Colony. This embraced the idea that the covenant with God extended to the children of the faithful unto a thousandth generation. This belief was greatly enhanced by the drama and trauma of the Great Trek and was held by President Paul Kruger, who accompanied the trek as a ten-year-old boy. President Kruger was more closely associated than any other leader with the concept of the Afrikaners as a chosen people, similar to the Hebrews who had a covenant with God to fulfil a divine plan.

After the defeat of Dingaan and the Zulus and the flight of Mzilikazi and the Matebeles to Zimbabwe, the Great Trek was compared to the exodus of the Israelites from Egypt and seen as a means to spread the Gospel and civilization to the wild tribes in the interior of South Africa as reported in De Zuid Afrikaan.[35]

---

34   Gilliomee, p. 177.
35   G D Scholtz, *Die ontwikkeling van die politieke denke van die Afrikaner*, Voortrekker Pers, Jhb,

The Voortrekkers had a sense of mission. In 1841, the Natal Volksraad wrote to Governor Napier at the Cape that they saw themselves as an instrument in God's hand to promote Christian civilization and to protect blacks from internecine 'murder, pillage, and violence.' The trekkers themselves, however, played no or little part in promoting Christianity among the Zulu.[36]

In the constitution of the Zuid Afrikaansche Republiek (ZAR) of 1858, it was stated that the burgers were not prepared to allow any equality between white and black either in the church or state (Art. 9, 1858 Grondwet van die Zuid-Afrikaansche Republiek).

A root factor in the Afrikaner mindset concerning apartheid and his adherence to it is an egoistic spirit which by nature is domineering, selfish, and without love. The Afrikaner's belief that apartheid was just, and based on God's will, is egoistic and is not of God.

Verwoerd maintained that the whites would triumph against the blacks' opposition as the blacks were instigated by Communists. He said the whites were to enter the future with courage and faith with the eye on God above, to God who planted the white man in this country for a purpose.[37] The Afrikaner Christians believed in this calling, and it served as motivation for their support of apartheid.

An unsuccessful assassination attempt was made on Verwoerd on 9 April 1960. He was shot twice in his upper jaw, and two bullets were removed. In a radio address after his convalescence, Verwoerd confessed that he believed a Higher Hand was stretched in protection over him with a purpose, a purpose that also served South Africa. He expressed the wish that it would be his destiny to faithfully execute that purpose. Verwoerd made it clear that he believed that God was protecting him to execute God's will – maintaining the supremacy of the white man in South Africa.[38]

This belief of Verwoerd can be traced back more than a decade. Early in 1947, Verwoerd wrote in *Die Transvaler*, an Afrikaans Johannesburg daily newspaper which he edited, that it was in accordance with God's will that different races and nations exist.[39] He wrote that the Afrikaner's survival struggle against millions of non-whites would become more difficult and the Afrikaners would prevail if they clung to this interpretation of God's will.[40]

The association of the white Christian Afrikaner with Israel of the Old Testament caused them to see themselves as a chosen people and a superior

---

1970 Volume 2, p. 489–505 in Gilliomee, p. 174.

36   Gilliomee, p. 166.

37   A N Pelzer, *Verwoerd aan die Woord*, p. 380.

38   Ibid, p. 372.

39   *Die Transvaler*, 16 February 1947. In Herman Gilliomee, *The Afrikaners*, p. 463.

40   Ibid.

race. Hence, the introduction of legislation on prohibition of mixed marriages, on separate amenities, and group areas.

Nelson Mandela had a clear understanding of the Afrikaner mentality of superiority. He wrote that "The lack of human dignity experienced by Africans is the direct result of the policy of white supremacy. White supremacy implies black inferiority. Legislation designed to preserve white supremacy entrenches this notion. Menial tasks in South Africa are invariably performed by Africans. When anything has to be carried or cleaned the white man looks around for an African to do it for him, whether the African is employed by him or not."[41]

Verwoerd indicated that the Afrikaners and other whites were confronted with threats against the future of their civilization and prosperity, also that the contribution of the white man of Africa as well as the struggle of the white man in Europe and America to maintain his supremacy in the world was not appreciated. He thought sacrifices should be made for Christianity to triumph, and nowhere is Christianity more threatened than in Africa. His reference to Christianity was set in a political framework. Indirectly he was saying that the "correct" political measures, that being separation, would protect Christianity from extinction.[42]

This belief would explain Verwoerd's motivation for clinging so strongly to his ideals and policies. He repeatedly made the statement that circumstances – due to political pressure – were difficult. He nevertheless believed that the Nationalists would survive because the tide of antagonism in the world against apartheid would turn. This was an unfounded optimism. The opposite was true, as events were to prove. Verwoerd had interpreted it wrongly. Today black Christians from African countries are missionaries and preachers in the UK and Europe, where the number of Christians has dropped dramatically.

Converting apartheid ideas into legislation was facilitated by the unification of the concepts of church and state in the Afrikaners' mind. Because of this, the Afrikaner functioned in the political system as Christian believer and held fast to his apartheid ideas in the church. He created machinery within the political system and the church to enforce his ideas. The two organisations that played a role in this regard were the National Party and the Broederbond. Cross membership between the Church, the National Party, and the Broederbond made it possible. This created the opportunity for entrenching the ideology, and exerting influence within the church and outside the church. The rejection by the Afrikaans churches of the Cottesloe Declaration in 1960, their withdrawal from the World Council of Churches,

---

41   Mandela, p. 353.
42   Ibid, p. 377.

and the ostracism of Rev. Beyers Naude indicated the strength of the NP's political influence at the time on the Afrikaans churches.

In his missionary endeavours the Afrikaner's thoughts were never directed towards outreach to the black people to build friendship encompassing a broader framework of individual, social, economic, and political relationships. This was not his motivation. He never contemplated active interaction between groups across the colour line – not with blacks, nor with coloured people. Verwoerd's direction was separation. Promoting contact was seen as integration and thus to be avoided. Thus opportunities were lost to create goodwill through group contact whether by churches or organisations in sport, business, and culture, and by youth or women.

During the treason trials Mandela observed that seeing prominent and educated white women discussing serious matters with a black man on the basis of perfect equality could only lead to the weakening of the women wardens apartheid assumptions.[43] 28 He wrote, "this is precisely why the National Party was violently opposed to all forms of integration. Only a white electorate indoctrinated with the idea of the black threat, ignorant of African ideas and policies, could support the monstrous racist philosophy of the National Party. Familiarity, in this case, would breed not contempt but understanding, and even, eventually, harmony"[44]

The Afrikaans churches were divided on the command in scripture to evangelise. Some decided to do nothing, others were committed to missionary programmes, and a third group had a lukewarm attitude. Missionary work took place within the broader political framework of separate amenities. Protestant churches were kept exclusively for white believers. Missionary work was generally an exercise in training a white missionary to do mission work in a black area with the objective of training black ministers or pastors. This was a one-way outreach. No room was allowed for two-way cooperation. Thus, missionary work was done as an exercise by a committee organizing an activity, and this soothed the conscience of church members that something was being done in obedience to scripture.

Another example of scriptural truth distorted was the interpretation by a professor in missionary work at the Potchefstroom University for Christian Higher Education. In his opening address at a meeting on missions work in King Williams Town in the early seventies, attended by the Free Church of Scotland, The Free Church in South Africa, and the Gereformeerde Kerk of East London, he said that the ladder Jacob saw in his dream while sleeping with his head on a stone at Bet-El, in practice meant that each church had its own ladder that gave them separate entrances into heaven. Members of the

43   Mandela, p. 236.
44   Ibid.

separate churches would one day meet in heaven. This unscriptural idea put a damper on fellowship and the work of the meeting.

Because of pressure to confess apartheid as sin and to deal with it, the Lutheran churches in South Africa withdrew from the Lutheran World Federation. An article on apartheid as a church-dividing ethical issue in the *Ecumenical Review* of the World Council on Churches in 1996 (Vol. 48, Issue 2) by Peter Lodberg, a lecturer at the Institute of Systematic Theology of the University of Aarhus, Denmark, gives insight on the issue from the perspective of the World Council of Churches, the Lutheran World Federation and the World Alliance of Reformed Churches.

The Cottesloe consultation in 1960 brought together delegates from the World Council of Churches, member churches in South Africa, representatives of the WCC from outside the country, ecumenical institutions, including the WCC, the Lutheran World Federation (LWF) and the World Alliance of Reformed Churches (WARC), who served as partners in the South African church struggle. In this process of moral and financial support a theology of church struggle was developed based on an analysis of the nature of apartheid as a state system and the possible theological response from the church.[45]

The conceptualisation of the struggle against apartheid in South Africa as a church struggle, involving a confessing church, originates from C. F. Beyers Naude. He was one of the leading figures at Cottesloe and had spent some time in Germany in the 1950s, studying the Kirchenkampf. Disillusioned by the failure of his church to accept the Cottesloe statement, which was a mild critique of the apartheid system, Beyers Naude established the Christian Institute to facilitate the true unity and witness of the church in South Africa and thus be the spearhead of a "confessing movement". The Christian Institute was later banned by the South African government, but a process of theological reflection in action was started that could not be stopped.

In South Africa, the Lutheran churches were organised along racial lines into black and white churches; fellowship in worship could not be shared in spite of common confessional heritage.

This meant that the unity of the Lutheran church was destroyed and the church had become the servant of apartheid. This was not only a confessional problem, but was important to the universal church, because it reflected a common problem in all South African churches.

The LWF said that opposing apartheid was a matter of faith. The integrity of the Christian faith was at stake, because of the ethical challenge posed by an evil social system.

---

45   .Peter Lodberg, Apartheid as a church-dividing ethical issue, *The Ecumenical Review*, Vol 48, Issue 2, World Council of Churches, 1996.

Fear as a factor motivating the Afrikaner's adherence to apartheid

Strange as it may seem, an important factor influencing the shaping of the apartheid ideology of the Afrikaner was fear. It is peculiar because Christian believers love other people. And scripture states that believers who have love do not have fear because God protects them.

The fear factor that was part of the Afrikaner's apartheid mindset is composed of interrelated elements concerning the white man's view of the black majority. It dates back to the late eighteenth century when black and white came into contact with each other for the first time in the Eastern Cape.

The white farmers' experience of attacks by certain Xhosa tribes who murdered white families and stole their cattle was the foundation of their determination to escape from such circumstances which were aggravated by the Cape Colonial government's unsympathetic attitude towards their plight. The Great Trek of Afrikaners from the Cape Colony in 1834 was motivated by the desire to find a new safe haven under own rule in the north.

The Cape Synod of 1837 expressed its concern over the 'departure into the desert, without a Moses or Aaron' by people looking for a 'Canaan' without having been given a promise or direction. *De Zuid-Afrikaan*, the only Dutch newspaper, was dismayed that the Voortrekkers had removed themselves from British authority.[46]

The element of fear not only relates to the threat of attacks by a majority of black people but also to the idea of blacks owning land among the whites in rural and in urban areas, to the idea of voting rights for a black majority that would rule over whites, and to the desire to maintain a pure white race. During the second half of the twentieth century the fear factor became more and more predominant in the Afrikaans society and also amongst a majority of the English speaking South Africans, and therefore also crept into the Christian churches.

A number of prominent politicians and leaders referred to this fear factor in the Afrikaner's apartheid mindset. Among many, references were made by general Hertzog; by an African Church leader, Rev. Z. R. Matabane; by Alan Paton, author of *Cry the Beloved Country*; by Dr. Verwoerd; by Mr G. P. Jooste, Secretary of Foreign Affairs; by President Mandela; by a psychiatrist, Dr. S. Kalinski; and by president F. W. de Klerk.

In the debate in parliament on the Bill on Black Administration Affairs in April 1917 General Hertzog, leader of the opposition National Party,

---

46   Gilliomee, p. 162.

declared that the bill was not far reaching enough because it did not, in his opinion, provide more powers than those provided in the *Glen Grey Act* of the Cape Colony. According to him, it protected the rights of the black man while it reserved land for blacks, and it did protect the rights of whites against intrusion by the black people.

In his words, the *Glen Grey Act* created the impression amongst white people that they had to protect themselves and their interests against the blacks. This was, according to him, the reason why the white population objected to voting rights for blacks. The white man was hard towards the black man because of fear of the black man. It was seen as an age old instinct of self protection. The result was that virtually nothing was done to promote the development of the black population.[47]

In his address at the opening of the Native Conference on 3 December 1925 in Pretoria, General Hertzog as prime minister concluded his speech on policies and legislation concerning black administration and land with a public acknowledgement that fear was the underlying motivation for the policies he explained to the conference. He said the search for a solution was the result of fear, and added that fear had its origin in reason and policy and not in cowardice.[48]

After the 1948 general election, Rev. Z. R. Matabane, President of the Interdenominational African Ministers Federation, remarked that apartheid sprang from two psychological sources, "a fear complex and a superiority complex." The fear complex revealed itself in the persistent anxiety about survival; the superiority complex in the constant racist references on the level of grass-roots politics during the 1950s.[49] This issue of survival was explained by Piet Cillié, a Nasionale Pers journalist from Cape Town. He wrote in 1952 that the Afrikaners' desire to survive was a far stronger and more indestructible feeling than race prejudice.[50]

The writer Alan Paton, a Christian and a leading liberal thinker, said in an interview with the *New York Times* in 1949 that South Africans also had a conscience. "But our fears are so great that our conscience is not so clearly apparent."[51]

A revealing aspect in Verwoerd's announcement to South Africa and the outside world that black nations in South Africa could develop to independence was his acknowledgement that he himself did not want it.

---

47   Debates of the House of Assembly, 21 April 1917, as reported in the *Cape Times*.
48   U G 17-1927. Report of the Native Affairs Commission for the years 1925-1926, p. 21.
49   L E Neam, History of Apartheid, p. 84 in H Gilliomee, the Afrikaners, Tafelberg, Cape Town, p. 471.
50   J C Steyn Penvegter : Piet Cillié in *Die Burger*, Tafelberg, Cape Town, 2002 pp. 68–72.
51   Harvey Breit, The Writer Observed, The World publishing company, Cleveland. 1956, p. 91 In H Gilliomee, *The Afrikaners*, Tafelberg, Cape Town 2002, p. 464.

According to him, it was forced on his government, apparently partly due to the hostility of the outside world and even of states assumed to be friendly. He stated that the government would unequivocally support development of the separate race groups into separate black states, even if it caused conflict.[52]

Verwoerd stated, "This is not what we wanted. It is a form of disintegration that we do not want to see happen if it were in our control to avoid. In the light of the powers descending on South Africa there is no doubt that it would have to be done eventually in order to buy the white man's freedom and the right to retain supremacy in an area that had been occupied for him by his forefathers."[53]

Verwoerd acknowledged in this statement that independence for black states was not a National Party aim and also not his own policy, and that the most important motivation for accepting the resolution as policy goal was the threat posed by hostile foreign powers.

Fear of an attack from abroad aimed at giving the black man the rights that were withheld from him by the National Party government was one of the most important motivations for Verwoerd's decision to grant independence to black nations.

He explained that he would have preferred that the white man be in control of white and black and not be endangered by blacks. He acknowledged that they had to take cognizance of a number of factors, including the latest views on human rights in South Africa and the growing knowledge and civilized status of non-whites, world opinion, and the Afrikaners will to maintain themselves.[54]

A fourth pronouncement concerning this fear factor was a contradictory statement by the leader of the South Africa delegation to the nineteenth session of the United Nations, Mr G. P. Jooste, Secretary of Foreign Affairs. In his speech to the General Assembly on 10 October 1963, he denied that fear was an influencing factor in his government's policy. "Equally wrong is the charge that the white South African nation is endeavouring to entrench its position because of fear. Let me assure this Assembly that fear is not an element in the motivation of our policies. Our government is confident that it will ultimately succeed in its task. Had it not been for this absolute confidence, based as it is on our knowledge of our own affairs, we could not have withstood, for so long, the incredible onslaught on us both in and outside this Organisation."[55] This statement that fear was not an element

---

52   A N Pelzer, *Verwoerd aan die Woord*, Speech by Verwoerd on the Prime Minister's Budget, 10 April, 1961, p. 531.

53   Ibid.

54   Ibid, p. 532.

55   Bierman, H H H, (Editor) *The case for South Africa, as put forth in the public statements of Eric H Louw, Foreign Minister of South Africa*, Mac-Fadden Books, Mac-Fadden-Bartell Corp, New

of the NP government's policy was palpably untrue. It would seem to be a message approved by the minister of foreign affairs (probably also by Prime Minister Verwoerd) stating that the South African nation was not afraid to implement its policies. Neither were they apprehensive of the black man in spite of violent opposition against the South African government.

Even President Mandela understood that the Afrikaner supporters of apartheid were motivated by fear. In his address to a press conference after his release from prison in February 1990 in Cape Town, Mandela commented on the fears of the whites. "I knew people expected me to harbour anger towards whites. But I had none. In prison, my anger towards whites decreased, but my hatred of the system grew. I wanted South Africa to see that I love even my enemies while I hate the system that turned us against one another"[56]

He added that he wanted to impress upon the reporters the critical role of whites in any new dispensation. He tried never to lose sight of this as they did not want to destroy the country before it was freed, as driving the whites away would have devastated the nation. He further said there was a middle ground between white fears and black hopes, and the ANC would find it. Whites were fellow South Africans, he said, and they wanted them to feel safe and to know that their contribution towards the development of South Africa was appreciated. Any man or woman who abandoned apartheid would be embraced in their struggle for a democratic, nonracial South Africa. The whites had to do everything they could to persuade their white compatriots that a new, nonracial South Africa would be a better place for all.[57]

Mandela was indeed making a profound statement of reconciliation by saying that any man or woman who abandoned apartheid would be embraced in the struggle for a democratic, nonracial South Africa. It was a statement totally unappreciated by the Afrikaner Nationalist leaders and followers. They should have conveyed their appreciation to the Truth and Reconciliation Commission in 1996–98 which was appointed by President Mandela. But it was not to be, and ten years later the majority of Afrikaners are still not responding as they should, with a public repudiation of apartheid and its injustice.

According to the psychiatrist Dr Sean Kalinski of the Valkenberg psychiatric unit, the basis of (legalized apartheid) was not a fear of communism. "We believed black people were not human; they were a threat, they were going to kill us all, and then waste away the country until it was nothing but another African disaster area," he said.[58]

York, 1963.

56   Nelson Mandela, *The Long Walk to Freedom* (Autobiography) Macdonald Purnell, Randburg, SA 1994.

57   Ibid.

58   Krog, p. 93.

F. W. de Klerk wrote that the dismantling of apartheid and accepting the new realities in 1990 required of the Nationalists to leave long cherished ideas behind, and to confront their fears and doubts and to press forward.[59]

The new dispensation proved these fears to be unfounded. A perception had been sustained which should have been eradicated by knowledge, intellect, honesty and compassion.

J H Hofmeyr's opposing views on segregation

Hofmeyr's views were liberal. They were honest, philosophical, universal, Christian, just and moral. In him and his views his biographer, Alan Paton, discerned a prophetic spirit. His views were ahead of his time but also timeless. He was a brilliant scholar who graduated from Oxford University and at a young age became vice-principal of the University of the Witwatersrand, the Administrator of Transvaal, and a minister in the cabinets of Hertzog and Smuts in the thirties and forties.

Some of the early political views Hofmeyr expressed in his book, *South Africa*, in 1931, from a white point of view whilst he was a member of the parliamentary select committee on Prime Minister Hertzog's Native Bills.

Hofmeyr's book and his comments thereon; both national and international, was discussed by Alan Paton in his biography, *Hofmeyr*.

Hofmeyr writes in his book, *South Africa*, that there was an uneasiness, a malaise in South Africa for three reasons, the first being the delay in achieving national union, accompanied by the waning of the influence of the English language and men of English speech. The second reason was economic, the race against time to industrialise the country before the demise of the mines. The third was the 'native problem', the white man's fear of the economic advance of the black man, and of the growth of his political rights, the fear of the black revenge which prevents the white man from making any concession of power, the fear that one day 'little brown children will play among the ruins of the Union Buildings'.[60]

Hofmeyr saw the task as that of making South Africa safe for European civilization without paying the price of dishonour to the highest ideals of that civilization. There are two 'white' answers to the question; the first is that only white power can preserve civilization, the second is that only shared power can do it. And each group finds the answer of the other dangerous.[61]

Although Hofmeyr had already used the phrase 'native problem' in the introduction to his book, he declared that he and his fellow-writers found

---

59 De Klerk, p. 390.
60 Paton, p.174
61 Ibid

it invalid, and that the problem was one of how white and black could live together in peace and harmony to their common advantage. [62]

Behind all the issues concerning blacks looms the problem of the land, wrote Hofmeyr, for self-development of the African depended on that. But complete territorial separation he ruled out as impossible, though he would have favoured it. 'Too late,' he wrote, 'and therein is South Africa's tragedy.' He wrote that if differentiation proved to be no longer practicable, 'then difficult, indeed, will be the path which South Africa must tread, between a policy of repression and subjection on the one hand and a policy of identity and equality on the other. It will have great need of vision and of faith, if it is to find the road.' [63]

But it was the *New York Times*, in its book review, that wrote most penetratingly. It said that Hofmeyr avoided the falsehood of extremes, while also evading their truth. It accepted Hofmeyr's statement that it was too late to apply a policy of differentiated development, and quoted his remark 'therein is South Africa's tragedy'. [64]

'The word *tragedy* shows how difficult it is for the Cape Dutch to emancipate themselves from the slaveholding sentiment of the past. The fact that the black has ceased to be a serf and refused to be a segregated captive, insisting on the position of co-worker in the building up of South Africa's economic life is not a tragedy but an opportunity. That opportunity, including education, is what the missionary, despite all his blunders, realised far ahead of time. [65]

To this comment, Paton added, "It is not only the Cape Dutch who find it difficult to emancipate themselves, it is almost every white South African. This is fear speaking here, the fear of the white South African whose mind cannot encompass and whose soul cannot rejoice in the idea of the liberation of his non-white fellow citizens from every restriction of true liberty." [66]

Hofmeyr disapproved of mixed marriages, but he objected to controlling them by law. One could not deal with every social evil by legislation, was his reply to a private bill on mixed marriages in parliament. [67]

To the students at the University of the Witwatersrand in Johannesburg in 1946 Hofmeyr explained the idea of freedom from prejudice. "We are as a nation to so large an extent the slaves of prejudice, while we allow our sense of dislike of the colour of some of our fellow South Africans to stand in the way of dealing with them. Prejudice means in South Africa the growing

---

62   Ibid
63   Ibid, p.180
64   Ibid, p.181
65   Ibid
66   Ibid, p.182
67   Ibid, p.259

tendency to describe as a Communist and therefore one who should be condemned, anyone who asks for fair play for all races, or who suggests that non-Europeans really should be treated as equals of Europeans before the law.

"The plain truth, is that the dominant mentality in South Africa is a Herrenvolk mentality – the essential feature of our race problems is to be found in that fact. The true solution of these problems must be found in the changing of that mentality." [68] "More and more South Africa is suffering because its policies and dominant attitudes of mind do not measure up to what are coming to be accepted internationally as standards of values. But our chief loss is a moral loss. As long as we continue to apply a dual standard in South Africa, to determine our attitudes towards, and our relationships with, European and non-European on different ethical bases, to assign to Christian doctrine a significance which varies with the colour of men's skins, we shall suffer as a nation from what Plato would have called the lie in the soul." [69]

Strong political or religious beliefs are a reality among many groups in the world. In many instances it is the political or religious mentality prevalent in peoples' minds that accepts absolute values or ideas as a true or unchanging state of affairs. One example is the Muslim population. In his book *Islam's Coming Crusade*, Martin Kramer commented, as reported in the *Jerusalem Report*, March 10, 2006: Hundreds of millions of Muslims who live alongside us and among us (in Israel) inhabit another mental world.

In the case of the Afrikaner Nationalist, Verwoerd's speeches suggested that the idea of co-existence in a common society should be rejected at all levels. Co-existence should only occur between black and white as neighbours each in a separate area.

During the debate on the Asiatic Bill in 1946, Hofmeyr said "I take my stand for the ultimate removal of the colour bar from our constitution." [70] He added that "if we act under the tendency of prejudice and fear we shall not save our white civilization in South Africa. We then abandon these principles which make European civilization worthwhile." [71]

In the election of 1948, the Nationalists and their Transvaal leader, adv Strydom, effectively used against Hofmeyr and his party, his declaration that he stood for the abolition of the colour bar in Parliament which prevented coloured people, Africans, and Indians from being represented by their own people. [72]

68   Paton, p.422
69   Ibid
70   Hansard, Col 4436, in Paton, p.424
71   Paton, p.425
72   Paton, p.441

Before he died at the end of 1948 Hofmeyr wrote that total separation was impractical, partly because white South Africa would never pay the price for it and partly because its realization would require the use of such force that it would cease to be a genuine liberal ideal. [73]

He saw clearly that complete apartheid was a myth and partial apartheid an injustice. He condemned white domination. He wrote, "The only real alternative to a policy of Christian trusteeship is a policy of repression – a policy of maintaining the white man's domination at all costs, including the surrender of justice and Christian principles. 'Such a policy, the world being what it is today, will as surely as night follows day, lead to disaster for the white man in South Africa. The alternative policy, which stands firmly by Christian principles, has a far better chance of ultimate success."[74]

The unfinished stage of the process of truth and reconciliation

In practical terms, reconciliation makes relationships and the improvement thereof possible between opposition parties and individuals. It fosters understanding, accommodation, compromise, empathy, and tolerance.

Deputy president Thabo Mbeki shared his thoughts on reconciliation with a circle of friends at the launch of the book *Reconciliation through Truth* by Kader Asmal, Louise Asmal, and Ronald Suresh Roberts as follows, "Apartheid forced the individual to abdicate his or her personal morality. The only thing that will heal this country is large doses of truth ... and the truth is that apartheid was a form of genocide and a crime against humanity". [75]

"The days of bending over backwards to accommodate (Afrikaners), of gritting the teeth in tolerance, are over. Reconciliation will only be possible if whites say that apartheid was evil and they were responsible for it, that resistance was justified, even if excesses occurred within this framework." Mbeki continued that if this acknowledgement was not forthcoming, reconciliation would no longer be on the agenda. [76]

The TRC reformulated its position on reconciliation after hearings on human rights violations. It then said that South Africa's shameful apartheid past had made people lose their humanity. It dehumanized people to such an extent that they treated fellow human beings worse than animals.[77]

---

73   Paton, p.520
74   Paton, p.520
75   Krog, p.58
76   Krog, p.58
77   Ibid

A difference emerged between the reconciliation concepts of Mbeki and Desmond Tutu. For Tutu reconciliation was the beginning of a transformation process and for Mbeki it was a step that could only follow after total transformation had taken place.

At a graduation ceremony of the University of Natal in Durban in 1996, Mbeki stated that given the history of the country, true reconciliation could take place only if South Africans succeeded in their objective of social transformation. Reconciliation and transformation should be viewed as an interdependent part of one unique process of building a new society. Regarding transformation, Mbeki quoted Chief Albert Luthuli. "There remains before us the building of a new land … a synthesis of the rich cultural strains that we have inherited … It will not necessarily be all black, but it will be African." Mbeki wanted black people to work together to transform the country and the continent. He talked about an African Renaissance. He wanted to show the world that black people can run a country and a continent successfully. For him reconciliation should take place among all black people with white people in peaceful coexistence.

The concept of transformation is in part derived from the ideals of the Freedom Charter, 1955, which is an approved ANC document. In practical terms it is enacted in legislation providing for black economic empowerment in public and private enterprise, commerce, industry, mining, agriculture, and land.

Apartheid had become history, although still a painful memory with black people. For the majority of Afrikaners the yet unresolved issue for repentance and demonstration of compassion for the victims remains. A further unresolved issue is that of perpetrators of violent acts from the security forces who did not come forward to testify and receive amnesty. This remains a bone of contention between the security police and their political masters who did not negotiate a better resolution to provide protection if they gave truthful evidence about atrocities. The national politicians, cabinet ministers, and leaders saved their own skin and ran away from their responsibilities.

It is significant that the majority of NP politicians did not attend the hearings of the TRC.
They did not want to know what price the common people paid to end apartheid and to bring about the new constitution. The black people in the audience at the TRC hearings were seldom upset.

They had known the truth for years. The whites were often disconcerted: they had not realised the magnitude of the outrage, the 'depth of depravity', as Tutu called it.[78]

A valid question was what the truth was and how it tied in with reconciliation and justice. Many people deliberately distanced themselves from the process of the TRC. This was done by merely not reading about it. Others did hear about it in radio news bulletins. These listeners reacted in a variety of ways. Some disassociated themselves from the perpetrators of violence. Others took offence at the reports or rejected it. But they did become informed.

Truth, when it came to torture, violent attacks, and death was something the Afrikaners ignored, pretended not to know, or did not want to know, although the security officers said it was done on the instruction of the cabinet and for the nation. That makes the Afrikaners as a nation to a certain extent co-responsible.

In an anonymous letter, an Afrikaner posed the question about the TRC, how was it possible that no one knew? The letter was read by Tutu at one of the early hearings of the Commission, "Then I cry over what has happened, even though I cannot change anything. Then I look inside myself to understand how it is possible that no one knew, how it is possible that so few did something about it, how it is possible that often I also just looked on. Then I wonder how it is possible to live with this inner guilt and shame ... I don't know what to say, I don't know what to do, I ask you to forgive me for this – I am sorry about all the pain and the heartache. It isn't easy to say this. I say it with a heart that is broken and tears in my eyes."

One commentator was of the opinion that reconciliation would only become possible when the dignity of black people was restored and when whites became compassionate. He said, "It was not about skin colour, culture, language, but about people who connected with their humanity."[79]

God says in his word, "If My people who are called by My name will humble themselves, and pray and seek My face, and turn from their wicked ways, then I will hear from heaven, and will forgive their sin and heal their land."[80]

One of the final chapters concludes with a discussion of the process of truth and reconciliation and the Afrikaners' involvement in its unfinished business.

---

78   Krog, p.111
79   Antjie Krog, p.45
80   Ibid, p.45

The five main unresolved issues concerning reconciliation are the impoverished conditions of black shack dwellers in urban areas; the spirits of fellow comrades that need to be laid to rest; the subjective, politicized and discriminatory manner in which Section 9 of the Constitution is applied that makes provision for affirmative action and black economic empowerment; the lack of information on political murders by the security and military forces of the NP government; and the great number of Afrikaners who did not participate in the TRC investigations and process of reconciliation and amnesty.

CHAPTER 2

THE UNION OF SOUTH AFRICA, 1910 AND EXCLUSION OF BLACK RIGHTS

The first statements on political rights for blacks after the Second War of Independence (Anglo Boer War) can be dated back to the peace agreement of Vereeniging. The eventual formulations of the clauses concerning voting rights for black people follow the draft drawn up on 20 May 1902 in Pretoria. According to the draft, Britain and the two republican governments agreed that the question of voting rights for blacks in Transvaal and the Orange River Colony would be raised for discussion only after the granting of self government to the two new colonies.

This stipulation that excluded granting of black voting rights was a concession to the Boers by the British minister of colonies, Joseph Chamberlain, at the insistence of Lord Milner, British high commissioner in South Africa, who was persuaded by the position of general Louis Botha, leader of the Transvaal delegates.

Chamberlain wanted to extend the Cape system, which did not recognise a political colour bar, to the defeated republics. General Botha had informed general Kitchener on 28 February 1901 in Middelburg that the Boers were opposed to voting rights for blacks but would be prepared to consider the issue after a representative government had been granted.[81]

---

81   L M Thompson, *The Unification of South Africa 1902-1910*, Oxford University Press, London, 1960, pp 11-12 – WAB, p63

The issue of voting rights for blacks was raised at the national convention in October 1908 in Durban where the four colonial parliaments deliberated on unification.

The view of General J. C. Smuts on the issue of voting rights before and at the convention was that the northern standpoint that did not provide for voting rights for blacks should be maintained.[82]

Nevertheless, Smuts had a pragmatic approach. "When I consider the political future of the natives in South Africa I must say that I look into shadows and darkness, and then I feel inclined to shift the intolerable burden of solving that sphinx problem to the ampler shoulders and stronger brains of the future. My feeling is that strong forces are at work which will transform the Afrikaner attitude to the natives."[83]

The standpoint of General J. B. M. Hertzog was that he saw great danger if the principle was accepted to grant voting rights to blacks.[84] In 1909, Hertzog warned that if given political rights, the numerical strength of the blacks would eventually overpower the whites in fifty or a hundred years' time which would result in the destruction of the Western civilization in South Africa.[85] Hertzog was an honest politician, but here he was displaying naïve and erroneous judgment on people who could well in fifty years develop to a higher level of civilization, as they did.

About fifty years after unification in 1910, Prime Minister Verwoerd did comment on the civilized status attained by black people that would justify attainment of voting rights. He said, "We must however take cognizance of the latest views on human rights also in our own country and among our own people (Afrikaners), the growing knowledge and civilized status of the non-whites, the world opinion, and our will to maintain ourselves."[86]

Britain wanted a qualified voting right to be approved for non-whites. This was conveyed to the convention by Sir Henry de Villiers from a letter he received from Lord Selborne, the British high commissioner in South Africa.[87] A qualifying voting right was not accepted. Black voters in the Cape Colony lost their right to be elected as members of the Union parliament as a result of the standpoint of Hertzog and Botha at the convention. The decision was taken that members of parliament had to be British subjects of European descent.[88]

82   Ibid., pp212-213 – Botha p. 64

83   Ibid.. p. 119, Smuts to Merriman, 3 April 1906., Botha p. 64

84   Ibid., p. 218

85   J F Preller, Die Konvensie Dagboek van sy edelagbare Francoise Stephanus Malan, 1908-1909, Van Riebeeck Vereniging, 1951, p. 13; W ABotha Thesis p. 65

86   Verwoerd, p. 532

87   L.M. Thompson, p.217, Botha p.65

88   E F W Gey van Pittius, Generaal Hertzog se standpunt in die Nasionale Konvensie, *Gedenkboek Genl J B M Hertzog*, SA Akamedie vir Wetenskap en kuns, Pretoria, 1965, p. 333. Botha p. 65

The existing voting rights in the Cape Colony and Natal were nevertheless retained with the condition that it could only be changed by a two thirds majority in Parliament.[89]

A new constitution with restrictions on blacks

Two unfulfilled promises of the negotiated settlement between the British government and the defeated Boer forces were that transfer of the protectorates to the Union of South Africa could be executed only with approval of Great Britain. Secondly the agreement beforehand of the two parties at the insistence of the former Boer republics that the extension of the voting rights of black people in the Cape Colony by the South African government to blacks in the whole Union should be considered at a later stage.

After a period of more than fifty years, the South African government under Verwoerd finally relinquished their aspirations for Britain to transfer the protectorates to South Africa (then the Republic of South Africa). This aspiration was part of a grand design of the South African premiers, starting with General Louis Botha, to Verwoerd, to use the protectorates as a base to incorporate Southern African black territories as part of a solution by separating blacks in black states from the white parliament.

It seems that as much as the South African governments desired this transfer of rule, they never understood the British reluctance to agree to it. Continuously postponing a decision to this effect actually meant that the British were not sympathetic to such a transfer and would never agree to it. Refusal meant loss of the ideal of realising greater viable black areas becoming autonomous. In reality, the effect of this loss of opportunity meant that the majority of black demarcated areas in South Africa would be small and that independent status was therefore unrealistic and in some cases unattainable.

The question of voting rights for blacks to be granted in the South African constitution became a struggle between the Nationalist Afrikaner standpoint to exclude black voting rights totally and the ANC, who increased their demands over decades, eventually to be supported by the United Nations as a whole.

The response to the creation of the Union of South Africa and exclusion of black voting rights was the establishment of the South African Native National Congress in Bloemfontein on 8 January 1912, which subsequently became the African National Congress.

In part the Nationalist emphasis on segregation strengthened the resolve of the British government to withhold transfer of the protectorates

89   South Africa Act, 1909, Articles 35 and 125

to South Africa. Before Verwoerd finally ended his government's desire for incorporation of the protectorates in 1964, the British Prime Minister Harold Macmillan visited South Africa in 1960. It was a year before South Africa became a republic and was forced to withdraw its membership of the Commonwealth due to the opposition from the new independent African states and India. Macmillan told the South African parliament that a wind of change was blowing over Africa. This was a warning that Britain had started granting independence to all its colonies and that its policy was actually favouring black majority rights against white minority interests.

Looking back at the two unresolved issues of the Union's constitution that concerned the protectorates and voting rights for blacks, the policies of the Afrikaner Nationalist lost out and the policy ideals of Britain were ultimately realised.

How the ANC began in 1912

Pixley Ka Izaka Seme, the founder of the African National Congress, was born in Natal of a Christian family. After receiving his university training at Columbia (New York) and Oxford (England), he was called to the bar at the Middle Temple, London. Seme's return to South Africa in 1910 was preceded by that of Alfred Mangena, who also studied law in London and was called to the bar at Lincoln's Inn. Mangena's arrival in South Africa paved the way for Pixley Seme and made it possible for him to be admitted as an attorney of the supreme court of South Africa. Altogether a group of four African lawyers – Alfred Mangena, Pixley ka I. Seme, D. Monsioa, and R. W. Msimang—returned to South Africa from overseas at this time.

The four lawyers, at the suggestion of Pixley Ka I. Seme, decided to call a conference of all the chiefs and prominent educated Africans to meet in Bloemfontein on 8 January 1912, two years after the establishment of the Union of South Africa. The chiefs came from the four provinces and the high commission territories.

Pixley Seme explained the purpose of the conference. The white people of this country have formed what is known as the Union of South Africa – a union in which we have no voice in the making of laws and no part in their administration. They have been called, to this conference, so that they can together devise ways and means of forming their national union for the purpose of creating national unity and defending their rights and privileges.[90]

The conference approved of the plan to form an organisation for the unification of the various tribes along national lines. That is how the African

90   Thema, Selope R. V., How congress began, *Drum*, Johannesburg, July 1953

National Congress, which at the time was named the South African Native National Congress, came into existence.

The first round of talks between the government and the ANC about a new constitution which would include black voters was held at Groote Schuur, an official government residence in Cape Town, in May 1990, seventy-eight years after the establishment of the ANC in 1912. Mandela pointed out that the meeting represented not only what the ANC had been seeking for so many years, but an end to the master/servant relationship that characterised black and white relations in South Africa. "We had come to the meeting not as supplicants or petitioners, but as fellow South Africans who merited an equal place at the table," he said.[91]

Mandela explained to his counterparts that the ANC from its inception in 1912 had always sought negotiations with the government in power. "Mr de Klerk, for his part, suggested that the system of separate development had been conceived as a benign idea, but had not worked in practice. For that, he said, he was sorry, and hoped the negotiations would make amends. It was not an apology for apartheid, but he went further than any other National Party leader ever had," Mandela said.[92]

---

91   Mandela, p. 570
92   Ibid., p. 570

CHAPTER 3

THE ROAD TO THE APARTHEID STATE, 1910–48

After unification, the newly established Department of Native Affairs and the Parliamentary Select Committee on Native Affairs immediately gave attention to the policy guidelines of the report of the South African Native Affairs Commission 1903–05, which recommended that blacks be restricted to purchase and rent land in allocated areas only to be determined by legislation. The principle of segregation was laid down by this decision, and it served as a guideline for future legislation.[93]

Native Land Act, 1913, and critique by Sol Plaatje

The Native Land Act, 1913 was the first part of a grand design of measures by the Afrikaners to establish segregation through legislation and to secure its hegemony over the blacks.

The Native Black Land Bill of 1913 was to a large extent based on a draft bill which was drawn up by General Hertzog before General Botha left him out of his cabinet on 20 December 1912.[94] This Botha did only six months after he had entrusted Hertzog with the portfolio of native affairs due to reshuffling of his cabinet on 25 June 1912. At that time Hertzog had

---

93   W. A. Botha thesis, p. 60
94   H. B. Kruger, Die Politieke Aspekte van general J. B. M. Hertzog se Naturellebeleid vanaf Unifikasie tot aan die einde van sy Parlementêre Loopbaan, unpublished thesis, Unisa, 1976, p. 48

already formulated a policy concerning blacks. Hertzog stated that his policy exactly matched that of General Botha, and that the prime minister after consultations requested him to take over the portfolio from minister Henry Burton and to start with the practical implementation of the policy.[95]

Concerning this appointment, Hertzog explained seventeen years later in 1929 that the Department of Native Affairs was handed over to him in 1912 with the object of implementing a policy of segregation. According to Hertzog, this was done with the knowledge and consent of Smuts who then supported the segregation ideal (*Die Burger*, 30 January 1929).

In the Native Land Act, Act No. 27 of 1913, specific restrictions were placed on legal transactions concerning land between natives and other persons pending an investigation by a commission. Except with the approval of the governor general, no native could enter into an agreement for the purchase, hire, or other acquisition of land with a person other than a native outside the scheduled native areas described in the schedule to the act. A person other than a native could also not enter into any agreement for the purchase, hire, or acquisition of any such land from a native.

The act provided for the appointment of a commission to be appointed by the governor general to enquire and report what areas should be set apart as areas within which natives would not be permitted to acquire or hire land or have interests in, and what areas would be set apart as areas within which persons other than natives were not to be permitted to acquire or hire land or have interests in.

On the question of occupation by natives of land outside the scheduled areas, no restrictions were placed on the number of natives who, as farm labourers, may reside on any farm in the Transvaal. In the Orange Free State the state law book remained in force, in particular the arrangement whereby a person, in consideration of his being permitted to occupying land, promises to render a share of the produce other than his own labour or any of his family.

The schedule to the act described the native areas per district in each of the four provinces, and the land areas reserved as native areas totalled 10.4 million hectares. During the debates in parliament on the Native Land Bill, the member for Tembuland in Transkei, Mr T. L. Schreiner, pointed out that the land in the scheduled areas was occupied by native tribes when the Voortrekkers conquered the country and reserved as trust land for their continued use by the government of the Zuid-Afrikaansche Republiek.

The act immediately caused an outpouring of protest from black organisations and leaders throughout the country including the South African Native National Congress. The actions of the congress secured its acceptance

---

95   Ibid

as a united African political movement. Sol Plaatje, the first elected general secretary of the South African Native National Congress, led the growing black opposition to the Natives Land Act in 1913 and 1914. Plaatje was extremely critical of clauses on occupation of land, and of the fact that natives who occupied land outside the scheduled areas without labour contracts had to move out of those areas. He also criticised the hardships suffered by these natives. He stated that the legislation would interfere with the economic independence of the natives and reduce them to a state of serfdom. [96] The congress under the leadership of its president, John Dube, and its secretary, Sol Plaatje, brought its protest before the minister of native affairs. But the government rejected it. The congress then decided to appeal to the British government in London. The elected deputation consisting of Dube, Plaatje, and three other members left for England in May 1914. Lord Harcourt, the British colonial secretary, did not accede to the request of the deputation to suspend the harshest clauses of the legislation, leaving the others in operation until the commission rendered its report. [97]

The report of the Native Land Commission, chaired by Sir William Beaumont, a retired judge, was published in March 1916. It found that the black population occupied 17.8 million hectares of land of which 4.1 million hectares were owned by whites. Whilst the Native Land Act, 1913, only demarcated 10.4 million hectares land as scheduled black areas, it was recommended in the report that the scheduled black areas be enlarged by 8.5 million hectares land (U.G. 19-1916, Report of the Native Land Commission).

The commission found it impossible to divide the land in the other three provinces into two large areas as was the case with Transkei in the Cape Province. The chairman, Sir William Beaumont, stated that it was too late for such demarcation because of the established pattern of property rights that had already taken place, with the result that any drastic measures to effect separation would lead to large scale removals, great costs, and widespread dissatisfaction (U.G. 19-1916, Report of the Native Land Commission, Additional report by the Chairman, par. 30–31). Some white areas had pockets of black owners and vice versa.

In his speech during the second reading of the Natives Land Bill, the previous prime minister of the Cape Colony, Mr J. X. Merriman, stated that the underlying principle of the bill could not be the separation of the two races as many members (mainly Afrikaners) thought, because the whites had been developing the country with black labour. The blacks had been advancing, and the two races had become mixed in an inextricable fashion.

---

96   Sol Plaatje p. 59
97   Sol Plaatje p. 194

According to Merriman, the main object of the bill was to do away with natives squatting in white areas. Natives increased in the Transvaal because of employment in the mines and in the Free State, despite the most stringent laws, because the whites found it best to evade these laws. The laws in the Free State were not carried out, and the natives flooded the country. Despite squatter laws the natives provided service as a labour tenant or as a labour servant, very much like the Russian serf.

The book, *Native Life in South Africa* by Sol Plaatje, was published in 1916 in London as a response to the Natives Land Act of 1913 and attacked the policy of segregation. It was the first book of its kind to have been written by a black South African and important as a political statement and testimony of its author and of African political activists. It explores the political and historical foundations of the policies of South Africa's government in the early part of the twentieth century that excluded black South Africans from political power. It also traced the development of African opposition to this process and gave an account of the early years of the South African Native National Congress.[98]

Solomon Tshekisho Plaatje was of Barolong origin and had been born in 1887 in the Boshof District of the Orange Free State. He was brought up on a German mission station at Pniel, near Barkly West, where he received a primary education. He moved to Kimberley in 1894 to take up a job as a postman with the post office. From 1904 to 1912 he was the editor of *Koranta ea Becoana*, a Setswana-English weekly in Mafikeng and thereafter edited the newspaper *Tsala ea Batho* in Kimberley.

Native Life in South Africa was referred to in debates in the South African Parliament. The minister of lands described it as a mean attack upon the Boers. Plaatje was also accused of trying to spread the belief that the Boer was the oppressor of the natives. General Botha's view of the book was more restrained. To him, Mr Plaatje, was a special pleader of native interests, and consciously or unconsciously had been somewhat biased in his denouncement of the government in regard to the Natives Land Act: he exaggerated incidents which told in his favour, and suppressed facts that should have been within his knowledge which showed the honest attempts made by the government to avoid the infliction of hardships in carrying out a principle which was sanctioned by the legislature. One of Plaatje's arguments was that only when that legislature was fully representative of the people of South Africa could its enactments be deemed justified and authoritative.[99]

The battle lines were drawn in 1913 between the program of the Afrikaners to enforce segregation through legislation and the supporters,

---

98   Sol Plaatje, p. 1
99   Sol Plaatje, p. 9

blacks and some whites, of the idea to create a common society through a democratically elected government.

Emily Hobhouse warning the Afrikaner against selfishness and racialism, 16 December 1913

In her Commemorative Speech over the National Dead, Emily Hobhouse said the heroic and innocent victims, women and children, who passed through the fire, the suffering of the concentration camps, during the Anglo Boer War died for freedom. The speech was read on Vrouedag, 16 December 1913 at the unveiling of the National Women's Monument in Bloemfontein. Emily Hobhouse had led an organisation in England that advocated improvement of the conditions in the concentration camps.

The occasion was not for pity but honour. Alongside honour of the sainted dead forgiveness must find a place. Only by forgiveness can one rise to full nobility of character and a broad and noble national life. Noble character forms a great nation. The suffering do not live as memories of sorrow but of heroic inspiration. Generations will hold the great thought of freedom won. It should not be maintained as a sacred gift but increased to include other races, she said.

Emily Hobhouse then came to the heart of her message, that the Afrikaner be merciful towards the weak, the downtrodden, the stranger. The Afrikaners are not to open their gates to the worst foes of freedom – tyranny and selfishness. These are traits that withhold from others in the Afrikaners' control, the liberties and rights which the Afrikaners had valued and won for themselves, she wrote.

British leaders, she said, were still struggling with the unlearned lesson that liberty was the equal right and heritage of every child of man, without distinction of race, colour or sex. She warned that a community that lacked the courage to found its citizenship on this broad base, becomes a city divided against itself, which cannot stand.

Miss Hobhouse said that the slogan of the French Revolution, "Liberty, Fraternity, and Equality", could be attached to the tombs of the women who died in the concentration camps. She asked whether justice and liberties, so well loved by the Afrikaner, should not extend to all people within South Africa's borders and whether community of interest, binding all people into one nation, would not root out racial animosity.[100]

These thoughts of Emily Hobhouse were, as far as the Afrikaner and South African politics were concerned, ignored and forgotten. Twenty-three

---

100 MCE van Schoor, pp. 30–34

years later J. H. Hofmeyr raised the issue of exclusion of black political rights in parliament in the debate on the bills of General Hertzog concerning land and voting rights for blacks.

The element of selfishness as characteristic of the Afrikaner concerning sharing of land and voting rights with blacks was mentioned by General Hertzog as a stumbling block in implementing legislation providing land for blacks. Dr Eiselen, secretary of native affairs also mentioned this problem when consolidation of black areas was planned under Verwoerd in the early sixties.

Legislation segregating land and voting rights : Hertzog vs. Hofmeyr

On 2 June 1926, Hertzog tabled four bills in parliament that had to be accepted as a whole. A bill on land for blacks, a council for blacks, parliamentary representation for blacks, and a bill on coloured rights. A two-thirds majority was necessary to change the existing voting rights for blacks in terms of the constitution. His aim was to legislate for the segregation of land and political rights between black and white. His predecessor, General Smuts, had done nothing about it while the union's first prime minister, General Botha, started the process with the introduction of the Black Lands Act of 1913.

The parliamentary representation bill was rejected by the native conference. The government was requested to leave the voting rights for blacks in the Cape Province unchanged and to start with the provision of voting rights for blacks in the Northern Province.[101]

A strong stand against political rights for blacks was taken by the NP of Transvaal in November 1926. It rejected voting rights for blacks in parliament, provincial councils, and municipalities. No voting rights were to be given to blacks in the Northern Province and voting rights for blacks in Cape Province should be taken away. The National Party was also not in favour of direct representation of blacks in parliament, even if their representatives had only advisory status.[102]

The bills were referred to a select committee after Hertzog had submitted it to parliament on 23 March 1927 for discussion. Smuts opposed the withdrawal of voting rights from blacks in the Cape Province. Hertzog

---

101   U.G. 17-1927, Union of South Africa, Report of the Native Affairs Commission for the years 1925 and 1926, p. 11. In W. A. Botha thesis, p. 211

102   *Die Burger*, 20 November 1926. In W. A. Botha thesis, p. 217

withdrew his bills when he could not obtain the required two-thirds majority vote in parliament.

The select committee recommended in its report in 1935 that the three bills on black affairs be reduced to two. After consultations, Hertzog amended the representation of natives bills in 1936 to allow the Cape African franchise to continue but to place all African voters on a separate roll and to allow them to elect three white representatives to the House of Assembly. Smuts and the United Party accepted it, except for J. H. Hofmeyr and ten other MPs.

Hertzog told the joint session of both houses of parliament that the two great fears of white South Africa were the intermingling of blood and black domination and rejoiced in the fact that Afrikaans and English representatives supported the legislation. He welcomed the appointment of a Natives Representative Council which would be able to bring complaints quickly to the attention of parliament.

Hertzog told those who opposed the bill on grounds of Christian principles that it secured the continued existence of the Europeans in South Africa and that it was a sacred principle, a Christian principle just the same as any other principle, and it was of equal importance. "I place that principle still higher, it is the only principle, that of self-preservation, that of self-defence, by which humanity itself and Christianity itself will ever be able to protect itself".[103]

Alan Paton commented that Hertzog's statement about the principle of self-preservation for a nation, the principle which causes everybody to sacrifice his life in time of war, was the most plausible of Christian heresies.[104] Paton wrote further that Hertzog placed the defence of the good higher than the good itself and made Christianity one of many warring factors, the survival of which was the last resort dependent on the use of power.[105] Christianity and the believers are protected by God himself.

The United Party MP for Johannesburg North and a member of Hertzog's cabinet, Jan Hofmeyr, decided to oppose the bill at its third reading on 6 April 1936. He was not only opposing both Hertzog and Smuts, he was opposing white South Africa; he was laying himself open to the half-contemptuous, half-fearful dislike of those who were told that what they believed to be politically magnificent was in fact morally wrong.[106]

Hofmeyr voted for the first reading of the Representation of Natives Bill in a purely formal way but decided to oppose it at a next reading after first discussing his position with Prime Minister Hertzog.

---

103 Paton, p. 224
104 Paton, Alan, *Hofmeyr*, p. 224
105 Ibid
106 Alan Paton, p. 225

Hofmeyr's interview with the prime minister was not characterised by the unpleasantness that he feared. Although Hertzog was renowned for his courtesy, he was cordial to very few people, and Hofmeyr was not one of them. Nevertheless, he told Hofmeyr that he would not regard opposition to the bill as a vote of no confidence. He said he was prepared to keep Hofmeyr in his cabinet, and Hofmeyr agreed to stay.[107]

In parliament Hofmeyr said the bill "proposed to put up an entrenchment of a two-thirds majority not only against any deterioration in the Natives' position but also against any improvement in the Natives' position. The National Convention did not think such a double entrenchment necessary. Because the white man was put in the constitution into an impregnable position. They thought there was no necessity to protect the White man. They did not think it necessary to protect the White man against the possibility of his own generosity. Today we are asked to do both". [108]

He added it reminded him of the first recorded definition of justice. "*Justice is the interest of the stronger*. I am afraid it is from that conception of justice that a good deal of the support of this bill is derived."[109]

Hofmeyr asserted that the bill "is called a compromise, but if we look back to 1926, then from the point of view of the Natives, it is the Natives who have done all the giving and none of the taking. Let us see what this Bill does. The central feature is to give to the Natives an inferior, a qualified citizenship which has the marks of inferiority in clause after clause of this Bill and which bears the added stigma that whatever may be the advance of the Native in civilization and education, to all intents and purposes he is limited for all time to three members in a House of 153. That surely is a qualified, an inferior citizenship."[110]

"I want to say, that once franchise rights have been given and exercised by a section of the community, then no nation save at the cost of honour and ultimate security should take away those rights without adequate justification."[111]

"Some have sought to find that justification in terms of high ethical and political principle. Some have used those blessed words and phrases, segregation, trusteeship, the Native developing along his own lines. The Native developing along his own lines – that means for most who use the words the same as the Native being kept in his place."[112]

---

107   Alan Paton, p. 221
108   Alan Paton, p. 226
109   Ibid
110   Ibid
111   Paton, p. 227
112   Ibid

Hofmeyr strongly objected to the principle of communal representation and regarded it as dangerous, "not least of all from the point of view of the European in this country". "Communal representation of different races implies a divergence of interests, and in South Africa there is no real ultimate divergence of interests between Europeans and non-Europeans. There is a far greater community of interests in this land. We have on both sides a contribution to make to the welfare of South Africa, and the weakness of this Bill, from my point of view, is that it emphasises the differences, it stimulates hostility, and it pays no regard to the ultimate community of interest."[113]

Hofmeyr gave a warning to the house, "By this Bill we are sowing the seeds of a far greater potential conflict than is being done by anything in existence today. Let me explain. To my mind, as I have always felt, the crux of the position is in regard to the educated Native. We have many educated and semi-educated Natives in South Africa. Many of them have attained and many more of them are advancing towards European standards. They have been trained on European lines, they have been taught to think and act as Europeans, we may not like it, but those are the plain facts. Now what is the political future for these people? This Bill says that even the most educated Native shall never have political equality with even the least educated and the least cultured White or Coloured man.[114]

This Bill says to these educated Natives, 'There is no room for you. You must be driven back upon your own people.' But we drive them back in hostility and disgruntlement, and do not let us forget this, that all that this Bill is doing for those educated Natives is to make them the leaders of their own people, in disaffection and revolt."[115]

The final vote on 7 April was 169 votes to 11, whilst only 127 votes of MPs and senators were required to change the franchise. When the count was announced members defied the rules, and a spontaneous cheering erupted in acknowledgement of Hertzog's achievement.

The *Rand Daily Mail* expressed its belief that history would be on the side of Hofmeyr. In 1936, the paper paid him tribute that has seldom been equalled either for its generosity of sentiment or its economy of words:

"New lustre has been added to the honoured name of Hofmeyr in South African politics by the speech of the Minister of the Interior on the final reading of the Native Bill. It was an utterance all compact of courage, and generations yet to come will hold his name in honour because of its deliverance. The making of such a speech in such an atmosphere was an

---

113   Ibid
114   Ibid
115   Alan Paton, pp. 226–228

exhibition of intellectual and moral integrity that had probably not been excelled in South Africa in our time."[116]

Twenty-three years later, in 1957, the Black Representatives Act of 1936 was repealed by Verwoerd with the Promotion of Black Self Government Act, which provided for the abolishment of indirect representation of blacks in parliament, and for the incorporation of blacks outside their homelands in the politics and administration of the homelands to which they had ethnical ties.

Verwoerd wanted to achieve complete political separation between black and white and said it was a logical extension of Hertzog's policy and compatible with it.[117]

Apartheid scripturally justified by the Dutch Reformed Church

Formulating a biblical basis for its views on race relations had already become important for the Dutch Reformed Church in the early 1940s.

The view heard at synodal assemblies of the time was that the policy of racial apartheid was consonant with principles laid down in the holy scriptures. Apart from references to, for example, Acts 17:16, the history of the Tower of Babel, the events at Pentecost, and texts about the "purity" of the people of Israel, the scriptural basis had not yet been spelt out clearly. Hence the need for a direct biblical justification of apartheid.[118]

The first official attempt by an assembly of the Dutch Reformed Church to put apartheid on a scriptural basis was in 1943, when the Council of Churches (the council in which the provincial Dutch Reformed Churches were represented before their amalgamation into a general synod in 1962) made the following statement, "This assembly has taken note of the increasing agitation for colour and racial equality in our country, but wishes to point out that in truth, according to the Bible, God brings nations into being thus, [119]each with its own language, history, Bible, and church, and that the salvation of the native tribes in our country should also be sought in sanctified self-respect and God-given national pride."[120]

In 1947 – the year before the general election – an important report on this matter came before the DRC Council of Churches. This document, drawn up by Prof. E. P. Groenewald, was the first comprehensive attempt to

---

116   *Rand Daily Mail* editorial, 8 April 1936, In Paton, p. 234
117   W. A. Botha thesis, p. 381
118   Journey
119   Gen 11:1-9, Acts 2:6, 7, 11
120   Proceedings, Council of Churches 1943. Journey

link pure principles from God's word with the reality of a practical historical situation in South Africa.[121]

Groenewald emphasised that (1) the scriptures taught the unity of the human race; (2) the dividing up of the human race was a conscious act by God; (3) the Lord wished separate peoples to maintain their separateness; (4) apartheid extended over every aspect of a people's life – national, social, and religious; (5) respect for the principles of apartheid enjoyed God's blessing; (6) in Christ a higher spiritual unity would come about; (7) the stronger had a calling in relation to the weaker.[122]

The Council of Churches adopted Groenewald's report as did the Natal and Free State Synods subsequently. The Transvaal and the Cape Synod affirmed it a little later.

Apartheid was incontrovertibly church policy, as is evident from a remark in the leading article of *Die Kerkbode* on 22 September 1948: "As a church we have .... striven constantly for the separation of these two national groups (white and black). In this regard one can correctly refer to apartheid as church policy." [translation].[123]

In terms of the Native Laws Amendment Act of 1957 – and specifically the so-called church clause – non-whites could be prohibited from attending church services in predominantly white areas. Following representations from the Dutch Reformed Church, amongst others, the section concerned was amended to put beyond all doubt that the bill did not envisage interfering with the individual's freedom to worship, provided that such freedom is not abused to disrupt good order in society.[124]

Various Dutch Reformed theologians who maintained that apartheid was not a biblical imperative or presumption were nonetheless prepared to accept it as a practical arrangement.

Hofmeyr's Native Education Finance Bill, 1945

In March 1945, J. H. Hofmeyr as minister of finance (he was also minister of education) presented his last war budget to parliament. In it he had created a new vote to be called Native Education and scrapped the old makeshift measure reserving the revenue from black taxation to the expenditure on black education. He furthermore proposed to increase the expenditure by an additional £255,000.

121   see P B van der Watt: Die Ned Geref Kerk 1905-1975, p. 88 Journey
122   van Rooyen, op. cit., p. 54. Journey
123   Journey
124   Journey

After the budget debate, Hofmeyr moved the second reading of the Native Education Finance Bill. It made provision for the funding of education of black children from general revenue; provided for a Union Advisory Board of Native Education with the secretary for native affairs as chairman and the Union Department of Education as its secretariat. Control of education was left to the provinces.

M. D. C. de Wet Nel, on behalf of the Nationalist opposition, protested against provincial control and wanted control in the hands of the Native Affairs Department. W. D. Brink, the Nationalist MP for Christiana, said that whites would work for their own decline by paying for black education. His colleague, General Kemp, also objected to paying for black education and promised the house that the Nationalist Party would one day repeal the act. His prediction came true after the NP won the 1948 general election and parliament passed the Bantu Education Act in 1953.

When Hofmeyr's Native Education Finance Bill was passed in Parliament, the education of African children was for the first time in South African history financed out of general revenue. In the debate, De Wet Nel and Kemp had drawn the battle lines of major changes to come with Bantu education when Verwoerd as NP minister introduced the Bantu Education Bill in parliament in September 1953. Later this issue became part of the black resistance to the apartheid government led by the Soweto youth in 1976.

A facet on which segregation failed and two election policies, 1948

Upon her return from London in 1947, Helen Suzman, having represented the Institute of Race Relations, made the following observation on two salient points of society in her report to the institute: "SA has a multiracial society, dominated politically, economically and socially by a minority group determined to maintain its supremacy. While the spirit of trusteeship is supposed to be the basis of policy, it is a trusteeship which operates on the assumption that the ward will never be of age.

"The primitive state of the rural African is not well understood by people living outside SA, while the rapid development of the urban native is not comprehended by people living in SA. Here, then, is our problem – guidance rather than criticism is urgently needed."

These extracts are from her original report, which is kept at the Cullen Library, Wits University, that Helen Suzman quoted in a letter to *The Star*, 10 August 2007, in reply to comments by Ronald Suresh Roberts and Siyande Mhlango as published in *The Star* and based on an original misquote.

The policy of segregation of political rights and land did not succeed in one important aspect. This aspect was indicated by Prime Minister Smuts in an interview with six members of the Native Representative Council in Cape Town in May 1947. Smuts told them that Hertzog's segregation policy as envisaged in the 1936 legislation (which he had supported) had failed because it did not succeed in putting a stop to the stream of blacks from the black areas to the white areas. The result was that these new arrivals had to be provided with land for residential purposes and eventually must have part of a form of political rights.[125]

Smuts's interview with the members of the Native Representative Council was in response to a unanimous resolution taken by the Council on 15 August 1946 to request the government to immediately scrap all discriminatory legislation pertaining to blacks in the country. The Council also refused to fulfil any further functions until the government reviewed its policies towards blacks in accordance with the council's requests.[126]

The resolution of 15 August 1946 brought the Native Representative Council into step with the African National Congress and the Indian National Congress.[127]

In the election of 1942, eighteen of the twenty-three members elected to the Native Representative Council were from the ANC.[128] Since then similarly worded resolutions were taken by the ANC and the Native Representative Council.[129]

After the interview in Cape Town, Smuts published his proposals for general information in *The Star*, 14 October 1947. Among others he proposed to increase the membership of the Council to fifty; in addition to its advisory powers it should receive additional powers on secondary legislation concerning black areas; income tax and expenditure; local and general councils should be black and subject to the representative council. But no parliamentary representation was given to blacks.

Both the working committee of the ANC in Transvaal and the Native Representative Council rejected Smuts's proposals.[130]

Before the general election in 1948 Malan said in a statement entitled "Colour Policy of the National Party" that the choice was between equality on the one hand, and on the other the separate development of racial groups,

125   W. A. Botha, p. 321 and p. 472
126   UG 30-1953, Union of South Africa, Report of the Department of Native Affairs for the years 1950-1951, p. 12
127   W. K. Hancock, *Smuts,* Vol. II, p. 485
128   Roth, p. 95
129   Roth, p. 84
130   Roth, pp. 496–497

each with national pride, self-respect, and respect for others.[131] Malan stated that the best way to achieve the happiness of all South Africans was to maintain and protect the white race, and that was to be the very root and foundation of Party policy. There would be residential, social, industrial, and political separation. Coloured voters would be placed on a separate roll and elect white representatives to parliament. All mixed marriages would be forbidden. The Native Reserves would become the fatherland of the native, and all important services, including education, would be provided there and not in the towns as at present. The native in the white urban areas must be regarded as a visitor. Movement from country to town would be rigidly controlled. Native education would be Christian-national, and the money spent on it must be in proportion to the contribution made to the state income. Natives' representatives in the lower house would be abolished, but retained in the senate. As for Indians, they were aliens. As many as possible would be repatriated, and those that remained would be subject to rigid separation and would not have representation in parliament. Family allowances to Indians would be abolished, and drastic steps would be taken against Indians who incited non-white people against whites.

Hofmeyr wrote in Afrikaans at the bottom of the Malan statement among his notes these words, "No longer a policy of uplift but one of oppression."[132]

Against Malan's programme, Smuts published the report of the Fagan Commission, which dealt particularly with the question of migratory labour and the pass laws and made many humane recommendations for reform. Nothing could have contrasted more vividly with Malan's programme than Fagan's report. Malan aimed at achieving the maximum racial separation in every department of life. Fagan aimed at recognising the fact of interdependence and adapting oneself to it.[133]

In his book *The Age of the Generals,* D. W. Krüger wrote on the 1948 NP election victory, "It was the last desperate attempt of Afrikanerdom to stem the rising tide of colour. The electorate believed that the salvation of the white race in South Africa lay in entrusting the National Party with the defence by every possible means of their White heritage. White South Africa believed that the racial estate it had inherited in 1910 could still be made solvent, disregarding the unfavourable balance sheet. For a century and more, Afrikanerdom had managed to preserve its life through heroic action. It now thought to prolong its existence by heroic thought against the whole world. Afrikanerdom would endeavour to maintain its existence through politicians.[134]

131   *Die Burger* 29/3/1948
132   Paton, p. 480
133   Ibid
134   Kruger, p. 226

CHAPTER 4

PURISTS AT WORK AND OPPOSITION FROM BLACKS, 1948–66

Apartheid Legislation and Bantu Education

After 1948 the Dutch Reformed Church frequently urged the government to implement the policy of apartheid, and many laws were instituted with the approval of the church. Van der Watt mentions the following laws which appeared in the statute book, or were amended, after representations from the Dutch Reformed Church.[135]

Act No. 55 of 1949, which prohibited mixed marriages between individuals of different race groups, was instituted chiefly as a result of sustained pressure from the Dutch Reformed Church (from as early as 1915). Later (1978) the church decided that the Bible did not explicitly oppose mixed marriages, but that they were still "extremely undesirable."

The Group Areas Act of 1950 (with subsequent amendments), which provided for separate residential areas for the different population groups, was adopted with the approval of the Dutch Reformed Church. In later years the Dutch Reformed Church criticised the indiscriminate enforcement of this act and requested that it be applied with discretion.

---

135 Journey

The Dutch Reformed Church commended legislation that provided for more land for black people and the improvement of Bantu education.

Major changes in education for blacks were introduced by Verwoerd in his speech on 30 September 1953 in the senate during the second reading of the Bantu Education Bill. He announced that a division of black education in his Department of Native Affairs would take over the control of the provincial government's administration of black schools in accordance with the constitution and the country's policy of segregation which provided for a Union Department of Native Affairs. The missionary schools were replaced by community schools with black school boards under the control of the government. Afrikaans was introduced in schools which did not previously provide for it along with English and mother tongue education in the first four primary school grades. The two official languages would receive equal recognition after mother tongue education. Children would be accepted in primary schools only from the age of seven years.

He criticised the mission schools with their English and westernised education. He preferred a Bantu orientated school system.

Facilities for advanced education would by preference be promoted in black reserve areas and not in white urban areas. Blacks would be guided to serve their own communities in total. They would not have facilities in white areas beyond a certain level of employment requirements. [136]

The Department of Native Affairs would take over and control the training of teachers. They would in the future be trained to teach both Afrikaans and English language subjects. The aim would be to eliminate white teachers in primary schools and to increase black female teachers to become a greater number than black male teachers. To accommodate more children he arranged for two sessions of two groups per day in the same school building.

The NP government had taken over total control of black education and separated it under control of the Department of Native Affairs, and later under the newly established Department of Black Education, a monopolistic measure.

From the point of view of requirements of well educated and skilled black labourers in the industrial sector of the white areas, the Verwoerd policy on Bantu education with its focus on promoting advanced education in the black reserve areas was a disaster. The idea that the black areas required advanced education and it not be offered in white areas was wrong and detrimental to the economy and to black advancement. Also the department's insistence on teaching Afrikaans as a compulsory official language along with English and also as medium of instruction of at least one subject would in the future

---

136   Pelzer, p. 59

create political problems. The industrial environment was predominantly English.

The administration of education services for the black population groups became controlled by the central government with their takeover in 1954. In the same year the cabinet resolved that the annual contribution from the government income account to the black education account be fixed at R13 million per year, and that further education services be financed from the taxes on black persons. The amount paid from general taxes on black persons annually in addition to the R13 million did not amount to much. When taxes on black persons were increased on 1 January 1959, the department expected that sufficient funds would be received. The blacks resisted paying taxes, and the expected increase did not materialize. From 1 April 1963 the full amount received from taxes on black persons was paid into the black education account.

This funding policy was changed by the NP government on 1 April 1972 when the department could for the first time budget according to the needs for black education and plan on a long term basis for education services for the black population.[137]

The black education account was established in terms of clause 20 of the Exchequer and Audit Act, 1956 (Act 23 of 1956) and stipulated that money in this account only be spent on education services for blacks in accordance with the Black Education Act 1953. (Act 47 of 1953)

Blacks took exception to the rejection of Western and English cultural values, particularly the reference in the Eiselen Commission Report (the Native Education Report 1949-51) that liberal ideas were taught by outsiders, and that mission schools have achieved nothing but the destruction of the Bantu culture and succeeded in making blacks imitation westerners. This statement was untrue. Compare the case of President Thabo Mbeki, who was educated at a missionary school in Lovedale, near Alice in the Eastern Cape, and studied for his masters degree at a university in England. At the inauguration of the new South African constitution he proclaimed as vice president that he was an African.

Opposition came from the ANC in the early fifties. The ANC set up an alternative education system, and many "backyard schools" were established. A shortage of funds, teachers, and facilities, as well as the government's insistence that all such schools should be registered, forced them to close down.[138]

---

137   Botha, H. J. Unpublished thesis. Die Administrasie van Universiteits onderwys vir swart bevolkingsgroepe in Suid Afrika, May 1988, p191 and p323

138   Education Training Development Practices – SETA, Study notes on Social Issues, Johannesburg, 2003

The Freedom Charter of 1955, listed education as one of the social issues that need to be improved amongst the demands for a free and democratic South Africa.

Freedom Charter, Kliptown, 26 June 1955

The Freedom Charter was adopted at the Congress of the People in Kliptown, Soweto, on 26 June 1955 by the Congress Alliance, which comprised of the African National Congress and its allies—the South African Indian Congress, the South African Congress of Democrats, and the Coloured People's Congress. It was later accepted by all four organisations.

The meeting was broken up on the second day by police. By then the charter had been read in full. Mandela escaped from this meeting disguised as a milkman, because at that time he was restricted by banning orders which limited his movement and to whom he could talk.

The charter was drafted by Z. K. Mathews, Lionel "Rusty" Bernstein, and others of the South African Communist Party.[139] The document is notable for its demand for and commitment to a nonracial South Africa, and this has remained the platform of the ANC. Members of the ANC with opposing Africanist views left the group after it adopted the charter, forming the Pan Africanist Congress. The charter also called for democracy and human rights, land reform, labour rights, and nationalisation.

The freedom charter resulted in the arrest of 156 activists by the government who accused them of treason, for which the penalty was death. The trial, known as the Treason Trial, was one of the longest trials in South Africa's history at that point. The Charter states, "We, the People of South Africa, declare for all our country and the world to know: that South Africa belongs to all who live in it, black and white, and that no government can justly claim authority unless it is based on the will of all the people; that our people have been robbed of their birthright to land, liberty and peace by a form of government founded on injustice and inequality; that our country will never be prosperous or free until all our people live in brotherhood, enjoying equal rights and opportunities; that only a democratic state, based on the will of all the people, can secure to all their birthright without distinction of colour, race, sex, or belief; And therefore, we, the people of South Africa, black and white together, equals, countrymen and brothers, adopt this Freedom Charter; and we pledge ourselves to strive together, sparing neither strength nor courage, until the democratic changes here set out have been won."

The slogans of the various sections are: The People Shall Govern!, All National Groups Shall have Equal Rights!, The People Shall Share in the

Country's Wealth!, The Land Shall be Shared Among Those Who Work It!, All Shall be Equal Before the Law!, All Shall Enjoy Equal Human Rights!, There Shall be Work and Security!, The Doors of Learning and Culture Shall be Opened!, There Shall be Houses, Security and Comfort! and There Shall be Peace and Friendship! The Charter concludes: These freedoms we will fight for, side by side, throughout our lives, until we have won our liberty.

In his address to the Supreme Court during his trial in the Rivonia case in April 1964, Mandela described the Freedom Charter as the most important political document ever adopted by the ANC. He said it is by no means a blueprint for a socialist state. "The ANC has never at any period of its history advocated a revolutionary change in the economic structure of the country, nor has it, to the best of my recollection, ever condemned capitalist society ...."[140]

Exactly thirty-nine years after the Freedom Charter was adopted on 26 June 1955 and its main goals were realised that the people should govern in a democratic state without distinction of colour, race, sex, or belief, that all national groups shall have equal rights, and that all apartheid laws and practices shall be set aside, de Klerk said in an interview with *The Star* 24 May 2007 and added that by the time Nelson Mandela became president in 1994, all discriminatory legislation had been removed from the statute books. The fact is, he received a clean slate, de Klerk stated.

If the Freedom Charter of 1955 is today still alive and well serving as a document to guide the ANC, the question is why at the date of its acceptance was it considered by the national government as a treasonous statement.

It was an ordinary political program of slogans and ideals. It was motivated by communist ideology as much as a reaction against a government which through legislation treated the black people as second class citizens.

The national government and the white electorate considered the Freedom Charter a dangerous document. Nobody on the National Party had a thought to accommodate these aspirations through dialogue, relationships, and reform.

When Mandela was acquitted in 1963 on the charges of treason in the supreme court in Pretoria before the Rivonia trial, the judges found that the Freedom Charter did not constitute treason.

In the agenda of the ANC's policy conference held in Midrand in June 2007 it was evident that the Freedom Charter is still alive and well. In a preview of the conference it was reported that reference to the Freedom Charter and its slogans about the people sharing in the country's wealth was to receive the main attention. The idea of a democratically shared economic

---

140   Mandela, p. 352

cornucopia was expected to be supported by all sides. The difference lay in the perceived means to the professed end.[141]

The discussion document of the conference, *Economic Transformation of a National Democratic Society*, summed up the issue. It stated, "The achievement of democracy in 1994 provided South Africans with the opportunity to pursue economic growth, development and redistribution so as to achieve a better life for all. Yet we are only at the beginning of a long journey towards a truly united and democratic country. Likewise, we are only at the start of a historic transformation of the South African economy; a transformation which aims to realise the Freedom Charter's vision of a society in which the people shall share in the country's wealth!"

The Freedom Charter, in which that vision was described, stated that it should be achieved through the nationalization of "the (mines), banks, and monopolise industries", but this did not remain the intention.

The charter is one of the contradictions that riddles the discussion documents, a clear indication of the degrees of difference that existed within the ANC. However, the balance seemed predetermined. As Cosatu General Secretary Zwelinzima Vavi complained, "If you don't have anyone sympathetic to your cause at the drafting stage, you know you're buried."

Cosatu and its allies did not have a hand in drafting the policy documents for debate. Drafting committees tended to be influenced by individuals such as Joel Netshitenzhe, head of the policy and advisory services in the presidency. He had stressed the multi-class nature of the ANC and condemned those (by implication, Cosatu and the SA Communist Party [SACP]) who tried to impose the interests of a single class. The conference of the ANC was not an alliance conference, so alliance members such as Cosatu and the SACP did not, in their own right, have much voice. However, members of both Cosatu and the SACP were also members of ANC branches, and many would have been among the 1,500 delegates. So too would be a small but vocal and well-briefed core of delegates who were part of state structures: senior civil servants who attended because they were "deployed cadres". They were expected to play important, if not dominant, roles. So the odds – for all the fact that the majority of delegates probably qualified as workers – were therefore stacked against any radical change of policy.

141   *The Star*, 26 June 2007

Announcement of independence for black territories, 27 January 1959

In his speech on 20 May 1959 during the debate in parliament on the bill promoting black self-government, Prime Minister Verwoerd announced that the policy of the National Party provided for the eventual total independence of separate black territories.[142]

Up to 1959, independence had never been part of the National Party policy, or for that matter of any other political party in South Africa. This was a radical change in policy that broke with the historical and traditional policy that blacks in South Africa were to be subjected to white authority.[143]

The process of granting independence to countries in Asia and Africa after the Second World War with the accompanying nationalism of the non-white nations compelled the Western countries to grant one-man-one-vote constitutions.

Verwoerd's chief motivation was fear of external pressure for the granting of political rights to blacks. His policy guideline of complete separation in all spheres of life is totally abstract and divorced from reality. By 1994 every trace of apartheid legislation had been withdrawn. An integrated society replaced the apartheid system. But in the sixties the majority white voters supported Verwoerd's unrealistic idea.

In his speech, Verwoerd referred to two reports in two British newspapers to support his arguments on the direction of events in Africa, which was not to be in South Africa. Quite remarkably, the predictions about the end of white rule in Africa and South Africa in these two reports eventually materialised. Also remarkable is that the two reports Verwoerd used to justify his policy directive of separate freedoms for all black territories in South Africa not being realised, proved how wrong Verwoerd was to try to oppose the forces of history instead of coming to terms with it by accommodation and negotiation.

Verwoerd started his argument by rejecting the policy of a federation in South Africa, propagated by Sir De Villiers Graaff, leader of the United Party opposition in parliament. He said the NP cautiously avoided encouragement of the idea of a federation, because he did not want a white government in his own area to be subjected to a higher federal authority under mixed control. He then firstly quoted from the *London Economist* of 22 October 1955, referring to events in Central and East Africa, "Lord Malvern has sagely told them (the whites) that a privileged class must yield privileges, but he did not

---

142   A. N. Pelzer, p. 254
143   W. A. Botha, thesis, p. 399

tell them at what rate. It is probably much faster than they think … It is not too much to hope that the Europeans will courageously face this sentence to constructive abdication … The art of being submerged without actually drowning may be difficult, but it can be seen practised in the West Indies where the black majority rules the polls, but the whites reign in society and enjoy the full influence conferred by education and business leadership…

"Together, if not overlaid by fear and security, they (black and white) can guarantee a comfortable and permanent home in Africa to those Europeans who can accept the idea that multiracial government can never be a stable political system, or a set of brakes; but rather a process for creating new modern states in which power will inevitably be in the hands of Africans."

Verwoerd then quoted from what he said the *London Observer* of 8 February 1959 thought of South Africa in terms of the same development, "The question is now being asked – what is the future of the white man in Africa, and has he a future at all? The answer is surely that he has a future, but not as a permanently privileged ruling class … In an interesting statement some days ago, Sir Roy Welensky, Prime Minister of the Central African Federation, said that while the white man may be doomed in the Northern territories of 'Black' Africa (including, though he did not say so, Kenya), in Central and South Africa the present concept of a multiracial society would become the rule.

"Is this really credible? It is obvious that the white settlers in South Africa (27 percent) and Central Africa (5 percent) may, alone or together, hold the privileged position much longer than in Kenya where there are only 2 percent or less. But can they really hope to hold out forever against a population which is beginning to organise itself and which cannot be sealed off from African Nationalist propaganda from other parts of Africa? The wiser answer is that the white man has a place in Africa only if he accepts the principle that in the end the African majority must and will rule."

Verwoerd added that full control by blacks as stated in the articles in the two British publications is also the stated ambition of the ANC and the "so called learned" black leaders.[144]

In his speech Verwoerd also motivated the decision to abolish the native representatives, who were white in parliament, in order to clearly separate the two systems of political development for whites separated from black territories. Any possibility of a common forum for debate was scrapped as well as the thought that black representatives from urban areas may attain representation in parliament despite the fact that they would have their own states.[145]

---

144   Pelzer, p. 273
145   Pelzer, p. 274

Nearly thirty years later, one of Verwoerd's cabinet members, President P. W. Botha, started to tamper with this issue by formulating changes in policy to accommodate blacks in urban areas through a power sharing mechanism that would allow representation of blacks in parliament.

His minister of constitutional development and planning, Mr Chris Heunis, in a speech before the Natal Chamber of Industries on 20 June 1985 said, "It is accepted without reservation by the government that reform and adjustment are necessary in regard to all our communities, including the black communities."[146] In that speech he recognised that urban blacks could not come into their own through autonomous and self-governing homelands.[147]

The Tomlinson Commission already in 1956 recommended accelerated development, consolidation of land, and substantial increase in funds for development. Verwoerd rejected it.

Verwoerd did not obtain formal approval from the National Party provincial congresses for his announcement of independent status for black territories.

In 1961, two years after Prime Minister Verwoerd's address in parliament on 27 January 1959 announcing independence as the political development goal of the administration of black areas, the Department of Black Administration drew up a memorandum together with an explanatory annexure to give effect to the new declared goal of Verwoerd.[148]

The title of the memorandum was General Principles and Constitutional Development Plan for the granting of Representative Government to Black Ethnic Units on a Homelands Basis in the Republic of South Africa and South West Africa. It is interesting that at this stage South West Africa was incorporated into the political development plan that provided for the country to be carved up into black administrative units which were also to attain representative status and thereafter independence.

The further constitutional development of the black homelands was aligned with what is stated to be the well known commonwealth framework in terms of the principle that the citizens of the developing homelands do not have representation in the mother parliament; that the present black territorial units considered to be legislative bodies in the first stage of a development process; and that evolutionary constitutional development takes place along the lines of representative, responsible, and independent government.

Borders: that the borders of the different homelands be demarcated, and that land in possession of whites within those demarcated areas be declared to be open.

146   Heunis, p. 127

147   Ibid

148   M. D. C. de Wet Nel collection, SA Archives, Pretoria University, Transkei Series, Band No. 3 in W. A. Botha thesis pp. 407–412

Citizenship: the citizenship of every black person would rest in his homeland, regardless of his present or future place of employment or residence, but with a common loyalty and bond with the Republic of South Africa.

Finance: local sources of income are identified and it is acknowledged that it would not be sufficient to provide for all government expenditure. Additional sources are suggested: customs and excise duties; tax on every employee working in the republic outside his homeland; grants and loans for agricultural and economic development.

Since Transkei had expressed the wish to attain responsible government status, it was decided that the process would start with that region. Within the following five years other homelands could obtain the same status if they requested it. The date for enactment of legislation for Transkei's new form of government was proposed as 1963.

Political independence was stated as the main goal and not economic independence. The homeland would have been economically dependent on the RSA although a stage of economic interdependence was foreseen.

In the explanatory note it was stated that approximately 1 651 332 hectares of land outside the declared open areas were to be found for the existing homelands. This required that finality had to be reached as soon as possible on the extent and boundaries of the homelands.

The current situation created uncertainty among white farmers who owned farms near existing homelands, and the minister and department were swamped with inquiries and offers. Public opinion required comprehensive demarcation of black areas as reflected in a request by the South Africa Agricultural Union that government should declare the final borders of the homelands and expedite purchase of farms.

Finality needed to be reached on the problem arising from the ownership of land by whites in so called "white pockets" in the Transkei. It was recommended that the "pockets" be declared open areas in terms of Act No. 18 of 1936.

Legislature: it was recommended that citizens outside their homeland be required to register as voters in their homelands where they were to vote, and that they could also register as candidates for electoral office in the homelands. White voters in the homelands were required to vote in constituencies outside the homelands.

Verwoerd's reply on 9 March 1960 to Macmillan's winds of change speech

At a joint sitting of the two houses of parliament on 3 January 1960 in Cape Town, the British prime minister, Harold Macmillan, discussed Britain's reaction to the winds of change in Africa, of the way in which Britain had done and would do her Christian duty in the face of the new challenges. He emphasised Britain's nonracial approach to these challenges, and he told the parliamentarians, "It may well be that in trying to do our duty as we see it, we shall sometimes make difficulties for you. If that proves to be so, we much regret it. But I know that, even so, you would not ask us to flinch from doing our duty. You too, will do your duty as you see it … as fellow-members of the commonwealth, we always try and, I think, we have succeeded in giving South Africa our full support and encouragement, but I hope you won't mind my saying frankly that there are some aspects of your policies which make it impossible for us to do this without being false to our own deep convictions about the political destinies of free men to which in our own territories we are trying to give effect. I think therefore that we ought to face as friends together – without seeking, I trust, to apportion praise or blame – the fact that in the kind of world of today, this difference in outlook lies between us.…

"The wind of change is blowing through this continent and, whether we like it or not, this growth of national consciousness is a political fact. We must all accept it as a fact, and our national policies must take account of it. … As I see it, the great issue in this second half of the twentieth century is whether the uncommitted peoples of Asia and Africa will swing to the East or to the West. Will they be drawn into the communist camp? Or will the great experiments of self-government that are now being made in Asia and Africa, especially within the commonwealth, prove so successful, and by their example so compelling, that the balance will come down in favour of freedom and order and justice?"

Macmillan's speech was reported throughout the world. It heralded the parting of the ways between South Africa and the West over South Africa's race policies.

In his reply Prime Minister Verwoerd said that South Africa was looking critically at some aspects of British policy in Africa. He maintained that it could contain great dangers that could defeat the very object they were aiming at.

On 9 March 1960, Verwoerd gave a more detailed reply to Macmillan's speech of the previous month. In a policy announcement, he said Western nations were abandoning the white man in Africa, and his response contained three aspects: his principles of no integration in any area of life, not in politics or any other, but coexistence; development to nationhood of the black man from the bottom up and not top down; a common bond between the white state and its black neighbouring states in a commonwealth in South Africa with economic relations.[149]

Sharpeville Massacre, 21 March 1960, and a lone Afrikaner voice of conscience

While the African National Congress, South Africa's long-time voice of black nationalism, planned its campaign against the so-called "Pass laws", the more militant, break-away Pan Africanist Congress announced its own campaign. This involved calling all members to leave their reference books at home and to present themselves at police stations for arrest. The slogan for the campaign was: No bail, no defence, no fine. The object was to embarrass the government by flooding its penal system. The demonstrators were told that, if the police refused to arrest them, they should return again and again until arrested. They were also told to ensure that no violence occurred. But violence there was—including the Sharpeville tragedy in which police gunfire killed 67 blacks and wounded 186. In disturbances in Cape Town people were killed and injured. Demonstrations and sporadic outbreaks of violence also occurred in other parts of South Africa.

The government reacted by banning public meetings in all relevant magisterial districts on 24 March 24 1960. On 28 March legislation was introduced to ban the PAC and the ANC. On 30 March a state of emergency was declared, and hundreds of people were arrested in different parts of the country in a pre-dawn police swoop. More disturbances followed on a wide front. It was a time of high tension for both white and black. Citizen force units were mobilised. Mandela was also temporarily detained and later went underground to lead a campaign for a national convention.

Although these events sparked off a great deal of White soul-searching and political re-thinking, the Verwoerd government continued its course and, armed with emergency powers, the authorities largely smashed the organisation behind the protests. These events strengthened Verwoerd's determination to take really tough action against subversive elements in South Africa.[150]

---

149   A. N. Pelzer, p. 343
150   D'Oliveira, p. 122

In the aftermath of the massacre at the anti-pass demonstration in Sharpeville, Ingrid Jonker, an Afrikaner poet, wrote a poem about an incident where a black child in Nyanga was killed by a soldier's stray bullet. The poem was read by president Mandela in 1994 in his first speech in parliament under the new democratic constitution.

The child is not dead the child lifts his fists against his mother who shouts Afrika! … The child is not dead Not at Langa nor at Nyanga nor at Orlando nor at Sharpeville nor at the police post at Philippi where he lies with a bullet through his brain … the child is present at all assemblies and law-giving the child peers through the windows of houses and into the hearts of mothers this child who only wanted to play in the sun of Nyanga is everywhere the child grown to a man treks on through all Afrika the child grown to a giant journeys over the whole world without a pass!

World Council of Churches, Cottesloe 1960 and Rev. Beyers Naude

The tragic insurrection at Sharpeville in March 1960, in which 67 people were killed, and the resultant state of emergency led the World Council of Churches to contact its member churches in South Africa. Amongst these churches were the Dutch Reformed Church of the Transvaal, the Dutch Reformed Church of the Cape, and the Church of the Province of Southern Africa (the Anglican Church). At the time the Dutch Reformed Church and the Anglican Church were involved in an ecclesiastical dispute. The archbishop of Cape Town sent the World Council of Churches an ultimatum: either the Dutch Reformed Church had to be expelled from the World Council of Churches on account of its stance on apartheid, or the Anglican Church would be obliged to withdraw from that body.

In spite of the many obstacles put in its path by the Anglican Church as well as the Dutch Reformed Church, the World Council of Churches succeeded in calling a conference of churches, and eventually eighty delegates of the South African member churches (including the Dutch Reformed Church of the Cape and the Dutch Reformed Church of the Transvaal) and six representatives of the World Council of Churches met for the conference, which was held at the Cottesloe hostel of the University of the Witwatersrand between 7 and 14 December 1960. Rev. C. F. Beyers Naude was one of the Transvaal DRC representatives.

A major crisis for the churches in South Africa was caused by the Cottesloe Declaration in December 1960 in Johannesburg. At this meeting the role of the church as regards racism was discussed by delegates of the

World Council of Churches and representatives of South African member churches. Far-reaching decisions were taken that resulted in a strong reaction from especially the Afrikaans churches. At synods held in 1960 the Dutch Reformed Church (DRC) and the Nederduitsch Hervormde Church of Afrika decided to resign from the World Council of Churches.

The Cottesloe Declaration read in part, "The general theme of our seven days together has been the Christian attitude towards race relations. We are united in rejecting all unjust discrimination. Widely divergent convictions have been expressed on the basic issues of apartheid. They range on the one hand from the judgement that it is unacceptable in principle, contrary to the Christian calling and unworkable in practice, to the conviction on the other hand that a policy of differentiation can be defended from the Christian point of view, that it provides the only realistic solution to the problems of race relations and is therefore in the best interests of the various population groups.

"The church of Jesus Christ, by its nature and calling, is deeply concerned with the welfare of all people, both as individuals and as members of social groups. It is called to minister to human need in whatever circumstances and forms it appears, and to insist that all be done with justice. In its social witness the church must take cognizance of all attitudes, forces, policies and laws which affect the life of a people; but the church must proclaim that the final criterion of all social and political action is the principles of Scripture regarding the realisation of all men of a life worthy of their God-given vocation."

They recognised that all racial groups who permanently inhabit their country were a part of their total population, and they regarded them as indigenous. Members of all these groups had an equal right to make their contribution towards the enrichment of the life of their country and to share in the ensuing responsibilities, rewards, and privileges.

In a period of rapid social change the church had a special responsibility for fearless witness within society. The church as the body of Christ was seen as a unity, and within this unity the natural diversity among men was not annulled but sanctified.

The declaration further stated that no one who believed in Jesus Christ was to be excluded from any church on the grounds of colour or race. The spiritual unity among all men who are in Christ was to find visible expression in acts of common worship and witness, and in fellowship and consultation on matters of common concern.

No scriptural grounds were found for the prohibition of mixed marriages. The well-being of the community and pastoral responsibility required, however, that due consideration be given to certain factors which could make such marriages inadvisable.

Attention was called to the disintegrating effects of migrant labour on African life. No stable society was possible unless the cardinal importance of family life was recognised, and, from the Christian standpoint, it was imperative that the integrity of the family be safeguarded.

It was widely recognised that the wages received by the vast majority of the non-white people obliged them to exist well below the generally accepted minimum standard for healthy living. Concerted action was required to remedy this grave situation. The then present system of job reservation had to give way to a more equitable system of labour to safeguard the interest of all concerned.

It was their conviction that the right to own land wherever a person was domiciled and to participate in the government of the country was part of the dignity of the adult man, and for this reason a policy which permanently denied to non-white people the right of collaboration in the government of the country of which they were citizens could no longer be justified. Also there could be no objection in principle to the direct representation of coloured people in parliament, and they expressed the hope that consideration would be given to the application of this principle as soon as possible.

Insofar as nationalism grows out of a desire for self-realisation, Christians were to understand and respect it. The danger of nationalism was, however, that it could seek to fulfil its aim at the expense of the interests of others, and that it could cause the nation to become an absolute value which would take the place of God. The role of the church was, therefore, to help to direct national movements towards just and worthy ends. European congregations were urged to cooperate by making their buildings available to non-white people for worship in urban areas.

Greater security of tenure in the provision of homes for non-white people was propagated, and that residential areas be planned with an eye to the economic and cultural level of the inhabitants.

The Cottesloe Declaration led to great tumult in Afrikaner ranks and intense controversy in the daily newspapers and church press. Many church councils adopted resolutions denouncing Cottesloe, and public meetings were held. The church delegates were sharply criticised. Leaders such as Dr A. P. Treurnicht, editor of *Die Kerkbode*, wrote that the Cottesloe delegates did not represent the voice of the church as a whole, and that the debate on matters such as the coloured vote was far from over.[151]

Prime Minister Verwoerd also entered the debate in his New Year's message on 31 December 1960 with his comment that a wrong impression

---

151   Journey, p. 11

had been created by opponents of the policy of separate development that certain churches (two synods of the DRC) had taken a stand against this policy. He observed that the churches had not expressed their opinion through their synods in which the church ministers and members were represented. They still had to make their voices heard.

He expressed the hope of a more united 1961 and that the nation and churches would find the true way forward. Personally he did not believe that any international organisation (UN or World Council of Churches) could make a lasting impression on the thoughts and actions of South Africans and their decisions on how justice for all could best be exercised in practice.[152]

With this statement, Verwoerd drew a line through the Cottesloe Declaration. He polarized the government and specifically the National Party against the church leadership.[153]

Early in 1961, Dr Piet Meyer (chairman) ordered an extraordinary Broederbond circular to be sent to all cells in which everyone was assured that the executive was monitoring the situation closely. There was no need for concern, as the synods of the NG member churches were to make the final decision. It was a clear hint that the synods dominated by the Broederbond would reject these "liberal" decisions and remain loyal to the apartheid policy of Afrikaner nationalism.[154]

With one exception, all the DRC Cottesloe delegates opted for withdrawal from the controversy and the debate about apartheid in the DRC. The one exception was Rev. Beyers Naude, who remained undaunted.

Prime Minister Verwoerd in his New Year's message and Dr Piet Meyer in his secret circular were right when they suggested that the church had not yet officially pronounced on the Cottesloe consultation, and that only the synods could do so. The various synods and synodal commissions met during the course of 1961 – and each and every one rejected the conference resolutions. The Cape and Transvaal Synods declared emphatically that the policy of differentiation was scripturally based and offered the only realistic solution to the problems of race relations in the country, and therefore best served the interests of all population groups. The general tenor and the joint testimony of the Cottesloe Declaration were unacceptable to the synods because they "impugn and undermine the policy of separate development".[155] Internal antagonism was expressed by politically motivated church members against anyone who dared agree with the Cottesloe report. It was historically a "high" point in intolerance. A lot of it was directed at Rev. Beyers Naude.

152   Pelzer, p. 404
153   Journey
154   *Ecunews*, March 1985
155   cf. FM Gaum: *Die kerk en die toekoms van Suid-Afrika*, p. 50., Journey p. 11

The reaction of the Dutch Reformed Church to the pronouncements of the Cottesloe conference caused a deep rift between the Dutch Reformed Church and many other recognised Protestant churches in the country. The Transvaal and Cape Dutch Reformed Churches resigned from the World Council of Churches and, when most other mainstream churches in the country came together in the South African Council of Churches, the Dutch Reformed Church (and the other Afrikaans sister churches) stood apart.

In this regard, Prof. Ben Engelbrecht remarked, "How political forces could succeed in driving the wedge so deeply between churches and Christians in our country will always remain a baffling mystery."[156]

Looking back on the Cottesloe resolutions it is apparent that they were all scripturally based, of common sense, sound judgement, and practical. At the time quite the opposite view was taken about them by the Afrikaans Protestant churches. Strong reaction against it followed. The Afrikaner's intolerance towards anybody with opposing views was reinforced. But no doubt, the seeds of doubt have been sown in many an Afrikaner Christian's mind, although still dominated by the Apartheid ideologies.

On 15 May 1962 Beyers Naude started a theological magazine, *Pro Veritate*, and became its first editor.

In April 1963 Beyers Naude was elected moderator of the Southern Transvaal Synod of the DRC and defied pressure from the Church hierarchy to end his association with *Pro Veritate*.

He took the initiative in the establishment of a formal ecumenical structure to demonstrate the unity of Christ's church across the boundaries of race and denomination. When the Christian Institute (CI) was launched on 13 August 1963, Naude accepted the post of its first full-time director. The DRC refused him permission to retain his status as minister if he accepted the position. On 22 September 1963 he announced his decision to leave his church to a packed congregation.

Making it clear that he rejected the DRC decisions concerning himself, the CI, and *Pro Veritate* he said, "For me there is only one way, to be obedient to God! It is God's word and God's way for me. Therefore I must go."

In November 1963 Beyers Naude gave a number of secret documents to a close friend, Prof. Albert Geyser, especially those which showed to what extent the church was bound by the Broederbond. He later said he was sorry he gave it to Prof. Geyser and apologized for doing so.

At the end of 1963, a series of sensational exposés of the Broederbond activities, based on Prof. Geyser's documents, appeared in *The Sunday Times*. For the first time, South Africa was shown how this organisation, which

---

156 . B. J. Engelbrecht: *Ter wille van hierdie wêreld – Politiek en Christelike heilsbelewing in Suid-Afrika*, p. 25, Journey, p. 12

was made up of the church, political, economic, and academic leadership of Afrikanerdom, was controlling the community and the church in particular.

There was uproar in government circles. Within days, an Afrikaans Sunday newspaper announced that General Hendrik van den Berg, the head of the security police, was personally investigating the matter.

At the beginning of November 1963, the security police raided the *Sunday Times* offices and confiscated the Broederbond documents. Two weeks later General van den Berg personally visited both Dr Naude and Prof. Geyser to question them about their role in the Broederbond exposures.

Because of these and other exposures in 1963 to 1970 and the later split in the National Party, the Broederbond had lost much of its influence and was no longer the dominant factor it had been in public life for more than forty years.

For his support of Cottesloe, Dr Naude and his family paid the price of ostracism in the Afrikaans Church and the Afrikaners cultural society, enduring a venomous smear campaign. At one of the regular prayer meetings of Christian friends held in Bedfordview near Johannesburg in the early eighties, Mrs Naude , in tears, told the group how they were ostracized and her husband, Rev. Beyers Naude, was belittled, insulted, and ignored by fellow Afrikaner Christians. After the exposure of the Broederbond he was denounced as a traitor and received death threats.

At a massive "volkskongres" on Christendom against communism, Dr Naude and the Christian Institute were branded as liberals who were the forerunners preparing the way for Communism. In the DRC there was a long campaign against him. His status as a minister was taken away, and the synodal authorities rescinded a church council decision in his new Parkhurst congregation to elect him as an elder.

The role of Dr Naude as the controversial director of the Christian Institute from 1963 to 1977 was restricted when both were banned. On 19 October 19 1977, the voice of Dr Naude and many other individuals and organisations were silenced when they were banned for five years. His own banning order was extended for three years in 1982 – until it was unexpectedly lifted after two years at the end of September 1984.

The first rejection by the Dutch Reformed Church of apartheid, as had been done in the Cottesloe Declaration by delegates of the World Council of Churches and South African Churches, was in 1986 with the confession by the Synod of the DRC, under the chairmanship of Prof. Johan Heyns, that racial discrimination and thus also apartheid was a sin. This was done with the acceptance by the synod of the document *Church and Society*. It was a complete vindication of the views of Rev. Byers Naude and the Cottesloe Declaration.

Republic of South Africa 31 May 1961; beginning of the armed struggle; and a new minister of justice

On 20 January 1960, Verwoerd announced in Parliament during the no confidence debate that a referendum would be held later that year on the issue of a republic. After India in 1949, Pakistan in 1953, Ceylon in 1956, and Ghana in 1960 became Republics they did not lose their membership of the commonwealth.

In his testimony in August 1960 during the treason trials, Mandela suggested in court that democracy could be achieved through gradual reforms. He said, "We demand universal adult franchise, and we are prepared to exert economic pressure to attain our demands. We will launch defiance campaigns, stay-at-homes, either singly or together, until the government should say, 'Gentlemen, we cannot have this state of affairs, laws being defied, and this whole situation created by stay-at-homes. Let's talk.' In my own view I would say, 'Yes, let us talk,' and the government would say, 'We think that the Europeans at present are not ready for a type of government where they might be dominated by non-Europeans. We think we should give you sixty seats. The African population is to elect sixty Africans to represent them in parliament. We will leave the matter over for five years, and we will review it at the end of five years.' In my view, that would be a victory, my lords; we would have taken a significant step towards the attainment of universal adult suffrage for Africans, and we would then for the five years say that we will suspend civil disobedience."

Mandela told the court that they believed they could achieve their demands without violence through numerical superiority. He said, "We had in mind that in the foreseeable future it will be possible for us to achieve these demands, and we worked on the basis that Europeans themselves, in spite of the wall of prejudice and hostility which we encountered, that they can never remain indifferent indefinitely to our demands, because we are hitting them in the stomach with our policy of economic pressure."

For its part the state was determined to prove that Mandela and his co-accused were dangerous, inclined to violence and pro-communists. Mandela's statements in court were made two months before the referendum in October 1960. The national government and Verwoerd took no notice of it since they were intent on opposing the ANC. Negotiations and universal suffrage were the opposite to their way of thinking. Verwoerd's and the Nationalists' intransigence led the way.

The referendum was held on 5 October 1960, and the majority of White South Africans and voters in South West Africa voted in favour of a republic.

Black, coloured, and Indian people were not allowed to vote. Both the United Party and the Progressive Party called on voters to vote against the Republic. The result was 850,458 in favour with 775,878 against: the referendum was won by 74,580 votes.

On 3 March 1961, Verwoerd left for England to attend the conference of commonwealth premiers held in London from 8 to 17 March 1961 and to submit the application of the Republic of South Africa to remain a member of the Commonwealth of Nations.

The Afro-Asian countries were especially critical of apartheid, with Nkrumah and Nehru leading the opposition. Canada was also critical of South Africa. The call was for South Africa to abandon her racial policy. Verwoerd refused and felt that nobody should have the right to dictate to South Africa what its policies should be. Verwoerd decided it would be best to leave the commonwealth and withdrew the application for membership on 15 March.

On 25 March 1961, Mandela made the main speech at an all-in conference in Pietermaritzburg organised to agitate for a national constitutional convention for all South Africans. It was a few days before his five years long ban restricting him to Johannesburg, not to attend meetings and not to be reported on, ended. It was also two days after adjournment of the Treason Trial in which he and other ANC leaders were accused of involvement in an ANC policy to overthrow the state by violence.

The verdict announced by Mr Justice Rumpff on behalf of a panel of three judges on 29 March 1961 was not guilty.

In the meantime, Mandela organised a three day stay-at-home starting on 29 May, to coincide with the Republic Day celebration of 31 May 1961. In the latter half of May the government took counter measures including a military call up, and Verwoerd warned that those supporting the strike, including sympathetic newspapers, were playing with fire.

On 31 May, South Africa became a republic, with her membership in the commonwealth simultaneously expiring. The choice of this particular day was of great significance for the Afrikaner. Republic Day (31 May) coincided with the end of the Second War of Independence (Anglo Boer War) in 1902, the date of the Union of South Africa in 1910, and the date when the South African flag had first been flown in 1928. The new constitution combined the old powers of the queen and the governor general and invested them in the new position of state president – a position without a political role and elected by the legislature. Equality between the English and Afrikaans languages was retained. Exclusive voting rights for whites remained unchanged.

The ANC organised country-wide stay-at-home for 29, 30, and 31 May 1961 was called off on the 30th for not succeeding as a sustained massive stay-away. Mandela informed press representatives that the non-violent policy of the ANC would cease. At a meeting of the ANC Working Committee in June 1961 he raised the issue of an armed struggle.[157]

The joint executive committee, including all the congresses of the ANC, thereafter authorised Mandela to form a new military organisation separate from the ANC which would retain its policy of non-violence.[158] The name of the new organisation was Umkhonto we Sizwe (The Spear of the Nation), or MK for short. Mandela recruited Joe Slovo and Walter Sisulu to form the high command under him as chairman.[159] On 26 June 1961, the ANC Freedom Day, Mandela released a letter to the South African newspapers from underground, calling for a national constitutional convention.[160] He also wrote a letter to Prime Minister Verwoerd to join in the convention.

Mandela wrote in the letter to the newspapers, "We of Umkhonto have always sought – as the liberation movement has sought – to achieve liberation without bloodshed and civil clash. We hope, even at this late hour, that our first actions will awaken everyone to a realization of the disastrous consequences to which the Nationalist policy is leading. We hope that we will bring the government and its supporters to their senses before it is too late, so that both the government and its policies can be changed before matters reach the desperate stage of civil war".[161]

On July 1961, Verwoerd offered B. J. Vorster, his deputy minister of education arts and science and of social welfare and pensions the portfolio of minister of justice. Vorster recollects that he said to Verwoerd that he should let him deal with the threat of subversion and revolution in his own way. He added that you could not fight communism with the Queensberry rules because you would lose. Verwoerd agreed with Vorster and said that he would leave him free to do what he had to do – within reason.[162]

A British newspaper reported on 3 August 1961 that a former pro-Nazi leader was now in the South African cabinet and commented, "The cabinet changes suggest an obstinate determination (on Verwoerd's part) to pursue the doctrinaire policy of apartheid uncompromisingly."[163]

According to Vorster and his security policemen, South Africa faced revolution. They reckoned if it were necessary to resolve a conflict between the interests of the state and the interests of the individual, the interests of the state would win. And if his policemen had to err, then he would prefer

---

157 Mandela, p. 259
158 Ibid., p. 261
159 Ibid., p. 262
160 Ibid., p. 263
161 Mandela, p. 274
162 D'Oliveira, p. 125
163 *London Daily Telegraph*, 3 August 1961, in D'Oliveira, p. 126

them to err in the direction of excessive zeal in protecting the interests of the state. Vorster recalls his thinking at the time, "In normal circumstances you can play the game according to the rules. But these were not normal times, the Communists were plotting revolution, bloodshed, violence and they were certainly not playing the game according to the rules. I realised that if the security forces had to play according to the rules it would be like fighting an implacable and vicious enemy with one hand tied behind your back. I was not going to send my men into battle with one hand tied behind their backs. I saw my way very clearly right from the outset because my own experiences during the war had given me a very clear insight into the whole thing."[164]

Since it was not normal times and the Communists were not playing the game according to the rules, neither would, in Vorster's own words, the security forces under his command.

As one of his first steps, Vorster signed a big number of banning orders under the existing Suppression of Communism Act.

Nearly all the non-white leaders in South Africa were restricted in their movements and activities. Most of them were called upon to resign their positions in the African National Congress or the South African Indian Congress. Many of them had been forbidden to attend any gatherings or to enter certain magisterial districts in the union. Albert Luthuli, president of the African National Congress, was forbidden to move away from his own district at Groutville, Natal.

Most of the bans were in force for two years, after which time they could be renewed. Some had already been renewed. The bans took affect under the Suppression of Communism Act of 1950. This allowed the minister of justice to prohibit from gatherings or organisations anyone suspected of furthering the aims of communism. Communism was defined under the act as aiming to bring about social economic or political changes in the country. Many of those convicted or "named" under the Suppression of Communism Act were not "Communists" in the usual sense of the term, but "statutory Communists" who came within the definition of the act.

Umkhonto chose 16 December 1961 for their first explosions, the day white South Africa celebrated the defeat of the Zulus under Dingaan at Blood River in 1838. Further explosions followed on New Year's Eve. The explosions took the government by surprise. They condemned the sabotage as heinous crimes while at the same time deriding it as the work of foolish amateurs. The explosions shocked white South Africans into the realization that they were sitting on top of a volcano. Black South Africans realised that the ANC was no longer an organisation of passive resistance.

---

164   D'Oliveira, p. 130

Umkhonto spurred a vicious and unrelenting government counter-offensive on a scale like never before. The special branch of the police now made it their number one mission to capture members of MK, and they would spare no effort to do so. They would show that nothing would stop them from rooting out what they saw as the greatest threat to their own survival.[165]

In January 1962, Verwoerd announced in parliament that South Africa intended to grant the Transkei self governing status, and it became a self-governing homeland the following year. The government had decided to accelerate the programme of separate development.

In the senate on 15 February 1962, Vorster announced far-reaching measures aimed at protecting the security of the state. This was his reaction to the new threat to state security in the form of acts of violence by Umkonto we Sizwe. On 12 May 1962, Vorster published details of the General Laws Amendment Bill (called the sabotage bill). Publication of the details of the sabotage bill sparked one of the longest and most heated political controversies in South Africa's history. Vorster remained implacable and unyielding.

The legislation made sabotage as serious an offence as treason, and it laid down a minimum penalty of five years and a maximum penalty of death. It was based on an extremely wide definition of sabotage, and it placed the onus on the accused to show that, if he wilfully committed one of the acts listed in the definition of sabotage, he was not guilty of it. It increased the state president's powers to ban subversive organisations and it provided the minister of justice with the power to order the house arrest of people he believed were a threat to the safety of the state. The minister's powers to prohibit people from attending gatherings (in terms of the Suppression of Communism Act) were increased, and it created a law on reporting on all people who were prohibited from attending meetings – nobody could henceforth publish anything said at any time by anybody who had been prohibited from attending meetings.

Vorster's elder brother, Koot, a theologian, tells the story of his brother John, who told him that he had underlined a passage in the Bible while still a student at Stellenbosch University.[166] During the period he was considering the issue of legislation to deal with sabotage he read the Bible, as he does every evening, and came to the underlined passage about Solomon and Shimei in 1Kings Chapter 2:36–46.

It reads, "And the King sent and called for Shimei, and said unto him, Build thee a house in Jerusalem and dwell there and go thee not forth any wither. For it shall be, that on the day that thou goest out, and passest over

---

165   Mandela, p. 275
166   as reported by D'Oliveira, p. 132

the brook Kidron, thou shalt know for certain that thou shalt surely die: thy blood shall be upon thy own head. And Shimei said unto the king, The saying is good: as my lord the King hath said, so will they servant do. And Shimei dwelt in Jerusalem many days. And it came to pass at the end of three years, that two of the servants of Shimei ran away unto Achish, son of Maacha, King of Gath. And they told Shimei, behold thy servants be in Gath. And Shimei arose and saddled his ass and went to Gath, to Achish, to see his servants: and Shimei went and brought his servants from Gath. And it was told Solomon that Shimei had gone from Jerusalem to Gath and was come again. And the King sent and called for Shimei and said unto him, Did I not make thee swear by the Lord, and protested unto thee saying, Know for certain that on the day thou goest out and walkest abroad any wither, that thou shalt surely die? And thou sadist unto me, The word that I have heard is good. Why then hast thou not kept the oath of the Lord, and the commandments that I have charged thee with? The King said moreover to Shimei, Thou knowest all the wickedness which thou heart is privy to, and thou didst to David, my father: therefore the Lord shall return thy wickedness upon thy own head. And the King Solomon shall be blessed, and the throne of David shall be established before the Lord forever. So the King commanded Benaiah, the son of Jehoiada; which went out, and fell upon him, that he died. And the Kingdom was established in the hand of Solomon".

A cynic could well ask the question, which Bible passage did Vorster find underlined when he was considering the ninety-day clause legislation?

In 1962 Mandela, who was operating underground at the time, left the country illegally for military training and to arrange training for other MK members. He was arrested on his return and sentenced to five years imprisonment for organising a stay-away and leaving the country without a passport.

At his trial in October 1962, Mandela questioned Prime Minister Verwoerd's private secretary, Neil Barnard, about the letter he wrote to Verwoerd at the end of March 1961 proposing a national constitutional convention. Barnard's answers were significant and revealing.

During questioning by Mandela, who was conducting his own defence, Barnard acknowledged that Africans did not vote in the South African parliament, provincial councils, and municipal councils. Barnard refused to agree with Mandela that in any civilized country in the world it would be scandalous for a prime minister to fail to reply to a letter raising vital issues affecting the majority of the citizens of that country. He explained that the tone of the letter was aggressive and discourteous, and for that reason the prime minister had not answered it. In a speech in parliament Verwoerd described the letter as arrogant.

During Mandela's trial at the end of October 1962 the general assembly of the UN voted in favour of sanctions against South Africa. At the same time acts of sabotage took place in Durban and Port Elizabeth, celebrating the UN vote and in protest at Mandela's trial.[167]

This issue of constitutional rights for blacks brings to the fore two leaders in a struggle for supremacy: Nelson Mandela and Hendrik Verwoerd. Both the ANC and the white government were prepared for violent conflict. Conflict was inevitable because of the intransigence of Verwoerd even to consider negotiations. The tragedy is that he had made up his mind to achieve separation or die. The new white republican government had no constitutional place for blacks.

A new phase of security enforcement started with Vorster's appointment of Hendrik van den Berg, a fellow inmate at Koffiefontein concentration camp for Ossewa Brandwag (pro-Nazi) activists during the Second World War. He was a senior officer in the security police and in the criminal investigations division. Lang Hendrik, as he was called, took office on 14 January 1963, as head of security police and later became head of the Bureau for State Security (called BOSS).

The Vorster–Van den Berg partnership led the NP government attack on the parties resisting apartheid through violent means. Van den Berg said that one of his conditions to take over security was that the security police force as it then existed should be disbanded, and that he would be able to draw to the new security police force the men he knew personally or knew as top policemen. He kept many of the old security policemen he knew, and brought in many more.[168]

He stated that they (security police) were fighting a revolution, and it was war. He saw the choice as being between revolution, violence, and bloodshed and the rule of law.[169]

Van den Berg became commissioner for police, and thereafter it was tradition to promote the head of security to head of the police force, with the exception of General De Witt. Also promotion in the police favoured security officials. If you refused service in the old Rhodesia, you skipped promotion. This came from the NP government which, after the 1948 elections, did not promote policemen who served in the Second World War beyond Africa.

Vorster told a NP meeting in Worcester on 20 April 1963, "That his new security bill was being framed in the full knowledge that South Africa's enemies did not play according to the rules. He added that he would ask

---

167   Mandela, p. 315
168   D'Oliveira, p. 141
169   D'Oliveira, p. 142

parliament for additional powers with which to fight subversion as often as he deemed this necessary – no matter how drastic these measures might be."[170]

Perhaps the toughest security legislation in South Africa's history was introduced by Minister Vorster in parliament on 23 April 1963 – the so-called ninety-days law.

Apart from closing certain legal loopholes and further excluding the courts from testing the validity of certain administrative actions, the General Laws Amendment Bill of 1963 gave the minister of justice the right to order the continued imprisonment without trial of certain people who had completed jail sentences for special crimes. It also gave all police commissioned officers the power to order the arrest and detention for up to ninety days on any single occasion of anybody suspected of committing an act of sabotage or any offence under the Suppression of Communism Act or the Unlawful Organisations Act, or anybody suspected of having information relating to the commission or intended commission of any such offence. The detainees were to be held incommunicado (except with permission of the minister of justice or a commissioned police officer) until such time as the commissioner of police was satisfied that they had answered all questions satisfactorily. No court of law would have the power to order the release of any ninety-day detainee. Many a detainee acknowledged privately that you could not hold out against the methods of interrogation during this time and gave the security police all the names of people with whom or activities with which they were involved against apartheid.

Vorster stated that the legislation was designed to break the back of Umkhonto and explained that the ninety day detention could be extended indefinitely.

Helen Suzman, the representative of the Progressive Party, cast a lone vote against the bill in parliament.

A storm of protest followed. The United Nations Special Committee on Apartheid called an urgent meeting to discuss this "new development". *The Times*, London, spoke of this "cruel and mind-breaking piece of administrative despotism" in a leading article on 24 April 1963. *The Star* headlined its editorial on 24 April ,"Guilt-edged security" and said that the legislation placed South Africans, as never before, at the mercy of the informer and the sneak.

Vorster told the house of assembly during the committee of supply debate on the justice vote on 12 June 1963 that Poqo, a black resistance group started in the Transkei, that attacked and killed whites had been knocked out, and that the ANC posed the biggest threat to South Africa. He told the house that, since the passing of the Sabotage Act in 1962, 126 people had

---

170   The *Rand Daily Mail*, 22 April 1963

been convicted, and none had received sentences of less than eight years. The courts were still dealing with a number of cases, and there were 511 persons awaiting trial on charges of sabotage. To date, 120 Poqo members had been convicted of murder and 77 were still in the process of being tried. Action had been taken against 670 persons in connection with continued membership of banned organisations. The number of active Poqo members arrested up to 5 June 1963 totalled 3246. There were certain incidents, and certain murders were committed ... but we can be grateful that there were only a few incidents, and it remained at those few incidents because measures were passed by this House to deal with the position, because the police had the necessary powers to take action when they were required to do so, and because the police, in the circumstances, were exceptionally efficient."

Vorster's reference to the murders committed by his security forces can only be described as euphemistic. In the measures he took, Vorster had the full confidence of Prime Minister Verwoerd.[171]

In 1995, the number of people who died in police custody had grown to 120, as reported at the public hearings of the Justice Portfolio Committee of Parliament concerning the Truth Commission Bill.

At the close of the parliamentary session in 1963 Mrs Helen Suzman, member of the Progressive Party, remarked that it was the most dangerous time in South Africa's history, and she

warned that attempts to enforce apartheid would mean the complete abandonment of the rule of law in South Africa. She said, "Any criticism is unpatriotic, recourse to the courts of the land is in defiance of the government ... the government bullies, threatens, and tries to intimidate anybody who offers it real opposition. And when this does not work, they resort to smear tactics."[172]

Mrs Suzman's prediction did in fact come to pass. Three times a state of emergency was declared in the years thereafter as the resistance to apartheid grew stronger, and the rule of law in South Africa had to be abandoned temporarily to enforce apartheid.

A reporter, Scott Haig, wrote in a Durban paper, "It is without enthusiasm that I comment on the parliamentary observers' automatic selection of Mr B. J. Vorster as the dominant ministerial figure of the session. For the first three years of his premiership, Dr Verwoerd lorded it loquaciously over the House of Assembly. Last session, and again this session, he lost his jaunty superiority and lost his ascendancy. More and more he has retired into the

---

171   D'Oliveira, p. 145
172   *Sunday Times*, 27 June 1963

shadows and, as the political stature of Mr B. J. Vorster has become enlarged perhaps grossly magnified out of his real importance."[173].

At the end of the 1963 parliamentary session Vorster was in full control of the police force. He had the prime minister's full confidence. Van den Berg had re-organised the security police, and the policemen were armed with greater powers than they had ever before had in peacetime. Poqo and the PAC had been smashed, and the security policemen had already begun effectively to infiltrate the Communist Party and the ANC.[174]

On 11 July 1963, the police raided Lillysleaf farm, the home of Arthur Goldreich, at Rivonia outside Johannesburg, and arrested seventeen people in terms of the ninety-day clause. Most were members of the high command of MK. One of them was the ANC leader Walter Sisulu, another was A. M. Kathrada, a listed Communist and leader of the Indian Congress. Also arrested was L. G. Bernstein, of the Congress of Democrats, Govan Mbeki of the ANC, Arthur Goldreich and his wife, Dr H. Festenstein, Dennis Goldberg, and Bob Hepple. Nelson Mandela was soon added to the list. Other arrests followed in different parts of the country, and Vorster commented grimly a few days later that "There is no doubt that the police were now tearing the Spear of the Nation apart."[175]

In an interview Vorster said that people must realise that the Communists were playing for very high stakes indeed. These were not men who play according to the rules. To try to combat them with conventional methods was just a waste of time.[176]

On 9 October 1963, eleven men appeared on charges of sabotage in the Supreme Court in the Palace of Justice in Pretoria. It was alleged that seven of them constituted the high command of the Spear of the Nation, and that the eleven men had conspired with others to commit a number of acts of sabotage which were committed in South Africa in preparation for guerrilla warfare and outside invasion. The case of the state against the national high command and others, known as the Rivonia Trial, served before Mr Quartus de Wet, judge-president of Transvaal. The name of the case was changed to the State against Nelson Mandela and Others.

One of the accused men was Abraham (Braam) Fischer, Q. C., Johannesburg advocate, son of a former Orange Free State judge-president, a respected member of Johannesburg society – and a dedicated Communist.

On 12 June 1964 all the accused were sentenced to life imprisonment by Justice de Wet.

---

173   *Sunday Times*, 7 July 1963
174   D'Oliveira, p145
175   *Die Vaderland*, 15 July 1963
176   The *Sunday Tribune*, 20 July 1963

Looksmart Ngudle, first to die in 1963 under the ninety-day clause

MK commander Looksmart Ngudle was arrested, tortured, and sixteen days later, on 4 September 1963, became the first detainee to die under the ninety-day detention law.

Looksmart Ngudle, from Kwa Zali village near Alice in the Eastern Cape, passed into

history just three months after the ninety-day detention act became law.

The police told the family that Looksmart had been arrested by the security police and had hanged himself with his pyjama cord in his cell in Pretoria. No one believed he had killed himself. They knew his captors had murdered him.

His history was reported by Shaun Smillie who undertook an intensive investigation to prove his story as reported in *The Star* on 5-7 June 2007. Smillie was assisted by a strong team including Madelein Fullard, head of the National Prosecuting Authority's missing person's task team in Pretoria, anthropologists Louis Fonderbinder from Argentina and Mosongwa Mosothuane from the University of the Witwatersrand, and surveyor Dirk Olivier. They uncovered what the committee set up by the TRC in 1996 failed to do.

The security police, especially the interrogators, welcomed Vorster's ninety-day detention act, which became law only three months before Looksmart died. No longer did they have to bring prisoners before courts within two days of arrest. No more defence lawyers. No more scrutiny of how they treated detainees. No more taunts from the enemy as they walked free. The new law gave them the power to arrest anyone for ninety days, and another ninety days, and another … "until eternity", as Vorster boasted. And it gave them the power to hold their prisoners in solitary confinement, hidden from the courts and their lawyers.

Looksmart joined the ANC in the 1950s and became actively involved in the struggle. He then joined the ANC's military wing, Umkhonto we Sizwe, and became an MK commander. He was helped by his friend Denis Goldberg, the organisation's technical officer. Mr Technico, as Goldberg's comrades nicknamed him, had kick-started the armed struggle in 1961 by making two bombs that had failed to go off on the night of apartheid's holiest day, 16 December, the Day of Covenant (previously known as Dingaans Day).

The police never caught Looksmart on one of their raids, but they had been watching him for years – not for what he did, but for what he said. In a document stamped GEHEIM (secret) an *impimpi* (informer) recorded

Looksmart's words at a gathering of the Cape Western Consultative Committee in Windemere on 18 January 1959. "Today our women must carry passes. We are divorced from our wives. We must fight here. We must free ourselves."

Memos on his movements, his speeches, and his associates landed on the desk of Justice Minister John Vorster. He was marked for action.

Given the date of his arrest, 19 August, and his departure from Caledon three days after his arrival there, he probably reached Pretoria by 23 or 24 August. From then until Tuesday, 3 September, there is no record of him.

On Wednesday, 4 September, Looksmart refused food and told an inmate, "This electric shock has really injured me." The next day, before breakfast, Govan Mbeki, a prisoner, heard a whisper from under his cell door, "They have killed Looksmart Ngudle."

Looksmart's body was buried in a desolate cemetery called The Field of the Hanged in Mamelodi, near Pretoria. In the 1960s and '70s this was the final destination of scores of condemned black political and criminal prisoners. The head of the missing persons task team of the National Prosecuting Authority in Pretoria, Madelein Fullard, traced Looksmart's remains to the Mamelodi cemetery. The surveyor found the exact position of Grave 5910, and DNA tests proved the remains were that of Looksmart, was Shaun Smillie's conclusion.[177]

Failed attempts to incorporate the British protectorates

One of the arguments in parliament from opposition party spokesmen against the Union of South Africa becoming a republic was that the possibility of incorporation of the British protectorates would be lost. Verwoerd's reply on 8 February 1961 in parliament was that it would be foolhardy to believe in incorporation after the failed attempts of Botha, Smuts, and Hertzog because Britain did not honour its word, as indicated by the developments in Africa and the constitutions Britain approved for the High Commission territories.[178] He said the black areas could attain political autonomy coupled with economic interdependence with South Africa in a commonwealth association and that the High Commission territories could join this association whether a republic or not.[179] With this announcement, Verwoerd did in fact give up on the idea of incorporation.

At a meeting of the Transvaal congress of the National Party in September 1962, Verwoerd declared that the incorporation of the protectorates was not

177   *The Star*, 7 June 2007
178   Pelzer, p.431
179   Pelzer, p431

possible and not wise. The republic was prepared to accept the protectorates as good neighbours and cooperation could be achieved if the protectorates sought friendship.[180] He would also have been thinking of the opposite possibility; that these territories could align themselves to the hostile independent African countries.

Three weeks later Eric Louw, the South African minister of foreign affairs, referred to the speech of Verwoerd in a policy declaration at the General Assembly of the United Nations on 24 September 1962 in New York. Louw referred to a statement in a resolution on Basutoland, Bechuanaland, and Swaziland, which was recommended to the General Assembly, expressing its profound concern if the Republic of South Africa were to annex these territories and condemning any attempt to jeopardize the right of the people of these territories to establish their own independent states.

Louw said that the prime minister declared in parliament on 9 February 1961 that the High Commission territories would not be incorporated into South Africa.[181]

Surprisingly, on 3 September 1963 Verwoerd, again at the annual congress of the NP of Transvaal, made an offer to Britain that South Africa administer the three British High Commission territories and lead them to independence in the same way it was busy doing with Transkei. He would steer them away from integration. Whites in those areas would become voters in the RSA and citizens of the High Commission territories living in the Republic would be voters in the protectorates.[182]

So serious was Verwoerd with this proposal that he had it printed and secretly distributed in the protectorates by the government, particularly to the chiefs. Nothing came of it.[183]

Britain rejected South Africa's offer. According to the *London Times,* no official notice was taken in British government circles of Verwoerd's proposal to take over the protectorates. The British standpoint was unchanged from the stand taken by the previous prime minister, Winston Churchill, in April 1954, in the Commons. He declared, "There can be no question of her majesty's government agreeing at the present time to the transfer of Basutoland, Bechuanaland, and Swaziland to the Union of South Africa. We are pledged, since the South Africa Act of 1909, not to transfer these territories until their inhabitants have been consulted and until the United Kingdom Parliament has had an opportunity of expressing its views." [184]

---

180   H. H. H. Bierman, p. 141
181   Ibid
182   *Die Transvaler,* 4 September 1963
183   WABotha, p. 432
184   *The Times,* London, 5 September 1963

The British ambassador to the United Nations again made it clear to the General Assembly in 1965 that the British government had no intention of transferring the protectorates to South Africa.

Thereafter Mr Cecil King, the British representative at the UN Special Commission on Colonialism, told the commission in July 1963, "I have the authority of my government to state that there is no question of these territories being incorporated in South Africa against the wishes of its peoples."[185]

At the Transvaal NP congress on 8 September 1964 in Johannesburg, Verwoerd reconfirmed that it was no longer possible or wise to incorporate the High Commission Territories.[186] Botswana and Lesotho became independent in 1966 and Swaziland in 1968 and Transkei only in 1976.

Verwoerd's assassination 6 September 1966 and a critical evaluation

A week after the police shot dead a number of terrorists who crossed into South West Africa with arms from Angola, Chief Leabua Jonathan, prime minister of Lesotho, made a historic visit to South Africa in September 1966. He was the first black head of government to visit South Africa officially. After more than three hours of private discussion, Verwoerd and Jonathan issued a joint statement pledging mutual friendship and nonintervention in their respective countries' internal affairs.

The day before Verwoerd was stabbed to death in parliament on 6 September 1966, newspapers speculated about the major speech which Dr Verwoerd would make when he spoke during the course of the debate on the prime minister's vote. It was expected that Verwoerd would pay particular attention to South Africa's relations with its black neighbours. It was also expected that he would deal with the issue of terrorism, which had added a new and potentially dangerous dimension to the South African security battle.

Verwoerd was fatally stabbed in parliament on 6 September 1966, by Dimitri Tsafendas. The official report did not reveal the reasons for the murder. No evidence of a conspiracy was found. Many questions remain unanswered. These include explanations for Tsafendas taking up residence in Cape Town; the reasons for taking up the job as a messenger in parliament; why he bought a knife; why he selected Verwoerd for the attack. Did he bear a grudge against the prime minister as a person or as proponent of apartheid?

---

185   Ibid
186   W A Botha, p.434

Did he have knowledge of and object to apartheid? If he was psychologically disturbed and unstable, was he not a subject of manipulation, and if so, by whom? Was he used by financial powers who wanted to end further entrenchment of apartheid? Investigation under General Hendrik van den Berg, did not provide answers to these questions.

Van den Berg, the head of security, questioned Tsafendas for forty-eight hours and reported that it was a one-man job, and that Tsafendas was not responsible for his actions.

Mr Justice Andrew Beyers, judge president of the Cape, after medical and psychiatric evidence, found that Tsafendas was mentally disordered and that he should be jailed at the state president's pleasure. He referred to Tsafendas as a lunatic with a mind so diseased that he could not find whether Tsafendas was guilty or not. Nobody explained how such a man came to be appointed as a messenger in parliament in the first place.

Something similar could be said of Verwoerd in much the same sense as remarked by the chairman of the Nobel Peace Prize committee at the presentation ceremony in Stockholm where President Mandela and President de Klerk received their awards, that these men were not saints. They are politicians in a complicated reality.[187] The two award winning statesmen succeeded in leading a process of peaceful transition, while Verwoerd tried to create a dispensation of separating whites and blacks by wanting to adapt reality to his ideology.

Verwoerd's policy of separate development was doctrinaire. He was seeking to apply his and the Afrikaners' doctrine of apartheid in all circumstances, even though it was theoretical and impractical. This was the difference between him and Vorster. Vorster was less doctrinaire. To a greater extent it was also the difference between him and P. W. Botha. But his two successors as prime ministers did hold fast to their belief that black majority rule could not be allowed.

Difficult to understand was Verwoerd's rejection of the recommendations of the Tomlinson Commission in 1954 to accelerate development with a great increase in capital expenditure for land purchases, agricultural and industrial development in the black areas. He caused a great opportunity to be lost to make political capital out of greater development of black areas.[178]

Verwoerd himself did nothing about consolidation of land in black areas. His minister of black administration and development, Mr M. C. Botha, said in an interview that he and one of his deputy ministers, S. Froneman,

---

187   Betty Glad and Rober Blanton, F W de Klerk and Nelson Mandela : a study in cooperative transformational leadership, *Presidential Studies Quarterly*, volume 27, Issue 3, 1997, p.11

literally had to dig the papers on consolidation out of the forgotten files and accept the issue as a task and an objective.[188]

Furthermore nothing was done about the elimination of white spots in the Transkei under Verwoerd, despite the fact that General Louis Botha had indicated this as a policy goal during the early years of union.[189]

When Transkei gained independence in 1976 not all the allocated land had been bought. The reason for this was that Verwoerd did not give priority to the program to purchase the land.[190]

Another issue was the slow pace of political development. The first expectations about representative government, which was granted to Transkei in 1963, was recorded as early as 1908. In his report of 1908, the chief magistrate of Transkei broached the subject of the expectations that already existed that the functions of the Transkeian General Council be expanded from advisory status to representative government, although not yet justified at that time.[191] Limited legislative and executive powers was granted only fifty-seven years later with the system of black authorities that was accepted in Transkei in 1955. In 1963, eight years later, Transkei received representative government. By 1966 virtually all the colonial countries in Africa had received independence.

In 1959 when parliament passed the Promotion of Bantu Self Government Act, which created eight separate ethnic Bantustans, the minister of Bantu administration and development said that the welfare of every individual and population group could best be developed within its own national community. Africans, he said, could never be integrated into the white community, which echoed Verwoerd's policy. Mandela called this Bantustan policy, whereby 70 percent of the people would be apportioned only 13 percent of the land, immoral. He said under the new policy, even though two-thirds of Africans lived in so-called white areas, they could have citizenship only in their own tribal homelands. The scheme gave blacks neither freedom in white areas nor independence in what was deemed their areas. Mandela said although Verwoerd thought that the creation of the Bantustans would engender so much goodwill that they would never become the breeding grounds for rebellion, in reality, it was quite the opposite.[192] Rural areas were in turmoil as in Zeerust and Sekhukhuneland.

Mandela's reference to two-thirds of the Africans living in white areas touches the heart of the failure of the apartheid policy. Since 1948, the policy outlined an eventual return of blacks from the white area to the traditional

188   W A Botha, Ibid
189   W A Botha, p.471
190   W A Botha, Ibid
191   W A Botha, p.471
192   Mandela, p.217

black areas. De Klerk wrote in his autobiography that Verwoerd and his advisors projected that the date of 1978 would see the return flow of blacks from the white areas back to the black areas. The early eighties proved this to be fictional and was one of the reasons that called for a rethink of policy.

Industrialisation in black areas was supposed to stimulate the outflow. It did not take place. Verwoerd refused capital expenditure for industrial development. He himself calculated that by the year 2000 only six million or seven million blacks would be living in the white areas, whilst it had grown to nearly twenty million.

The idea of incorporation of British protectorates and a realignment of African areas for independence also failed because the UK rejected it.

Smuts was the leader who said to the Natives Representative Council in 1946 that a form of political rights should be formulated for blacks in white areas. Verwoerd refused this idea and had the new minister of justice, B. J. Vorster, develop a security framework of laws and security police to deal with resistance from blacks with force. Political rights for blacks in white areas had no place in his policies.

Verwoerd's emphasis that schools for blacks be oriented and focused towards the black community was coupled with his rejection of Western and English culture in the school system. This was a one-sided and imbalanced approach to general education. English and Western culture had many elements of philosophical and cultural value that were universal. It was wrong to base the new system exclusively on the black community's culture and needs, and also to effect a monopolistic take over of schools catering for blacks; through a new process of registration funding and teacher requirements.

The belief among blacks grew that the requirement of the Afrikaans language as a medium of instruction in at least one subject in schools should be rejected because it was the language of the oppressive Afrikaner apartheid government. Apartheid was associated with the Afrikaner government and the Afrikaans language. To enforce it was asking for opposition and resistance. It sparked the uprising in Soweto schools in 1976 and was further instigated by the black consciousness movement.

In providing for advanced education in the black areas Verwoerd was ignoring the needs of the blacks and industry and commerce in white urban areas. It was wrong to limit technical education to a certain level of employment in white areas. Verwoerd was not realistic in thinking that the black areas exclusively needed black people trained at advanced levels and that this need did not exist in the white areas also. This idea was tied to his belief that black areas would become a draw card for blacks, and the stream of black workers from the black areas to the white areas would be reversed. It is difficult to understand how this would happen if in the very next year he rejected the Tomlinson Commission report to invest R207 million in a development program for black areas.

Another negative aspect of the NP government's education policy was to peg the annual budget for black education to R13 million and to rely on taxes from black people for additional funds. It soon became inadequate, and later had to be supplemented by state income. Without sufficient funds, the provision of education was restricted and retarded.

The failed state of KwaNdebele – a Verwoerd concept

KwaNdebele, designated to be a separate state adjacent to Bronkhorstpruit, near Pretoria, was the smallest political unit in the apartheid system. Locations and neighbouring black towns adjacent to cities were referred to as dormitory towns because the men were away working in the week and were at home only on weekends. KwaNdebele could be referred to as a dormitory state. Visitors to the area on a weekday saw empty streets and only women and children at home. The men were bussed out on Mondays in great numbers to places of work in Pretoria, Vanderbijl Park, and further.

The system of apartheid uprooted thousands of people, resettled them 100 kilometres from their jobs and then subsidised their travel to work by the amount of R1500 per person per year. Such was the case of some 20,000 KwaNdebele workers. During 1987, the government spent R280 million subsidizing bus transport for black commuters who had been relocated more than 100 km from their work.[193]

As a prelude to independence, P. W. Botha attempted to consolidate the so-called KwaNdebele state by incorporating the Moutse areas, which were traditionally part of Lebowa. After 150 people were killed in protest against the annexation the KwaNdebele legislature rejected independence. On 29 March 1988, the appeal court in Bloemfontein declared the attempt to incorporate the Moutse areas unlawful. The court ruled that by attempting to incorporate 120,000 Pedis, or North Sothos, into a Ndebele or Nguni homeland, Botha had used his powers for a purpose for which they were not intended. KwaNdebele was one of four black territories which refused to accept independence.

In the case of KwaNdebele the doubling of its size was simply a weak attempt to make the miniscule state look a little more respectable. In the process, Botha rode roughshod over the wishes of the Pedis and mocked his own principles.[194]

---

193   Rhoodie, p.247
194   Rhoodie, p.150

Tribute by Laurence Gandar, editor of the Rand Daily Mail

The most perceptive evaluation of Verwoerd, the politician, was given by his most vigorous critic, Gandar, who wrote in the *Rand Daily Mail* of 10 September 1966, "This was a man making his mark on the times because of an outlook which he, more than any other, symbolized and upheld in all its startling, abrasive unorthodoxy …. In his mind and in his speeches, the National Party's policy of 'baasskap', white supremacy, refined and rationalized into the policy of separate development with vertical rather than horizontal lines of division. He visualised a series of ethnically-organised African homelands, sustained by border industries and gradually evolving into independent states which would one day enter a confederation of friendly, co-operating white and black states in Southern Africa. This was his grand design for the future. I have been amongst the many who have criticised this policy, but I recognised its political significance in that, at a time of continuing turmoil in Africa, Verwoerd came to be widely regarded as the one man who had a positive plan for South Africa which the Whites found acceptable and which seemed to them to be fair to the non-White as well … The point was that he came to be recognised as the principal architect and driving force behind separate development. This was national policy, ostensibly endorsed at the polls and he was fully in charge of it … But it is in the sphere of foreign policy that Verwoerd made his most singular and personalized contribution. For, although he stood for a policy at home that ran completely counter to the main currents of world thought, he nevertheless had a lively sense of international realities and could judge with great shrewdness how far he could go and when to hold back. Early on, he managed to take South Africa out of the multiracial Commonwealth and yet retain Britain's friendship. He was coldly critical of the United Nations, yet stiffly correct in his dealings with it. He confidently predicted the collapse of democracy in Africa and was proved largely correct. Racial disorders in the United States and Britain strengthened his belief in the incompatibility of White and Black living in the same society. At the same time, he was busy proving his point at the time of his death that separate White and Black states could enjoy friendly relations in Southern Africa. But it was for his handling of Rhodesia that he was seen at his skilful best. From the formal posture of neutrality, he gave enough help to

Rhodesia to keep her going (thereby showing sanctions to be less than immediately effective) and yet not quite enough to provoke an open clash with Britain. He knew the risks but he was prepared to take them because of the high stakes involved and because he knew the strengths and the weaknesses of the parties involved, such as the United States, Britain, the African states and the United Nations."

The most serious of Verwoerd's beliefs that could be called to question was that it was God's will that he should uphold apartheid as leader on behalf of the Afrikaner Nationalists and the country. It was founded on the misguided interpretation of the Dutch Reformed Church that apartheid was scripturally justified. Twenty years after Verwoerd's death, the DRC Synod confessed to the biblical truth that apartheid was a sin.

CHAPTER 5

CHANGE AMIDST GROWING RESISTANCE, 1966–89

Prime Minister Vorster started with a lie and President Vorster ended with a lie

Just two years into his term as prime minister, Vorster showed the colours he earned as minister of justice and political head suppressing black resistance to white domination, by using General Van Den Berg and the security force to investigate an anonymous Afrikaans pamphlet deriding the NP politicians and policies by portraying their change in emphasis from Verwoerd's hard-line conservative standpoint as liberal. It was a parody and could be compared to newspaper cartoons. The second of two pamphlets was a film review.

They were written by two theology students and a part-time student at the University of Pretoria. The theology students were later ordained as ministers of religion in two of the Afrikaans Protestant churches. Mr Vorster was convinced that his own right-wing members of parliament had written it, although without any evidence, and instructed General Van Den Berg and the security police to find the authors. The security police questioned two of the authors at the police headquarters in Pretoria, according to a published sworn affidavit by the students, and told them they were instructed by the prime minister to do so. The students had acted on their own initiative with this political prank without anybody else involved, as was subsequently discovered by the security police. General Van Den Berg referred to them as lesser lights. No charges were laid. No law was transgressed. The state security was not threatened.

Nevertheless, Prime Minister Vorster, after receiving General Van Den Berg's report of his investigations, immediately made an astounding announcement, which was given prominent front page coverage by *Die Burger* on 29 June 1968. Prime Minister Vorster was delivering the opening address at the youth congress of the National Youth Council of the Federation of Afrikaans Cultural Organisations (FAK) at the University of Pretoria.

He said that pamphlets had recently been distributed by Afrikaner sons in Pretoria. "I know who everyone of them is. They are good sons who could have had a good future but were used by older people who did not have the courage to do it themselves or say what was written in the pamphlets. They had directly and indirectly misused those sons," Mr Vorster said. He was telling a lie in public and was in fact warning everybody what he would do to anybody who in the slightest had different thoughts on policy, particularly his own party members. This was a display of intolerance at its best, but ridiculously unbecoming a strong leader of government. Significantly, the party followers accepted Vorster's and the security police's actions and conduct with silent acquiescence. This mentality of a group following its leader led them into following President de Klerk in abdicating white supremacy in favour of black majority rule in 1994, based on de Klerk's promise of group rights.

At the beginning of 1970, Mr Vorster's government, worried by deteriorating relations with key Western states, had decided to add covert activities to its efforts to improve the image of South Africa abroad. Secrecy was Mr Vorster's forte.

Establishing *The Citizen* newspaper was the riskiest project of all, and, finally, produced the heaviest political fall-out, fatal to the careers of both Dr Mulder, a cabinet minister, and Mr Vorster. It was not so much the concept of financing a new newspaper with taxpayers' money which was so dangerous, as the fact that it could have been and was seen, maliciously, as simply an effort to bolster the National Party in the Transvaal, led by Dr Mulder. The idea that the NP would be favoured by a new English language newspaper is what people were later led to believe. That idea is what the Erasmus Commission found, and that idea is what ultimately ended Mr Vorster's career. In the eyes of the press and the Erasmus Commission, *The Citizen* project was the core of the information scandal.[195]

Mr Vorster's handling of the entire drama of the information scandal and *The Citizen* newspaper contract showed him to be a man who had lost

---

195 Rhoodie, p. 39

control of the situation and who feared using his massive public standing to defuse the issue. He decided that it was time to move to the safety of the presidency.

On 20 September 1978, Mr Vorster announced his retirement as prime minister and leader of the NP at a press conference in the Union Buildings, Pretoria. The NP caucus then elected the minister of defence, P. W. Botha, as leader of the NP and prime minister. After Judge Anton Mostert disclosed to the press in October 1978 that *The Citizen* newspaper was secretly funded by the Department of Information, under Minister Mulder, Transvaal leader of the NP, P. W. Botha appointed a judicial commission of inquiry. The commission consisted of two government officials and a judge from the Orange Free State division of the Supreme Court, known as the Erasmus Commission. The two officials who sat with Mr Justice Rudolph Erasmus were career public service officials: Mr Justice Lategan (having been promoted in the interim) and Mr Smallberger. Mr Justice Lategan told a public audience in Paarl that when they had to weigh the evidence of General van den Berg (Vorster's crony) they did not know whether they were dealing with "a liar or a madman." General van den Berg sued the judge. In the out-of-court settlement, Mr Lategan had to pay compensation and apologise in writing.[196]

About two months before Mr Vorster's resignation as state president in June 1979, Mr P. W. Botha had told Mr Louwrens Muller, leader of the house and the man who sat next to him in parliament, several times that Mr Vorster would have to go. "We will have to get rid of Mr Vorster as state president so that there will be an end to the attacks on the government because of the information affair," he said. During the no-confidence debate, he had also said, "We won't be able to put a stop to the information affair as long as Mr Vorster remains state president."[197]

If the report of the Erasmus commission on the information scandal had not sullied Mr Vorster's honour and integrity, he would never have resigned. Mr Vorster was made out to be a liar in the report. No person with self-respect could remain state president. He resigned on 4 June 1979.[198]

So the question is, what political developments or changes occurred under the Vorster term? First he got rid of a right-wing faction in the NP under Dr Hertzog and Mr Jaap Marais and crushed their new opposition party in a general election that left them without parliamentary representation. He continued loosening Verwoerd's strict anti-integration stance in sport and liquor laws pertaining to sport amenities. In 1975, he withdrew the South

---

196   *The Cape Times*, 7 December 1978

197   Rhoodie, p.79
198   Rhoodie, p.82

African police serving in the old Rhodesia and took a neutral stand in the negotiations between Britain and the Smith government.

After first announcing in Windhoek at a National Party congress that legislation was being prepared that would more closely link South West Africa with South Africa and integrate the administrations which started under Verwoerd, Vorster changed course. Instead of drawing SWA closer to South Africa, he started working hard for the territory's self-determination and ultimate independence. Questioned on this course of action, Vorster replied by pointing to a statement in the government-published *Survey of South West Africa* for 1967 which said quite clearly that it was the people of SWA who would decide on their own future. He said his whole strategy on SWA was two-fold: to get the people in the territory to realise that they would have to take the initiative in solving the SWA question and to buy time for this process to be completed.[199]

Vorster's next step in the field of security was the creation of the Bureau for State Security which the opposition and the English-language newspapers quickly dubbed BOSS, to the annoyance of both the bureau and the government. Vorster was creating a South African CIA which would, *inter alia*, take over foreign intelligence from the country's military intelligence service.

Hendrik van den Berg, who had been selected as the next commissioner of the South African police, was appointed head of the bureau and security adviser to the prime minister. What few people realised at the time was that Van den Berg's major function would be the creation of contacts in Africa and the establishment of lines of communication between Pretoria and African capitals.[200]

In fact, this whole outward movement initiative was, as far as Africa was concerned, led by Van den Berg and in cooperation with the Department of Information with its secret projects under Dr Eschel Rhoodie. No doubt Van den Berg could also operate his security operations under this guise, spying on ANC activities in African countries.

Vorster paid a state visit to Malawi in 1970, and President Hastings K. Banda of Malawi made an official visit to South Africa in 1971, the first African head of state ever to do so. During this period, South Africa claimed to have established relations with a dozen African countries. For the most part, however, African nations remained aloof. Apart from Malawi, no African nation had established diplomatic relations with South Africa, who had hoped that a clear divorce could be made between economic and political issues. However, its internal racial policies remained an insuperable

199   D'Oliviera, p. 223
200   D'Oliviera, p.241,242

obstacle to diplomatic rapprochement on the African continent. Senegal's former president, Leopold Senghor, was quoted as having said in 1971, "I am not against dialogue, but I believe in dialogue at the right time. South Africa must take the first step. She must prove that she has had dialogue with her own people."[201]

The OAU officially opposed dialogue with South Africa in 1971, effectively silencing the movement. In the mid-1970s, however, contact resumed. In 1974, Vorster met with Houphouët-Boigny in the Ivory Coast, and in 1975 with then-president William R. Tolbert in Liberia. All publicly acknowledged discussions between South Africa and the other northern countries of Africa ended abruptly with South Africa's foray into Angola in 1975, which unified Africa in a call for South Africa's isolation.[202]

In 1970, the OAU began a campaign for an effective arms embargo against South Africa. This embargo was adopted by the United Nations as a recommended action in 1975 and as mandatory policy by the Security Council in 1977. In 1973, OPEC imposed an oil embargo against South Africa. These particular efforts have had only minimal effect.[203]

Vorster resigned as president in June 1979 before new constitutional arrangements could be implemented. The NP approved a legislative structure of three parliaments for whites, coloured, and Indians. Nothing was approved for blacks, but the approval was a step in the direction of power sharing. It was pursued under Vorster's successor, Prime Minister P. W. Botha, but with major changes leading to the new 1983 constitution.

At this time most Afrikaners doubted that radical reform was either necessary or desirable. Most rejected any genuine power-sharing arrangement in a common society, and most believed that the status quo, with some modification, would best serve white political, economic, and social interests. Underlying all these attitudes was their deep-seated belief in the racial superiority of whites and a fear of the consequences of black rule.

The DRC document : Race, People, Nation, 1974, affirming apartheid

In 1974 the document Race, People (Groups) and Nation of the DRC was accepted by the General Synod of the DRC held in Cape Town, 16-25 October, 1974. The document concluded with appreciation of the stance and actions of the central government and other government authorities, its cabinet ministers, departments, and officials, and with its successful progress

201   *SA Time running out*, p.295
202   Ibid
203   *SA Time running out*, p.297

in finding solutions to the problems of a multinational state. These words of appreciation were an acceptance of the apartheid dispensation and a rejection of the main issue of voting rights for black people in parliament. The document addressed the position of the church and other churches within a political framework of race (biological), volk (cultural) and nation (constitutional). This document was a rejection of the reality of a multiracial, multicultural, multinational state, and of the worth of the individual in South Africa.

In the introduction, the document was associated with the farmers in the eastern districts of the Cape Colony and the Voortrekkers (before 1834). The concept of separate languages, cultures, and levels of civilization developed from the expansion of the Great Trek and led to separate churches for the different population groups. It was further stated that this natural development had blessed results and in no small measure influenced the later constitutional development and political thought in South Africa. In essence, a statement was made that the DRC contributed to and was partly responsible for the ideology and the system of apartheid.

The document claims scripture as the basis of the central theme of its message, namely to proclaim the way of salvation in Christ and the coming of the Kingdom. It should be noted that the method of proclaiming the message of salvation was to be done in separate churches to separate racial groups. Secondly, it proclaimed that the Kingdom of God was to be expected. There are different interpretations of this concept. The expected Kingdom of God could refer to the expected coming of Christ. Another interpretation is that the believer on earth is already a subject of the Kingdom of God, which is in heaven and on earth at the same time. The believer is a subject of God's Kingdom on earth and shares it with believers from all other groups, peoples, and races. [Matthew 6:33, Romans 14:17, Luke 17:21]

The document does not refer to any of the declarations of previous synods in which apartheid was justified on theological and biblical grounds. It does express a new justification of apartheid not based on scripture by calling the policy a practical solution. This also reiterated, although indirectly, the rejection by the DRC of the declaration by a meeting of the World Council of Churches in Cottesloe in 1960 against apartheid, which was supported by Rev. Beyers Naude.

The church with this declaration of 1974 was not leading the way nor was it ahead of its time with regards to a movement in the direction of change away from the belief in apartheid. On the contrary, it was strengthening the entrenched position of the Vorster government regardless of changed circumstances, growing opposition, and resistance to the maintenance of the apartheid system of exclusion of voting rights for blacks and of restrictions on black and white association at all levels.

By the amazing grace of God, a great number of blacks in South Africa were converted to Christianity. They are also part of the Kingdom of God and they form the natural allies for better relationships between blacks and whites. To them also Afrikaner Christians owe an apology for apartheid.

The United Nations rejects Transkei's independence 1976

A day before the Transkei parliament approved legislation to become independent on 26 October 1976, the UN Special Committee against Apartheid approved a resolution in which the establishment of Bantustans by the South African government and the sham independence of Transkei was condemned because it consolidated the inhumane policy of apartheid, would destroy the territorial integrity of South Africa, would prolong the supremacy of the white minority, and withhold the inalienable rights from the blacks.

The independence of Transkei was rejected and declared invalid, and all governments were called upon to deny any form of recognition of the so-called independent Transkei and to avoid any relations with Transkei and the other black areas.[204]

On the same day, the UN General Assembly accepted a resolution in which it called on every government and organisation to boycott any black area that became independent from South Africa, nor give recognition to it, and to inform the South African government that the international community would never accept that Transkei or any other black area should become a separate political entity.[205]

The standpoint of the British government concerning independent black states in South Africa was expressed in a declaration of the British embassy: "We wish to see a just and free society in South Africa based on racial equality, and to that end we are doing all that we can to encourage the policies of internal reform. We along with all other independent states, except South Africa, do not recognise the so-called independent homelands. These states are not fully independent and we see them as an intrinsic part of the policies of apartheid and separate development policies which we reject and abhor. We, therefore, have no contact with the independent homelands."[206]

---

204 Republick of Transkei, Debates of the National Assembly, 29 October 1976, p.7 in W
      A Botha thesis
205 Ibid
206 *Daily Dispatch*, 7 April 1980

The result was that Transkei as a nation did not receive any international recognition. As regards diplomatic ties it was totally ignored except for relations with South Africa.

Resistance to Bantu education and Steve Biko's death, 12 September 1977

A lull had developed in the ANC's ongoing actions of resistance to the apartheid government because of effective security measures. This inaction was not to the liking of the young black people. They decided to demonstrate their dissatisfaction by agitating against the government's school system for blacks.

Resistance to Bantu education continued during the 1960s and early 1970s. However, it did not have much impact until 1976 when the Soweto student uprising occurred. The 1976 Soweto uprising became one of the most significant events in contemporary South African history.

In a letter written on 8 May 1976, Desmond Tutu, then serving as the Anglican dean of Johannesburg, warned Prime Minister John Vorster that the political climate was "rapidly deteriorating." Reviewing the "blatant injustice and suffering" from such practices as forcing African men to leave their families to work as migrants, detention without trial, and police harassment, he professed "a growing nightmarish feeling that unless something drastic is done very soon then bloodshed and violence are going to happen in South Africa almost inevitably." Vorster dismissed the letter as "propaganda."

Officials later blamed the Soweto uprising of 16 June and the months of unrest that followed on Communist agitators. But Judge Pieter Cillie, serving as a one-man investigatory commission, finally reported on 1 March 1980 that the outbreaks of violence were largely attributable to government policies and the insensitivity of officials. Racially discriminatory policies, he said, "did not only cause dissatisfaction, but among many, a great hate. This dissatisfaction and hate was one of the foremost creators of a spirit of unrest."[207]

The reasons for the uprising by Soweto students in June 1976 included the system of Bantu education, and in particular that Soweto schools had to learn Afrikaans as one of the official languages, and that Afrikaans was a medium of instruction in at least one subject.

The students were in rebellion against the apartheid government, and the Afrikaans language issue was a cause for action. They were becoming

---

207 *S A Time running out*, p.181

increasingly impatient with their elders' more passive than active approach. The black consciousness movement further fuelled rebellion.

Stephen Bantu Biko was a nonviolent anti-apartheid activist in South Africa in the 1960s and early 1970s. Stephen Biko was born in Ginsberg in King Williams Town in the Eastern Cape Province on 18 December 1946. He was a student at the University of Natal Medical School. Initially he was involved with the multiracial National Union of South African Students, but after he became convinced that black, Indian, and coloured students needed an organisation of their own, he helped found the South African Students' Organisation (SASO) in 1968 and was elected its first president. The SASO evolved into the influential Black Consciousness Movement (BCM).

Since Biko's death in police custody, he has been called a martyr of the anti-apartheid movement. His writings and activism attempted to empower blacks, and he was famous for his slogan "black is beautiful", which he described as meaning: "man, you are ok as you are, begin to look upon yourself as a human being." His concept of black consciousness was explained by Vuyo Jack in an article in *The Sunday Independent* (2 September 2007). He wrote that Biko defined this concept as follows: "The philosophy of black consciousness expresses group pride and determination by blacks to rise and attain the envisaged self."

Vuyo Jack wrote that Biko defined integration as "the free participation by all members of a society, catering for the full expression of the self in a freely changing society as determined by the will of the people."

Echoes of this view and the following statement by Biko, quoted by Jack, correspond with the declarations in the Freedom Charter. Biko said: "We believe that in our country there shall be no minority, there shall be no majority, just the people. These people shall have the same status before the law and the same political rights."

Two declarations in the Freedom Charter that correspond with Biko's statements are: that South Africa belongs to all who live in it, black and white, and that no government can justly claim authority unless it is based on the will of all the people, and that only a democratic state, based on the will of all the people, can secure to all their birthright without distinction of colour, race, sex, or belief. It further proclaimed that all national groups shall have equal rights, all shall be equal before the law, and all shall enjoy equal human rights.

In an interview, one of the amnesty applicants at the TRC, Joe Mamasela, a Vlakplaas (secret security organisations centre) informant told SABC reporter Antjie Krog about Biko's writings. At school in Soweto, Mamasela was involved in student politics. In 1976, after the student riots, he became secretary general of the South African Student Movement at his school in

Jabavu. He said he became a student activist at a very young age and was given the SASO books of Steve Biko by a young man from the then-called Turfloop University, Donald Mashigo. In it Biko wrote under the pen name Frank Talk. Mamasela remembered one of the quotes related to Hegel's theory of dialectic materialism about which Biko said, "Since the problem is white, we need a very strong black force to counterbalance the state," with which Mamasela agreed.[208]

The Department of Bantu Education made a major mistake by deciding to retain the two official languages, Afrikaans and English, as subjects with an African language as optional in

accordance with government policy and the regulations of the matriculation board, and also to retain Afrikaans as a medium of instruction in at least one subject. This decision was a mistake. The obvious, reasonable decision in the circumstances was to rule that any two of three languages could be selected and Afrikaans be scrapped as medium of instruction. The Department of Education was filled with members of the Broederbond, including Dr Andries Treurnicht, the deputy minister for Bantu education who later broke away from the NP to form the Conservative Party. At the last day of the 1976 parliamentary session, Treurnicht, in reply to a motion on the Soweto student unrest, maintained the status quo. The officials were caught unawares by the student uprising and decided to uphold the status quo and not to give in to the demands of the students. The Department of Black Education remained insensitive to the issues and political implications. The Department's officials preferred to take a hard line against concessions to black students because they were determined to hold their views unchanged and enforce it upon the school system. This they did regardless of reports and advice from the security forces that they should expect trouble and should accommodate the wishes of the students. They ignored all these reports and maintained a hard line to the detriment of relations with black people and unnecessary hardship caused to blacks, the school system, and relations with security forces, not to mention the injuries and deaths. Within weeks, parliament closed the Department of Black Education in Pretoria advised schools in Soweto and elsewhere that the school boards and communities could decide on changing the policy on languages and Afrikaans as medium of instruction.

"Soweto" had come to mean not only the 16 June uprising but also a whole series of subsequent events: school boycotts and strikes; marches of tens of thousands; demonstrations extending into downtown Johannesburg; the burning or sabotage of symbols of white oppression, including government

---

208 Krog, p.173

offices, beer halls, and liquor stores in African townships; and clashes with police.[209]

Biko and the BCM played a significant role in the lead up to the protests during the Soweto uprising on 16 June 1976. The uprising was crushed by armed police shooting at protesters.

Mandela wrote about the Black Consciousness Movement while in prison on Robben Island. "My roots are in the movement," Achmat Dangor, the CEO of the Nelson Mandela Foundation, reported. He added that 2007 marked the thirtieth anniversary of a comprehensive discussion paper on the Black Consciousness Movement that Nelson Mandela wrote on Robben Island.[210]

Mandela observed that the Black Consciousness Movement helped fill a vacuum among young people. Black consciousness was less a movement than a philosophy and grew out of the idea that blacks must first liberate themselves from the sense of psychological inferiority bred by three centuries of white rule. Only then could the people rise in confidence and truly liberate themselves from repression. While the Black Consciousness Movement advocated a nonracial society, they excluded whites from playing a role in achieving that society.[211]

The ANC, however, was extremely hostile towards Biko and the Black Consciousness Movement from the 1970s to mid-1990s, although it had later reluctantly included Biko in the pantheon of struggling heroes.[212]

In 1973, Biko was banned by the government and restricted to his hometown of King Williamstown. Between 1975 and 1977, Biko was detained and interrogated four times. On 18 August 1977, Biko was arrested outside Grahamstown at a police roadblock under the Terrorism Act. He suffered a major head injury while in police custody. On 11 September 1977, police took him to Pretoria. He died the next day on the floor of the Pretoria central prison cell on 12 September 1977. He had been detained in August under the now infamous S29 (Section 29, referred to as S29), kept in detention at Walmer police station in Port Elizabeth, and regularly taken to security police headquarters in North End for interrogation.

"During one such interrogation he 'banged his head against a wall' during a 'scuffle' with his interrogators and sustained the head injury that eventually led to his death. The post-mortem examination showed brain damage and necrosis, extensive head trauma, disseminated intravascular coagulation, renal failure, and various external injuries. The failure of the two doctors – Benjamin Tucker and Ivor Lang, both district surgeons – to provide proper

209　*S A Time running out*, p.183
210　*The Star*, 17 July 2007
211　Mandela, p.472
212　*The Star*, 10 September 2007

treatment was subsequently described by a Supreme Court judge as 'callous, lacking any element of compassion, care or humanity.'"[213]

The inquest findings were referred by the presiding magistrate to the SA Medical and Dental Council (SAMDC), on the grounds that there was a prima facie case against Lang and Tucker.

The SAMDC took two-and-a-half years to respond by initiating a preliminary enquiry, in which it was found that the doctors had no case to answer. This decision was ratified by the full council. The SAMDC enquiry took place in 1985 only because it had been ordered by the Supreme Court to re-examine the case, finding Dr Tucker guilty of improper and disgraceful conduct on three counts and Dr Lang guilty of improper conduct on five counts.

Tucker was struck off the roll but reinstated some years later, Lang was suspended for three months, but this suspension was conditionally suspended for two years.[214]

When preparing for the truth commission hearings into the role of health professionals in human rights abuses, Dr Wendy Orr was given access to Steve Biko's S29 file, kept at the department of justice in Pretoria. This file contained all the records of his final detention. Regulations at that time required that S29 detainees be visited weekly by a magistrate and a doctor. (In Biko's case this was either Tucker or Lang.) After the visit, a report was sent to the regional police commissioner and the Department of Justice. Government officials used the existence of this statutory requirement to maintain that detainees were well looked after.

The standard reporting form has a section headed, "*Die aangehoudende het die volgende klagtes geopper.*" (The detainee made the following complaints.)

In this particular report from August 1977, Steve Biko is quoted, in neat black-and-white type framed by quotation marks, as saying, "I ask for water to wash myself with and also soap, a washing cloth and a comb. I want to be allowed to buy food. I live on bread only here. Is it compulsory for me to be naked? I am naked since I came here."

In a submission to the TRC health sector hearings, the Department of Health said, "(District surgeons had) a firm belief that the detainees were the enemy of the state, and that it was the right thing to do to assist the police in getting the information out of the detainees, as they were trying to overthrow the government.

"The country was fundamentally racist, and this included many district surgeons. The ideology was such that it was regarded as completely normal

---

213   *The Sunday Independent*, 9 September 2007
214   *The Sunday Independent*, 9 September 2007

not to give black people the same services as whites and to treat black people as second-class citizens."

Professor Maharaj, on behalf of the University of Natal (as it was then), stated that "Apartheid was a process of dehumanization. It reduced the majority of our people to objects or physical entities. Imperceptibly, medicine also became dehumanized."

Dr Wendy Orr concluded her article on Biko with comments on the current hospital situation. She wrote, "We might read this and think complacently that things are different now, that if this were to happen in 2007, Steve Biko would not have died. But I wonder if that is true.

"The current state of the public health sector is no secret – there are almost daily reports of appalling conditions, long queues, critically ill people turned away and unnecessary deaths. Health professionals themselves are not safe, as the recent rape of a medical student at Chris Hani-Baragwanath showed.

"In 2007, are we producing health professionals who uphold human rights and respect basic human dignity? I'd like to believe we are, but the challenge of doing so under current circumstances is immense.

"Another question is whether the SAMDC, now reconstituted as the Health Professions Council (HPC), would act differently, given the same evidence, in 2007? Again, I'd like to believe so.

"My challenge to health professionals, to the Department of Health, to health sciences faculties, to the HPC and to the SA Medical Association is: How do we make sure that the prospect of doing nothing is simply not contemplated by South Africa's health professionals in the twenty-first century?"

Dr Orr asked, "How do we live up to the principles of the Declaration of Tokyo, which states: "It is the privilege of the medical doctor to practice medicine in the service of humanity, to preserve and restore bodily and mental health without distinction as to persons; to comfort and to ease the suffering of his or her patients. The utmost respect for human life is to be maintained even under threat, and no use made of any medical knowledge contrary to the laws of humanity."

Dr Orr asked how we would realise Steve Biko's words, "In time, we shall be in a position to bestow on South Africa the greatest possible gift – a more human face."[215]

The death of Steve Biko while in the custody of the security police on 12 September 1977 was suggestive of the government's implacable and enduring hostility toward black militants. Bernard Levin of *The Times* of London commented that Biko was the forty-fourth black South African to

---

215   *SA Time running out*, p.183

die since September 1963 while in police custody on security grounds and "in circumstances sufficiently suspicious to warrant investigation."[216]

When Biko died the then minister of police, Jimmy Kruger, was quoted as saying, "Biko's death leaves me cold." He made this press comment in Pretoria at the time of the annual meeting of the congress of the NP of Transvaal. It showed an attitude of a leader in government without remorse, without empathy, no compassion. Kruger's remark was altogether distasteful. The minister also explained that Biko died while on a hunger strike.[217] The chief magistrate of Pretoria, Martinus Prins, found that the circumstances of Biko's death were inconclusive, and death was attributed to a prison accident.[218]

News of Biko's death spread quickly, opening many eyes around the world to the brutality of the apartheid regime. His funeral was attended by hundreds of people, including a number of ambassadors and other diplomats from the United States and Western Europe. The editor of the *Daily Dispatch* of East London, Donald Woods, a personal friend of Biko, photographed his injuries in the morgue. Woods later fled South Africa for England, where he campaigned against apartheid and further publicized Biko's life and death, writing many newspaper articles and the book, *Biko*.

The Truth and Reconciliation Commission reported in 1997 that five former members of the South African security forces had admitted to killing Biko, who died a year after the Soweto riots. These five former security force members applied for amnesty.

On 7 October 2003, the Department of Justice announced that the five policemen who were accused of killing Biko would not be prosecuted because of insufficient evidence, and because the time span for prosecution had elapsed.

Strong feelings of identification with Biko and his cause and against the government had been stimulated among the black population in the Eastern Cape and the country as a whole.

Although the government crushed the Soweto student uprising with force, this did not stop the protest and resistance to the Bantu education system. A boycott started in Cape Town in 1980 that spread throughout the country. Students demanded an end to what they called "gutter education". Throughout the 1980s education in many South African schools was disrupted. Many teachers and students were arrested and kept in jail, army patrols were sent into schools, and there were public meetings and other forms of protest.

216   *The Sunday Independent*, 9 September 2007
217   *The Star*, 10 September 2007
218   Ibid

Two popular slogans were "Liberation before education" and "Each one teach one". The second slogan was used by COSAS (the Congress of South African Students). By it they meant that education should be for all people and that everyone had a responsibility to help others by sharing their knowledge.

In June 1980, MK set off bombs at the Sasolburg refinery, power stations in Eastern Transvaal, police stations on the Reef, and the Voortrekkerhoogte military base. The government response was the militarization of the country to counteract the armed struggle, called the total onslaught under General Magnus Malan, minister of defence, and supported by President P. W. Botha.

The US influence on the power sharing policy of P. W. Botha

In 1981, Dr Chester Crocker, US assistant secretary of state, and Professor Sam Huntington of Harvard University submitted confidential memorandums to the Rockefeller Foundation Study Commission on US policy and South Africa. The Rockefeller report was published in 1981 following a visit to South Africa in 1980 by an eleven-member team from the foundation consisting of six blacks and five whites. Though the Rockefeller Foundation spokesman, John Stremlau, said that the study was not designed to tell South Africa what to do, the final product contained proposals and objectives which P. W. Botha seems to have followed during the next four years.[219]

The first and most important objective listed in the Rockefeller report was to promote genuine political power sharing in South Africa by systematically exerting influence on the South African government; a commitment to genuine power sharing, plus an extension of meaningful political rights to all groups, while providing protection for the basic rights of all segments of the population; and to create a forum for negotiations of power sharing with provision for urban black representation and a wide range of formal and informal consultations.[220]

Mr Botha did implement power sharing mechanisms but not of course representation for blacks in parliament.

Another (secondary) objective in the Rockefeller report was reversing the policy that denied South African citizenship to blacks from the independent homelands living in South Africa. Another was the extension of urban

---

219   The SA Foundation News, Vol. 7, June 1981, Rhoodie, p.134
220   Ibid, p.135

black administration; multiracial consultative bodies; communal political institutions for coloured and Asians; legislation to broaden the base of the electorate; and adoption of a system acceptable to black South Africans, with constitutional protection of the basic rights of all groups; changes in property ownership, and residential restrictions; large-scale implementation of the ninety-nine-year leasehold programme; rejection of race as a criterion in allocation of resources; formulation of timetables for equalization in expenditure on health and education; elimination of race as a structure in the industrial relations system; elimination of job reservation; registration of black and multiracial trade unions; decriminalisation of the pass laws; abolition of influx control; elimination of restrictions on black business; the ending of prohibition on mixed marriages and inter-racial sex.[221]

Five years after publication of this article, all of the above proposals became official NP and government policy. But no NP newspaper or National Party MP had advocated any of these major steps at the time the Rockefeller group wrote these suggestions. The Huntington-Crocker-Rockefeller package was designed and packaged in 1980–81 before most NP Members of Parliament even thought that these things were possible.

In 1982 Mr F. W. de Klerk told the Transvaal congress of the NP that the prime minister had undertaken that power sharing was not NP policy. NP members voted for Mr F. W. de Klerk as leader of the NP in the Transvaal. The Rockefeller worksheet for South Africa was submitted long before anyone else in South Africa who had a back door entrance to the government, such as the Broederbond, spelled out in such clear language what Mr Botha should do.[222]

Many people have asked who or what brought about this volte-face on Mr Botha's part after 1980. Was it something born from inner conviction, or because of some detailed study conducted by the brains trust of the National Party? The Broederbond? After all, the National Party was not in trouble in 1980. In fact, Mr Botha was riding high. Perhaps the answer can be found in an address by Dr Sam Huntington, a professor of political science at Harvard University in the USA, on the strategies for change in South Africa.

Professor Huntington is a very prominent scholar, a man frequently consulted by the American State Department. He was also a man who spent a great deal of time with Mr Pik Botha when the latter was Ambassador in the US. In 1981, at the urging of Mr Pik Botha, Professor Huntington paid a visit to South Africa and spoke at length to the Political Science Association of South Africa. Professor Huntington made such an impression on Mr P. W. Botha's top advisers that they brought the two of them together

221   Ibid
222   Politikon, Pretoria, Vol 8, No 2, 1981 in Rhoodie, p.131

for discussions which, in total, lasted several hours. Subsequently, Professor Huntington's lecture became compulsory reading for the prime minister's entire inner circle.[223]

Four years later, Tertius Myburgh of *The Sunday Times*, a man who has shown some belief in Mr Botha and his policies, wrote that there was an uncanny resemblance between the Huntington thesis on reform strategy and the pattern of political developments during the following three years, in many respects as if his script was being followed almost to the letter.[224]

Professor Huntington's thesis stated that for the reformer it is of the essence that he must

employ ambiguity, concealment, and deception concerning his goals. The successful politician, said Huntington, is always a master politician, and the highest priority should be given to devising strategies for achieving transition to a post-apartheid political system. It was less important to know where one was going than to know how one can get there, said Huntington. The political leader must shift allies and enemies from one issue to the next, to convey different messages to different audiences, and to hide his ultimate purpose behind his rhetoric. The reform programme, according to Huntington, is broken up into various components and presented one at a time, as if there was no linkage, minimizing the significance of each step and implying that each one would be the last.[225] According to Rhoodie, Mr Botha's methods and statements were in line with the Huntington thesis.

Each reform, said Huntington, should be drafted in secrecy and revealed to only a few political leaders whose support is essential. Reforms can then be dramatically unveiled. To use this method, he said, requires a high concentration of power and in South Africa the road could well be through some form of autocracy. Violence is also to be expected when reform comes, but the smart politician will use the violence to generate a broad enough coalition to push through some more reforms. In Rhoodie's view Mr Botha followed this pattern.

What is also important, said Professor Huntington, is to do what the Italian master of deceit, Prince Machiavelli, wrote: whoever wishes to reform an existing government in a free state should at least preserve some semblance of the old forms. Hence adherence to the homeland policy will make it easier to introduce political representation for the coloured and the Indians. According to Rhoodie, the foregoing resembles what happened in South Africa between 1982–88.[226]

---

223 Ibid
224 Ibid
225 Rhoodie, p.132
226 Ibid

Finally, Professor Huntington said that fundamental change in South Africa appears to be waiting for its Lenin, the leader who would give the same attention to the strategy and tactics of reform as Lenin devoted in the wake of the fall of czarist Russia to the tactics of revolution.[227] According to Rhoodie, it is a description of Mr Botha's role because when the "verligtes" (enlightened) toppled the pro-apartheid conservative elements in the NP, Mr Botha led the country and the NP from apartheid to a form of power sharing in five years, but excluding blacks from parliament, a crucial issue.

The duo of Professor Sam Huntington and Dr Chester Crocker had long and in-depth discussions and strategy sessions with Pik Botha in the USA during 1979–80, and with President Botha in South Africa in 1981–82. Thus Crocker was able to state in 1980 that Chris Heunis was to be given the portfolio of constitutional affairs and that the process of change included the isolation of Dr A. P. Treurnicht. What is significant about this move is that the new portfolio of Mr Heunis was announced only in 1982, the same year that Dr Treurnicht and the conservatives were forced out of the NP by Mr Botha. Dr Crocker's article had been written two years earlier.[228]

With equal foresight Dr Crocker also wrote that "We are entering a period in South Africa ... what amounts in practice to power sharing, no matter how it may be camouflaged." It is precisely what Professor Huntington advised both Mr Pik Botha and Mr P. W. Botha: camouflage your real intentions.[229] In structuring the presidency into an all-powerful executive office by way of the 1983 constitution, Mr Botha did what Professor Huntington had advised him to do two years earlier.

In an article in the US publication *Foreign Affairs*, Dr Crocker signalled that the people in Pretoria were slowly falling into line. "It is not inconceivable," he wrote, "that narrowing the scope of political participation may be indispensable to eventually broadening that participation. The arguments that it will be necessary to replace entrenched white democracy with enlightened despotism and the increased role of the State Security Council, the enhanced decision-making powers of cabinet committees, and the expansion of the role of the Prime Minister's office, are perhaps evidence of a tendency in this direction."[230] Dr Crocker indicated accurately what needed to happen in South Africa, using the same phraseology as Professor Huntington, that it is not "the ultimate goal" but the "process" which is important.

Dr Crocker wrote in 1980, "Too often our focus is the wrong issue: the ultimate goal, instead of the process of getting there. The dismantling

227   Ibid, p.133
228   Ibid
229   Ibid, p.133
230   Ibid

of apartheid and the creation of a new nonracial order is not going to take place through a sudden dramatic act, or result from one concession in one deal. Hundreds of decisions, drawn-out negotiations and, quite probably, a combination of violence and politics will precede the dawn of a new age for South Africa."[231]

It seems unbelievable that these two American experts could predict with such accuracy what should happen and what would happen in South Africa between 1982–88, when the NP press and even the NP academics failed to come up with the same analysis. Dr Crocker also had key talks with Mr Alwyn Schlebusch, a Botha cabinet member, and with Mr Chris Heunis on the same topic.[232]

It is plausible that the American brain trust put together by the US State Department turned Mr Botha around and pointed him in a new direction they favoured. That is the direction Sir de Villiers Graaff and the United Party wanted to go. The Americans also speeded his decision to finally indicate his idea of power sharing between black and white as a political goal.[233]

The Rockefeller Foundation had in the meantime financed another study report on US policy toward South Africa. It was published by the Foreign Policy Study Foundation, University of California, Berkeley, in May 1981, which recommended a policy to the US government: to make clear the fundamental and continuing opposition of the US government and people to the system of apartheid, with particular emphasis on the exclusion of blacks from an effective share in political power.

Further, to promote genuine political power sharing in South Africa with a minimum of violence by systematically exerting influence on the South African government.[234]

According to Washington insiders, President Reagan never intended that the policy of "constructive dialogue" would simply be an empty dialogue without any specific objective. The president is believed to have said that the dialogue should produce something constructive. In an address to congress, Mr Reagan said the US stood on the principle that the South African government "must" achieve justice and freedom for all its citizens. "We have a major stake, both moral and strategic, in encouraging a peaceful transition." Mr Pik Botha subsequently presented both Dr Chester Crocker and Professor Huntington with copies of the draft 1983 constitution more than a month before parliament in South Africa had a chance to look at the proposals.[235]

---

231   Rhoodie, p.132
232   Ibid
233   Ibid.
234   Ibid
235   Ibid.

Dr Neil Aggett, first white cell death 1982

Towards the end of 1981, more than sixty young men and women of all race groups and ethnic origins were detained under the Terrorism Act by the security police.

Many of them were post-graduate students actively involved in the struggle against apartheid. Close association between black and white activists was enough to elevate suspicion to proof of complicity in acts of terrorism. The more affluent parents among the affected families approached counsel to petition for their children's release, failing that, visitation rights or medical inspection.

They struggled to accept that the court's jurisdiction was excluded and that there was nothing counsel could do for them. The Rabie Commission report was published during this period, on 3 February 1982, and the then minister of police, Louis le Grange, was well pleased with the finding.[236]

The minister's security police had said that the information they obtained by means of interrogation in detention was the most powerful and to a large extent their only weapon of anticipating and combating activities which were planned and organised outside the borders of the Republic which endangered the state, and that without it they would not have been able to carry out the task which they had to perform in the interests of the security of the country.[237]

In response, the minister told Parliament that the detainees in police cells or in prisons were being detained under the most favourable conditions possible.

"All reasonable precautions are being taken to prevent any of them from injuring themselves or from being injured in some other way or from committing suicide. Surely honourable members are aware of the serious circumstances in the past [a reference to Steve Biko's death]. We were all faced with this, but during the past two-and-a-half years there has not been a single case of this nature."[238]

On 5 February 1982, two days after the minister's announcement in parliament, Dr Neil Hudson Aggett was found hanging from the bars of the steel grille in his cell in John Vorster Square police station. The police quickly announced that Dr Aggett had committed suicide. Many disbelieved them. The media reported that Aggett was a doctor and a trade unionist. Although he had been in detention for seventy days already, he was an idealist and not likely to have committed suicide.

---

236 Ibid
237 Ibid, p.134
238 Ibid

Aubrey Aggett believed that his son was killed by the security police. To the surprise of the family, Neil's funeral became a high-profile political event taken over by activists, particularly from the university and the trade union in which he had held a senior position. Tens of thousands marched from the cathedral to the cemetery.

When affidavits and documents regarding Neil's death were filed by the police, Denis Kuny and George Bizos were briefed to represent the Aggett family.

Among the papers was a statement made by Neil to Sergeant Alletta Gertruida Blom the day before his death, complaining of ill-treatment. There was also evidence that he had been deprived of sleep for more than seventy hours at a stretch and that he was expecting another such session.[239]

The Aggett magistrate gave a lengthy judgment, but he too disbelieved everything critical of the police and accepted their fanciful stories. He theorized that the injuries of at least one detainee were probably self-inflicted. This person knew that he was to be detained and could use the self-inflicted wounds to falsely accuse the police. He pointed out that the detainee was subjected to electric shock torture.[240]

The long list of those disbelieved by Magistrate Petrus Kotze included Dr Liz Floyd, Neil Aggett's companion.

Judgment in the inquest was given three days before Christmas 1982. After she heard the magistrate's finding, Liz Floyd commented, "If the security police say they dealt with Neil in the way they did, then why is he dead?"[241]

Even the government-supporting paper, *The Citizen*, commented, "Why indeed?" and added, "The magistrate in the Aggett case exonerated the police. He could not exonerate a system. Thus, only the end of the system and a return to the normal proceedings of the law will suffice if we are to have no more Aggetts or Bikos or other detainees whose death shocked all people who believed in the rule of law."

Michael Hornsby wrote in the *London Times*: "The parade of ex-detainees, black and white, through the witness box to tell under oath their tales of beatings, strippings, electric shock torture, sleep deprivation, third-degree interrogation techniques and worse, gave the press a rare opportunity to report on conditions in security police custody. Rarer still was the spectacle of the policemen themselves, normally beyond the reach of the law, being cross-examined by counsel on their own interrogation techniques."[242]

---

239 *SA Time running out*, p.140
240 Rhoodie, p.134
241 George Bizos, *Odyssey to Freedom*, Random House, Cape Town, *The Star*, 21 May 2007
242 Ibid

The Internal Security Act of 1982 and labour union exemptions

In a desperate attempt to force their hand on historical events, the government of P. W. Botha drew up new internal security legislation. They tried to do what had always seemed to work (i.e., "social engineering", or deciding what is best for the population) without taking into account the internal forces driving society or understanding that social engineering had never and could never provide a lasting solution. Botha wanted to control events, dictate and enforce his will.

As the groundswell of resistance grew into strikes and riots that threatened the income, security, and power pedestals of big business, the government passed the Internal Security Act, Act 74 of 1982. The bill was drafted by young advocates in the police force on personal instructions of P. W. Botha. According to a senior security officer, Botha had insisted on its draconian provisions that gave the minister of law and order virtual unlimited powers to act in the interest of state security. Even individual rights established under the common law could be overruled in terms of these powers.

The most effectively used sections of this act (as amended until repealed) were those dealing with the virtual supreme powers vested in the minister of law and order to declare both persons and organisations as unlawful if he was "satisfied" that they "engage in activities which endanger or are calculated to endanger the security of the State or the maintenance of law and order" as well as the sections enabling the minister to declare certain magisterial districts, which later included the entire country, as affected areas under what is termed a "state of emergency". But a caveat was enshrined in the Internal Security Act, that no regulation could be applied with "relation to an employers' organisation or trade union registered under the Labour Relations Act, 1956 (Act No 28 of 1956)". This caveat appeared no less than three times in the original Internal Security Act, Act 74 of 1982.

The South African Labour Relations Act, 1956 (Act No. 28 of 1956), as amended was at that time by far the most democratic apartheid legislation, safeguarding the right of employees to organise themselves into trade unions and their right to strike. This act followed the recommendations of the Wiehahn Commission of Inquiry chaired by Prof. Nic Wiehahn. It served as a motivating factor for foreign countries to maintain relations and trade with South Africa, but only up to a point, when in 1986 the US Congress imposed sanctions through the Anti Apartheid Act.

Whilst the act and its provisions were intended to ensure the prolonged existence of the status quo, the caveat included in the act indicated the politicians scant knowledge of the underlying Marxist-Leninist principle regarding the role and manipulation of the working class (especially organised labour), but also their ignorance of sound strategic reasoning. It further indicated the diehard attitude of P. W. Botha and his cabinet, who as politicians did not heed the advice to negotiate given by the council of military and strategic advisors.

With avenues of organised resistance against the state effectively blocked by the Internal Security Act, and the act leaving the door open for legal anti-apartheid activities within the trade unions, it was natural for the ANC's Revolutionary Alliance, consisting of the ANC, the SA Communist Party, and the SA Congress of Trade Unions (which had by then changed its name to the Congress of S. A. Trade Unions and was then a legal entity ironically protected by the Internal Security Act), to utilise this golden opportunity to, in tandem with the United Democratic Front and other organisations, apply pressure on the government through strikes, riots, and actions such as civil disobedience which *inter alia* made some areas ungovernable.

Minister Vlok held regular meetings of the State Security Council in Byron Place, Schubart Street, Pretoria with the generals from the military and security forces and their advisors to assess and plan operations. At one of these meetings in July 1984, also attended by deputy minister Roelf Meyer, at the time of the greatest and longest black uprising that started in the Vaal Triangle, one of the senior security officers was asked by Minister Vlok what should be done. He told the meeting that the labour unions have protection under the Internal Security Act. He said that nothing could be done against trade unions except under martial law. But the problem was that there was no reason to invoke such drastic measures since no hostile forces were crossing the borders of the Republic. Thus, the only thing left was to amend the Internal Security Act. But their was no time for that.

At this time the Congress of South African Students (COSAS), the Federation of S. A. Trade Unions, and the UDF organised the longest stay-away in South African history. All told, there were 469 strikes that year. In terms of the state of emergency in 1985, COSAS was banned and many UDF leaders arrested. But the security forces did not act against the trade unions. The newly formed governing body for the trade unions, COSATU, organised a nationwide strike the next year, and a new state of emergency was declared in 1986. COSATU's membership quickly grew to 500,000.

By 1990 the unrest, the sanctions, and the rejection by the DRC of apartheid as sin led de Klerk as new state president to make the decision that negotiations with the black people for a constitutional settlement was imperative.

Measures uplifting apartheid restrictions but not its four cornerstones

In the eighties, President Botha and his government embarked on a course where logic and common sense dictated that a true multiracial government with a black majority could emerge. The changes effected by the government are listed here, except for the 1983 constitution with a three chamber parliament, which is discussed separately.[243]

Sport

All sporting associations in South Africa were free to engage in multiracial sport. Sports grounds and stadiums could be used by all race groups. In Conservative Party controlled councils multiracial sport had been banned.
—*Group Areas Act No. 36 of 1966, as amended in 1982*

Anybody, irrespective of race, may attend any sporting event free of any restriction in any area.
—*Black (Urban Areas) Consolidation Act 1945, as amended by the Black Communities Development Act of 1983*

Sporting clubs could admit anybody, irrespective of race, to their membership, premises, and facilities.
—*Liquor Act No. 87 of 1977, as amended in 1981*

Civil defence

All races are represented in the Interdepartmental Civil Defence Committee, which is a policy-making, coordinating and monitoring committee.—*Department of Development Planning*

Labour

All racial restrictions on trade unions have been abolished. Statutory discrimination in employment based on race had almost entirely been eliminated. Legislation was introduced in 1986 to eliminate the only remaining restriction, which was in the mining industry. An industrial court had been established which was empowered to carry out the functions of a

---

243 Rhoodie, pp 165-168

court of law in regard to disputes arising from the administration of the laws of the Department of Manpower.
—Industrial Conciliation Amendment Act, 1979; Labour Relations Amendment Act 1984

Statutory wage discrimination was being abolished at a steady pace. The abolition of remaining salary disparities for personnel at colleges and schools as well as nurses and paramedical personnel had been approved by the government.
—Statement by Minister E Louw, 30 May 1986

Education

Acts of parliament have provided for the opening of tertiary educational institutions to all races on the basis of equal opportunities and equal standards.
—Universities Amendment Act No. 83 of 1983; Advanced Technical Education Amendment Act No. 84 of 1983

Legislation had been passed giving full membership and voting rights to blacks on the Committee of University Principals, and the Committee of Technikon Principals.
A multiracial South African Council of Education had been formed consisting of twenty-six members who would advise on general education policy.
—Announcement by Minister F. W. de Klerk in September 1985

A dramatic increase in the enrolment of black students at universities had occurred during the period 1955 to 1986. The figure had increased from fewer than 500 in 1955 to over 51,000 in 1986. This is itself testimony to the improvement in black school education over the same period. All previously white universities were open to all races.
—Official South African Yearbook-1986

The government's declared objective had for some time been equal educational opportunities for all. A ten-year plan had been announced to accelerate progress towards this end.
—Announcement by Minister F. W. de Klerk in 1986

Places of entertainment

Almost all South African theatres have been fully integrated. The law had been changed to allow cinemas to admit patrons of all races.
—*Announcements by Minister Marais Steyn in June 1978 and Minister Piet Badenhorst in October 1985*

Public transport

Although much remained to be done in this field, many previously segregated forms of public transport and associated facilities (waiting rooms, restaurants, toilets) were opened to all.

Hotels and restaurants

An increasing number of hotels and restaurants have, for some years, been multiracial. During 1985 amendments to the Liquor Act were introduced in parliament ending all forms of racial discrimination. Hotels and restaurants could admit anyone, irrespective of race and without prior permission having to be obtained.
—*Liquor Act No. 87 of 1977, as amended by Act No. 31 of 1985. Statements by Minister D. de Villiers in parliament during February and May 1986*

Recreation

The majority of local authorities opened libraries, museums, parks, and beaches to all races.
In Cape Town all beaches and municipal swimming baths became multiracial while in Durban five beaches and the municipal swimming bath on the main beach front were also free from discriminatory restrictions.
—*Announcement by Minister John Wiley in November 1985*

All official hiking trails were opened to all races.
—*Department of Environment Affairs*

Interracial marriage

The previous ban on interracial marriage had been abolished.
—*Prohibition of Mixed Marriages Act No. 55 of 1949, repealed by Act No. 72 of 1985*

Interracial sex

The provision prohibiting interracial sex had been scrapped.
—*Article 16 of Immorality Act No. 23 of 1957, abolished by Act No. 72 of 1985*

Political activity

Party political activities could be organised along multiracial lines. Political parties were free to accept members of all races.
—*Prohibition of Political Interference Act No. 51 of 1968, as amended by Constitutional Affairs Amendment Act No. 104 of 1985*

Population resettlement

The South African government had suspended all forced resettlement of communities under the homelands consolidation programme. All removals, therefore, took place with the consent of each individual person.
—*Statement by Minister Gerrit Viljoen, February 1985; Financial Mail April 11, 1986*

Property ownership

Previously, blacks were legally regarded as temporary residents in urban areas. Government policy had for some years recognised the black community as permanent and had legislated in favour of black urban freehold rights.
—*Black Communities Development Amendment Bill, 1986*

Pass laws

Blacks-only passes were abolished. All population groups were issued with a common identity document from 1 July 1986, with no reference to race or ethnic group.
—*Announcement by State President P. W. Botha on April 18, 1986; White Paper on Urbanisation 1986; Identification Bill 1986*

Freedom of movement

The Cooperation and Development Bill published in parliament in 1985 allowed freedom of movement for blacks wishing to enter urban areas. Urban blacks were enabled to move to other towns to follow employment opportunities.
—*White Paper on Urbanisation, 1986; Abolition of Influx Control Act 1986*

Citizenship

A bill had been published whereby South African citizenship would be restored, upon request, to citizens of the independent states of Transkei, Bophuthatswana, Venda, and Ciskei.
—*Restoration of South African Citizenship Bill, 1986*

Provincial government

When white voters in 1983 approved the tricameral constitution by referendum, they did not realise that, three years later, their vote would be taken as a mandate to get rid of the old provincial system. The central government could impose its will on city councils even if the majority of the elected members in that council supported another political party. The central authority could tell local government who could live where and tell private enterprise where it could or could not establish itself.[244]

As of 1 July 1986, the new system of provincial government had executive committees with executive powers which included members from all race groups appointed by the state president. The all-white provincial councils were abolished.
—*Provincial Government Bill No. 96 of 1986*

Regional government

All leaders in the different regions had the opportunity of addressing jointly regional problems affecting their communities. A Joint Executive Authority (JEA) for Natal province and the self-governing territory of KwaZulu had

---

244 Rhoodie, p162

been established as a starting point for further regional developments. The JEA represented an important step in power sharing on a regional basis.
—*Announcement by Minister J. C. Heunis in September 1987*

Group areas

"Open" group areas had been accepted. Legislation was planned for 1988 to give communities the opportunity of deciding on a local level whether they wanted their area to be declared "open" to individuals of other groups. New residential areas could be declared "open" before anybody settled there.
—*Bureau for Information, October 1987*

Business property

A new amendment had created free-trading areas where all races could acquire ownership of business, commercial, and professional properties. This move was designed to allow all traders and businessmen access to city centres. Sixty-six of these areas had already been approved.

Local government (a failed attempted reform)

To extend local government to the third level and to link up with municipal structures, Regional Councils were introduced in 1986. A Regional Services Council (RSC) was designed to provide joint services in a particular region and to upgrade poorly-developed black townships. It was an umbrella body for existing autonomous local bodies and city councils of the four main racial groups. Each local authority or city council which fell within an RSC had representatives on the council.

Although the local authorities would continue to manage so-called soft services such as parks, traffic control, libraries, sanitation, etc., the RSC would administer the "hard services" such as transportation, roads, housing, water, hospitals, etc.

For an RSC to work, municipal bodies needed to be in existence for all. The government had to convince Indian, coloured and black groups to accept the idea of autonomous municipal systems separate from those of the whites. Most blacks, Indians, and coloured saw it as a perpetuation of residential segregation and continued segregation of schools. In the Eastern Cape alone, nearly 70 percent of the fifty black councils were non-functional because they had been totally rejected by the people.

To overcome this resistance, the government tabled the Black Local Authorities Amendment Bill transforming these community councils into own town committees with municipal autonomy. Acceptance of this situation made the October 1988 local elections important. Those who participated in the election (only about 25 percent of eligible voters) believed that the system could be integrated from the bottom up. Those who boycotted the elections (75 percent of eligible voters) wanted to have integration imposed from above by a multiracial parliament.

The non-whites also objected to the fact that the Regional Service Councils were not elected. Members were nominated by the local authorities, while the provincial administrator would appoint the chairman.[245]

In 1987 Dr Sam Motsuenyane, president of the National African Federated Chamber of Commerce and Industry, remarked on the idea of a free market economy, that the whole idea of free enterprise was ridiculous as long as apartheid laws such as the Group Areas Act, the Population Registration Act, and the Land Act existed. "We are ... observing growing disenchantment in the ranks of the black youth and intellectuals for what is called capitalism or free enterprise by the government in South Africa because the system is not recognised to be free at all."[246]

Professor Marinus Wiechers said at the UNISA School of Business Leadership in Johannesburg in 1986 that change had not created a favourable atmosphere for negotiations "because most of the population believed the government's intention was to perpetuate white control." He added that "looking negatively at the changes ... one could say that all the reforms have created more instability and acrimony than all the aforegoing years of hard-line apartheid".[247]

The Botha option, Harald Pakendorf wrote, is to drive towards a society where colour will not count "as long as we all agree with those who currently exercise the power. A sort of non-racial autocracy." Pakendorf observed that the president has become increasingly intolerant of disagreement. In effect, he said, Mr Botha was saying they should get rid of apartheid as long as the instruments of power remained in white hands.[248]

The long list of legislation and measures dismantling apartheid still left the four cornerstones of the system intact: separate amenities, population registration, group areas, and no voting rights for a black majority.

---

245   Rhoodie, p.160
246   Rhoodie, p.172
247   Rhoodie, p.180
248   Rhoodie, p.169

The 1983 constitution and Botha's failed power sharing policy

On 22 February 1982 Prime Minister Botha called on his cabinet to agree that the idea of separate sovereign parliaments for coloured and Indians approved by the NP in 1977 could not be created because there could be only one central government authority in the country, thus one parliament with three chambers. Dr Treurnicht disagreed because it recognised power sharing between the two groups and the whites within the same constitution. In protest, Dr Treurnicht and a number of MPs walked out of a NP Transvaal Head Council meeting at the end of February 1982 in Pretoria. He and sixteen MPs founded the Conservative Party and became an opposition party in parliament. F. W. de Klerk was elected in place of Treurnicht as the leader of the NP in Transvaal.

In the advance towards power sharing, the coloured, Asian, and white communities enjoyed autonomy and self-determination expressed through one multi-chamber parliament under the new 1983 constitution. General business was carried out in multiracial standing committees consisting of members from all three chambers. Each group was responsible for all questions relating to its own community, and all groups were jointly responsible for matters of common concern. As this structure did not meet the political aspirations of the black community, the South African government regarded it as an interim arrangement in the move towards power sharing with black people. Botha personally worked on mechanisms to this effect, but it excluded black majority rule.

In the referendum on the new constitution in November 1983 the NP received a two-thirds majority with the support of the liberal Progressive Federal Party. The Conservative Party canvassed the one-third no vote. An election to the new houses of parliament followed the next year, but only about 20 percent of the eligible Indian and Coloured voters took part.

De Klerk wrote in his autobiography that despite all its flaws, the tricameral constitution was a symbolic beachhead for change and represented a major stride forward in the constitutional development of the country. For the first time, South Africans from the three communities gathered together in parliament to consider matters of common concern. There was genuine political interaction and accountability.[249]

After Chief Minister Mangosuthu Buthelezi of KwaZulu refused independence for this homeland and so also four remaining self-governing black territories in the early eighties, together with the fact that the black

---

249   De Klerk, p.96

influx did not turn back as predicted by Verwoerd's ideologies, in 1978 the government had to consider a new constitutional framework to accommodate blacks.

P. W. Botha established a special cabinet committee in February 1983 to promote multilateral cooperation between the South African government and the governments of the independent and self-governing black states. The chairman was Chris Heunis, minister of constitutional development.

A new organisation, the United Democratic Front, was formed in 1983 to coordinate the activities of all those who were opposed to the tricameral constitution. A wide spectrum of more than 700 organisations affiliated to the UDF and a wide variety of grievances became the subject of UDF mass demonstrations supported by these groups.

These campaigns soon became a vehicle for ANC involvement, and in 1984 and 1985 UDF instigated unrest that spread throughout the country. Youth groups took the leadership in many areas against Bantu education, in support of boycotts, and against so-called collaborators. They were attacked and murdered, both men and women, many by the method of "necklacing" – burning a tyre around their necks. In the hearings of the TRC, Queenstown in the Eastern Cape was called the "necklace" capital of the world. The actions of the young people against so-called collaborators led to disruptions, civil unrest, non-payment of rent and services, and making many municipal areas ungovernable.

P. W. Botha became the first executive state president in 1984 and reorganised the State Security Council established under John Vorster into a "securocrat" management system. The council developed strategies and action plans which were ratified by the cabinet. The strategy, called the total onslaught, started earlier under General Malan, became part of the new system. A partial state of emergency was declared in 1985 and a national state of emergency was declared in 1986. An unconventional war developed with murder and killings on both sides as reported by the TRC.

The first major fruits of the special committee's labour were revealed during President Botha's opening speech to parliament on 31 January 1985. In it the government acknowledged the permanence of the large black population in the white areas and the need to accept the political implications of this reality. Botha accepted that he could not force the remaining six non-independent black homelands to accept independence and acknowledged that closer cooperation with them on matters of common concern was necessary. President Botha also offered to release Nelson Mandela, provided he unconditionally rejected violence as a political instrument. He extended this offer of release to all political prisoners. In reaction, Mandela wrote that he was surprised at the conditions that the government wanted to impose on him. "I am not a violent man …. It was only then, when all other forms of resistance were no longer open to us, that we turned to armed struggle. Let Botha show that he is different to Malan, Strijdom, and Verwoerd. Let him renounce violence. Let him say that he will dismantle apartheid. Let him unban the people's organisation, the African National Congress. Let him free all who have been imprisoned, banished, or exiled for their opposition to apartheid. Let him guarantee free political activity so that people may decide who will govern them."[250]

At this time Mandela received a visit from Prof. Samuel Dash, a professor of law at Georgetown University in the US, authorised by the new minister of justice, Kobie Coetzee. Mandela told him that a future nonracial South Africa should be a unitary state without homelands, nonracial elections for a central parliament, and one-person one-vote.[251]

In 1985 the End Time Handmaidens in the US forwarded a prophecy to the Christians in South Africa in which God warned the people to repent of their sins. The Afrikaners were mentioned as stiff-necked people who specifically needed to heed this warning to avoid a new government hostile towards them being raised up in the country.

At its National Consultative Conference in Kabwe, Zambia, in June 1985 the ANC decided that the time had come to lead the people in raising the level of struggle to that of a people's war for the seizure of power.[252]

President Botha's power-sharing policy was doomed to failure in August 1985 at the Natal NP congress in Durban when he refused to commit to negotiated democratic elected black voters as agreed to by his special cabinet committee.

"Crossing the Rubicon" speech disaster, 1985, and the end of Botha

If ever there was a real test of the greatness of a statesman in South Africa, it was the issue of granting political rights to the black majority.

The second half of 1985 presented such an opportunity to President Botha when he was to address the Natal congress of the National Party in Durban. Many changes had been made by scrapping apartheid restrictions in the preceding five years. Also, negotiations had been taking place in South Africa among many role players and even with influential policy advisors of the US government. President Botha's own special cabinet committee on

250 Mandela, p.510
251 Mandela, p.508
252 De Klerk, p.111

constitutional affairs had discussions with him on the important issue of facing up to the goal of accommodating black

voters. But the crux of the change in the apartheid policy through Botha's idea of power sharing did not necessarily mean black majority rule.

P. W. Botha's infamous Rubicon speech at the Natal congress of the National Party on 15 August 1985 was a personal and national disaster. Viewed from another perspective, it can be seen as an important turning point in South Africa's political history inasmuch as Western governments, which still resisted sanctions against South Africa, finally lost faith in Botha's capacity to bring about meaningful reform in South Africa. This in turn led to pressure from the entire international community, most importantly the Western countries, which finally persuaded F. W. de Klerk when he replaced Botha as president to release Nelson Mandela and others, unban the ANC, and engage in negotiations which resulted in a fully democratic South Africa.[253]

P. W. Botha convened a meeting of the cabinet, deputy ministers (who were not members of the cabinet), and the chairpersons of the President's Council's committees at the Military Intelligence College in a converted observatory in Pretoria. The meeting took place on 2 August 1985. Botha was due to address the Natal National Party congress on 15 August 1985 and wanted to use the opportunity to announce new constitutional guidelines.

A debate followed after Minister Chris Heunis addressed the meeting. It was decided that black people would be accommodated in the cabinet as an interim measure pending the outcome of negotiations with black South Africans to reach agreement on their accommodation in a new constitutional dispensation. This was particularly significant because it recognised the fact that blacks would inevitably have had to be accommodated at central government level in South Africa, and that the homelands were no answer to blacks' political aspirations.[254]

According to de Klerk, these new guidelines signalled nothing less than the demise of the whole ideology of grand apartheid. We thought that these new announcements would, if properly presented and marketed, capture worldwide attention and convince the international community that things were really beginning to move in South Africa. We also hoped that the proposed initiative would open the door for negotiations with, at least, non-revolutionary black leaders.[255]

F. W. de Klerk's recollection, as set out in his autobiography, is that Botha asked cabinet members to suggest ideas for the speech he was due to deliver

---

253   Heunis, p.75
254   Ibid, p.77
255   De Klerk, p.102

on 15 August. According to de Klerk, Minister Chris Heunis drafted extensive suggestions which he sent to the president, as did the Department of Foreign Affairs. The Department of Foreign Affairs had also been authorised to brief leading Western governments on the speech and to urge them to respond with messages of encouragement and support. To this end Pik Botha went on a special mission to Europe, where he met senior representatives of various governments and informed them of the new direction that he expected P. W. Botha to announce.[256]

Pik Botha met US State Department officials in Vienna on 8 August. According to Chester Crocker's *High Noon in Southern Africa*, Pik Botha suggested an urgent meeting to discuss the road ahead as early as 2 August. At the meeting, according to Crocker, he "was at his thespian (dramatic) best …, walking out on limbs far beyond the zone of safety to persuade us that his president was on the verge of momentous announcements. We learned of plans for bold reform steps, new formulas on constitutional moves, and further thinking relative to the release of Mandela."[257]

After the special cabinet meeting, P. W. Botha asked Minister Heunis whether he would prepare a draft speech for him, based on the decisions that had been taken, so that he could announce them at the opening of the Natal congress of the National Party the following weekend. After reviewing it, P. W. Botha phoned Chris Heunis to tell him that he had no intention of delivering the Prog speech (at the time considered to be the liberal white element in the South African parliament) which he had prepared. Heunis told him that it was not a Prog speech, and that it simply reflected the decisions which had been taken at the Military Intelligence College.[258]

P. W. Botha's performance in Natal when he made his speech claiming to have crossed the Rubicon perhaps did more to undermine his personal credibility than any other single act. Mr Pik Botha had briefed ambassadors of European countries, (the British, US, and West German governments) and spoke to American senators and the press and created the expectancy that P. W. Botha would unveil the answer to what structure and ratio power would be shared at the highest level. The president's office told the press off-the-record that a major policy statement could be expected. But whereas Caesar crossed the Rubicon in 48 BC, Mr Botha failed to cross his in August 1985. Mr Botha, who had himself labelled his speech the final part of his own manifesto, chose to launch a vituperative, misinformed, and baseless attack on the press for putting words in his mouth in advance. With the entire world watching, P. W. Botha shredded his own credibility.[259]

256   De Klerk, p.103
257   Heunis, p.78
258   Ibid, p.79
259   Rhoodie, p.180

De Klerk wrote that in the speech, President Botha accepted the need for negotiations with the leaders of the black population to devise such institutions. However, he aggressively dismissed the United Democratic Front and the banned ANC (with whom the government would one day have to negotiate) as barbaric Communist agitators and even murderers who perpetrated the most cruel deeds against their fellow South Africans because they were on the payroll of their masters. He also warned his audience that our readiness to negotiate should not be mistaken for weakness and made it clear that his bottom line was the need to protect minorities. He warned that he was not prepared to lead white South Africans and other minority groups on a road to abdication and suicide.

For many of those who watched the speech, President Botha's aggressive attitude undermined the credibility of his and the government's simultaneous commitment to genuine negotiations – which would have presupposed a more conciliatory attitude.[260]

The result of the speech was catastrophic. Between the end of June 1985 and September 1985, the rand plummeted from R1.97 to R2.48 to the US dollar. The former governor of the South African Reserve Bank, Dr Gerhard de Kock, estimated that the speech had cost the country several billion rand – perhaps more than a million rand per word.[261]

The main points of Pik Botha's suggestions for the speech, which was called the president's Durban Manifesto, were :

- "Our readiness to negotiate should not be taken for weakness. Reform through a process of negotiation is not weakness.

- "How do we build a better future out of cultures, values, languages which are demonstrably real in our heterogeneous society?"[262]

It read further: "We are committed to do so in two fundamental ways. Firstly, by letting the people speak ... through their leaders ... it is not for the government to prescribe who the leaders of the black people are ...

- "Secondly, we depart from the basis that we all hold certain inalienable beliefs and values which ought to outweigh all other considerations ...

"The only way forward is through cooperation and co-responsibility.

- "Working together we shall succeed in finding the way which will satisfy the reasonable economic, social and political aspirations of everyone.

- "The government now accepts the principle that all our population groups must be jointly responsible for decision-making at all levels of

---

260   De Klerk, p.105
261   Ibid
262   *Beeld*, 21 June 2007

government in matters of common concern, without domination by any one population group over another...

- "A variety of black leaders have again approached me in connection with Mr Mandela. It is their conviction that Mr Mandela would not engage in the planning or implementation of violent acts. They are respectable men whose views are deserving of serious consideration. If I can from any of these leaders ... receive satisfactory indications that he will conduct himself in a law-abiding manner, I will in principle be prepared to consider his release."

Pik Botha wrote that the following background points motivated the above wording:

- "The government accepts the principle of a common South African citizenship for all South Africans...

- "So far as the independent national states (TBVC states) are concerned ... if their governments should decide to negotiate ... on the conferment of South African citizenship on their citizens, they will be welcome to do so...

- "The government is ... abolishing discrimination based on colour and race and is promoting constitutional development with a view to meeting the needs and aspirations of all our communities...

- "As violence diminishes ... and the process of dialogue ... acquires greater momentum, there will be little need to keep those affected in detention and prison...

- "The implementation of the principles I have stated here today, can have far reaching effects on us all. I believe that today we are crossing the Rubicon. There can be no turning back. We now have a manifesto for the future of our country."[263]

In this rendering of President Botha's proposed speech an important note on the security situation which had been given to him by Mr Adriaan Vlok, the minister of police, is overlooked. The report he rendered to the president was requested from each cabinet minister and had to be short. Minister Vlok said that the reports of the police and military were in agreement that the situation at that time was very serious. It was described as a government sitting on the lid of a boiling pot upon a red hot fire that could not be handled because it was going to explode, and that negotiations were the only solution.

A senior security officer commented on this report that the situation was indeed serious, not only by virtue of the president not heeding the counsel of

---

263 *Beeld*, 21 June 2007

his securocrats, but due to the stoic stance of the Botha government regarding the will of the black masses and learned opinions of academics and theologians (most of whom were declared enemies of the state). Heeding the advice of the securocrats could have assisted in not only saving the day, but also saving innocent lives.

When called for questioning by the TRC, the leader of the Freedom Party, General Constand Viljoen, told the commission that the army had begged the government for years to find a political solution to the conflict of apartheid because it was the sort of war the army could not win.[264]

P. W. Botha's inability to compromise and his stubbornness not to accommodate blacks as voters cost the whites their bargaining power when F. W. de Klerk started negotiations in 1990.

Professor Willem de Klerk, former editor of *Rapport*, said: "The speech, with its style of arrogance and aggression, damaged prospects for black-white negotiations … the government has

wasted its chances and it has often done so. It now has a huge credibility platform and there is widespread pessimism." Professor de Klerk's views were echoed by many others. Dr Ockie Stuart, director of economic research of Stellenbosch University, Professor Hermann Barratt of the Institute of International Affairs, and Professor Hermann Giliomee of the University of Cape Town counted among them. Professor Barratt said the speech "was a disaster of the greatest proportions and it came at a critical time."[265]

The *NRC Handelsblad* newspaper in Rotterdam, Holland, wrote in an editorial of 23 May 1986 what most other European newspapers had also declared: that the Botha regime was threatening to become the victim of a dilemma of its own creation. To master a situation as disease-ridden and complex as South Africa required, in the first place, credibility. And where it concerned the seriousness and scope of the reformist proposals, credibility was even more important.[266]

The real loss to every South African caused by the Rubicon speech disaster was the lost economic opportunity, which would have included the end of sanctions and of a rundown economy, a new wave of foreign investment, an inflow of capital, a growing international trade, a decrease in unemployment, and support from abroad for humanitarian projects. The above would have been possible because of the keen interest and goodwill of Western governments in the development of South Africa as they cherished the goal of the United Nations and the whole world to end the discrimination and

---

264   Krog, p.172
265   Rhoodie, p.181
266   Ibid, p.180

injustice of the blight of apartheid and by installing a democratic government with black majority rule.

A turnaround as described above was possible because of the reported scenario that negotiations could take place within a framework of all parties participating, including Mandela, due to his early release from prison with other political prisoners and detainees, supported by guarantees from Western Nations. The international community, as supporters of the process of negotiations and of the new democracy, would for a ten-year period guarantee peaceful transition. This was a promise for a prosperous new future, but the Nationalist government and the NP chose to ignore this opportunity, with the result that the government under de Klerk was largely left to its own devices when negotiations started. Thus, the Afrikaners lost a golden opportunity to work out a new future together with their fellow black citizens and participate in the opportunities available to all. Instead they let them be led by de Klerk, who clung to the concept of consensus, the new word of the Broederbond and himself to replace the discredited idea of power sharing under P. W. Botha, which did not accommodate blacks politically and democratically.

Condemning P. W. Botha for his Rubicon speech is to ignore the responsibility of his cabinet. The other guilty party was his meek cabinet colleagues who accepted his rule and decision to ignore a special cabinet resolution to execute the formulated announcement of starting an initiative for negotiations towards accommodating black voters. Botha's cabinet members did South Africa a disservice. P. W. Botha's affront to their integrity should have resulted in his overthrow, but they lacked resolve. They were divided, some left leaning and some right leaning. The cabinet was therefore also not able to cross its Rubicon.

The Rubicon speech showed P. W. Botha to be a narrow-minded egoist.[267] Botha reneged on what was decided by his special cabinet committee under his chairmanship. Some say he abandoned the speech based on the cabinet resolution because he was angry about the fact that its essence was reported in the newspapers a week before he was due to announce it. He castigated the press for their premature reports on his speech. But a man's anger cannot be enough reason for such a catastrophic step if he is supposed to act in the country's interest. In fact it was just a political ploy, a ruse to take attention away from his meek reform plans.

The real reason for his refusal to announce reforms lay in Botha's remark to Chris Heunis when he read the draft that Heunis had prepared based on the cabinet's resolution. He told Heunis on the phone that he had no intention

---

267 Heunis, p.84

of delivering the Prog speech.[268] It had apparently only then struck him what the real significance was in the cabinet's resolution to accommodate blacks in parliament – not his version of restricted power sharing but something real and more substantial. When it became clear what had to be done about black political aspirations, P. W. Botha turned against Heunis. Heunis's son Jan, himself a state legal advisor, wrote, "I know .... He was never in favour of sharing power with black South Africa"[269]

The truth is that the majority of the Botha cabinet was not genuinely reform minded and in fact did not act against Botha because they not only accepted his decision to abandon the resolution but agreed with his actions.[270] Cloete called them die-hards and included F. W. de Klerk in this group. F. W. de Klerk finally resolved to take up the issue of black majority rule when Botha fell ill, and he was elected as NP leader to become state president. Only then did he lead the cabinet and NP in real reform.

The test of de Klerk's stand on the Rubicon speech issue is contained in his observation about the great damage Botha had caused the country and its economy with his recalcitrance. De Klerk's criticism was the severest. So why did he then not do something about his leader's irresponsible action? He chose to play the waiting game, to wait for P. W. Botha's retirement or, figuratively speaking, Botha to hang himself.

De Klerk himself explained his position in a speech he made six months later in the debate that followed the opening of parliament in February 1986. His speech was not reformist at all. He said that recognition of the existence of different groups was not discriminatory. He believed that it was a God-given reality, and added that certain fundamental issues were inextricably linked to group security. These included the right of every community to its own neighbourhood, its own schools, and its own institutions within which it would be able to maintain its own character and promote its own interests.

De Klerk emphasised that the National Party was committed to the principle of group security, the effective protection of minorities, and also the prevention of group domination. He rejected the contention that the protection of group security could be equated with the simplistic concept of apartheid.[271] In other words de Klerk was at that stage a die-hard conservative.

Botha's proposed National Statutory Council of January 1986 to serve as a forum for negotiations with blacks came to nothing. No black leader of stature was prepared to talk with the government without the ANC. In

---

268   Heunis, p.79
269   Heunis, p.125
270   Prof Fanie Cloete, *Die Burger*, 16 February 2006
271   De Klerk, p.108

fact, led by Buthelezi, they insisted on the release of Nelson Mandela before considering constitutional talks.

In May 1986, the Eminent Persons Group of the commonwealth met Mandela in prison on a fact-finding visit. Mandela told them he favoured the ANC beginning discussions with the government. He said, "Various members of the group had concerns about my political ideology and what a South Africa under ANC leadership might look like. I told them I was a South African Nationalist, not a Communist, that Nationalists came in every hue and colour, and that I was firmly committed to a nonracial society. I told them I believed in the Freedom Charter, that the charter embodied principles of democracy and human rights, and that it was not a blueprint for socialism. I spoke of my concern that the white minority should feel a sense of security in any new South Africa. I told them I thought many of our problems were a result of lack of communication between the government and the ANC, and that some of these could be resolved through actual talks" [272]

In August 1986 the Federal Congress of the National party in Durban accepted a new policy formulated by the special cabinet committee under Chris Heunis that rejected apartheid and racial discrimination. The proposals accepted the principle of one united South Africa; one person, one vote; the eradication of all forms of racial discrimination; the protection of minorities against domination.

The Synod of the DRC approved a similar resolution two months later in the publication: *Church and Society*: racial discrimination and apartheid were rejected as unrighteous.

The stringent and severe measures of the most hostile legislation imposing sanctions against South Africa was now effective, called the CAAA: the Comprehensive Anti-Apartheid Act of the US Congress. It also contained strict conditions which South Africa would have to comply with before the sanctions could be removed. The US sanctions did have a negative impact on the economy and did influence reform-minded whites to consider negotiations with blacks as reasonable.

A further development on the road seeking to grant rights to blacks was the government's announcement that it was looking at a bill of rights. In 1986 Mr Kobie Coetsee, minister of justice, said that a bill of rights is a method by which the individual could turn to the courts for restitution of rights and announced that he had instructed the Law Commission to investigate the possibility of drawing up such a bill of rights.

When the chairman of the commission, Mr Justice Olivier, pointed out that a bill of rights is normally associated with the individual's rights, Mr Botha said it was not possible to talk about the protection of individual

---

272 Mandela, p.517

human rights unless one also talked about protecting minority rights, and only if group rights are guaranteed. Mr Coetsee then stated that the Law Commission would have to look at both human rights and group rights.

Group rights, however, are something which are protected in a constitution itself, such as language rights, not in a bill of rights, which deals with the rights of humans or individuals. Mr Justice Bekker, judge-president of SWA, made the point in 1984 that the fundamental approach is "that every person is entitled to the natural rights relating to his person or to his civil liberties unless such rights are limited or taken away by legislative enactment or regulations... "[273]

Professor Dion Basson, director of the Centre for Constitutional Research at the University of Pretoria, said in 1987 that in deciding where the government stood on real constitutional reform through meaningful negotiations, the debate on a bill of rights offered worrying insights. On the positive side, government rhetoric sometimes included a willingness to protect human rights, observed Professor Basson. The actions of the government, however, to a great extent belie these honourable intentions. Firstly, it comes after a long period of fierce resistance against the idea of a bill of rights and at a time when human rights were infringed upon as never before, especially with the state of emergency security measures – an onslaught on individual freedom for which the government was wholly responsible. Secondly, the government also did not hesitate to enforce the strictest security legislation through the non-elected President's Council in the face of fierce resistance against and without the consent of two of the houses of parliament (with the assent of only the government-controlled majority of the white house). Thirdly, and perhaps most important, was the stand taken on the protective, controlling constitutional role of the judiciary.

Professor Basson identified an alarming trend where the government strove vigorously to exclude the jurisdiction of the courts in security measures by making use of so-called "ouster" clauses. This trend also manifested itself in the actions taken by government to make the security measures even more severe every time the courts succeeded in controlling excessive government power within the narrow confines of judicial review.

These actions, Professor Basson concluded, revealed a grossly unsympathetic attitude towards the adequate protection of individual rights and freedoms, and if one took note of the fact that the Law Commission has been expressly given the task of investigating group rights, one could not help but conclude that the government intended to use the bill of rights merely as a ploy to entrench the political privileges of the ruling group. Group rights, Professor Basson pointed out, were totally irreconcilable with the true

---

273 Nestor and others vs. Minister of Police and others. In Rhoodie, p.162

purpose of a bill of rights to lend protection to individual human rights. The introduction of a fully liberal and individual bill of rights, in order to obtain a free and just society, was *not* in the cards as far as the government was concerned at that time.[274] A bill of rights did become part of the new constitution in 1994, and this debate did enlighten the voters to its merits.

Although the formulation and the real essence of power sharing was an element on which Botha with his manipulative designs failed, various opinion polls in South Africa indicated that whites supported the objective of power sharing. A 1986 survey for *Rapport* revealed that 67 percent of whites accept power sharing between black and white as inevitable. More than 54 percent believed the government should negotiate directly with black leaders. In the following year, a nationwide survey by the Human Sciences Research Council found that an overall majority among people of all races, and a majority among each racial group, supported the concept of power sharing between black and white. In a 1988 poll conducted for the Johannesburg *Star* newspaper by Marketing and Media Research, it was revealed that for every person in the Pretoria-Witwatersrand area who wants the Group Areas Act retained, almost two wanted it abolished immediately. The poll, whose statistical margin of error was about 3 percent, indicated that 52 percent of the people wanted the act either abolished immediately (36 percent) or abolished in time (16 percent), while only 18 percent favoured retaining the act.

The election of May 1987 was fought on the new policy approved by the NP Federal Congress the previous year. The NP won with a reduced majority against the growing opposition of the Conservative Party. A great number of apartheid laws were scrapped, but by 1988 the main pillars of apartheid still remained: race classification, separate amenities, group areas, and a constitution without black representation.

In August 1988, the government ignored the 1983 constitution (which required that all three houses must jointly consider decisions on general matters) by trying to push through the assembly a trilogy of laws affecting housing, squatters, and the Group Areas Act. The Progressive Federal Party walked out of the house. The Indian and coloured chambers refused to consider the laws. In the end the government backed down, faced by among other things a Labour Party threat to take their actions to court, but the harm had been done. The credibility of power sharing and consensus politics as viable policies suffered a body blow.[275]

In Washington, a senator of the Foreign Relations Committee, moderately sympathetic to the plight of South Africa, observed, "I admit your president

---

274   Rhoodie, p.164
275   Ibid, p.182

has publicly set a goal which, in previous years, during Malan and the others, even Vorster's time, would have won massive foreign support. Certainly our support. Yet Mr Botha remained on the apartheid team roster for another two decades and now, presto, he reveals himself to be a democrat. At least on paper. No-one is buying that. Everyone here is waiting for him to leave."[276] Apparently this also held true for some members of Botha's cabinet.

Mr Kurt von Schirnding, former South African ambassador to the United Nations and director-general of the South Africa Foundation, said in September 1988 that the previous eight years of the Reagan presidency had been squandered and were disappearing with enormous consequences for the future. If South Africa had the political will to move with purpose towards a new South Africa they needed courageous, visionary leadership to guide them along that road. The outside world was greeting their efforts abroad as too little too late because they placed no credibility on their willingness to reform.[277]

The US Congress Comprehensive Anti-Apartheid Act of 1986

This act was passed by the United States Congress on 2 October 1986. It is not for nothing that the act was called comprehensive. It was severe and covered every aspect of the US relations with South Africa. Its objective was to remove the system of apartheid and to establish a nonracial democracy in South Africa. It required the US to adjust its actions towards South Africa to reflect progress or lack of progress to achieve the aims of the act.

The act was drawn up in six chapters or titles that dealt with the following aspects or areas: policy of the United States with respect to ending apartheid; measures to assist victims of apartheid; measure by the Untied States to undermine apartheid – prohibiting imports from South Africa; multi-lateral measures to undermine apartheid – declare that it was US policy to seek international co-operative agreements with other industrialized democracies to end apartheid; future policy towards South Africa – declare that it was US policy to impose additional measures against South Africa if substantial progress had not been made within twelve months of enactment of this act in ending apartheid and the establishment of a nonracial democracy; and enforcement and administrative provisions of the act.

The policy of the United States with respect to ending apartheid outlined in the act required the establishment of a nonracial democracy in South Africa.

---

276 Ibid, p.183
277 Rhoodie, p.180

It set forth actions that the United States was to encourage South Africa to take, including releasing Nelson Mandela and establishing a timetable for the elimination of apartheid laws. It required the United States to adjust its actions toward South Africa to reflect the progress made by South Africa in establishing a nonracial democracy.

It declared that US policy toward the African National Congress, the Pan African Congress, and their affiliates be designed to bring about a suspension of violence that would lead to the start of negotiations. It required the United States to work toward this goal by encouraging such organisations, through diplomatic and political measures, to: (1) suspend terrorist activities; (2) make known their commitment to a free and democratic post-apartheid South Africa; (3) agree to enter into negotiations for the peaceful solution to South Africa's problems; and (4) re-examine their ties to the South African Communist Party. It required the United States to adjust its actions not only to reflect progress or lack of progress made by South Africa in establishing a nonracial democracy but also to reflect progress or lack of progress made by such organisations in bringing about a suspension of violence.

It declared that US policy toward the victims of apartheid was to use economic, political, diplomatic, and other means to remove the apartheid system and to assist the victims overcome the handicaps imposed on them by apartheid. It set forth actions the United States would take to help the victims of apartheid.

It declared that US policy toward the other countries in the region would be designed to encourage democratic forms of government, respect for human rights, political independence and economic development. The act set forth actions the United States would take toward such countries.

The act expressed the sense of the congress that the president should discuss with the African "frontline" states the effects of disruptions in economic links through South Africa.

The act declared that it is US policy to promote negotiations among representatives of all citizens of South Africa to determine a future political system.

It expressed the sense of the congress that high-level US officials should meet with leaders of opposition organisations in South Africa and should, in concert with other interested parties, try to bring together opposition political leaders with South African government leaders for negotiations to achieve a transition to the post-apartheid democracy envisioned in the act.

It declared that the United States would encourage all participants in the negotiations to respect the right of all South Africans to participate in the political process without fear of retribution. It further required the United States to work for an agreement to suspend violence and begin negotiations through coordinated actions with the major Western allies and with the governments of the countries in the region.

It expressed the sense of the congress that the achievement of such an agreement could be promoted if the United States and its major allies would meet to develop a plan to provide multilateral assistance for South Africa in return for South Africa implementing: (1) an end to the state of emergency and the release of political prisoners; (2) the unbanning of groups willing to suspend terrorism and to participate in negotiations and a democratic process; (3) a revocation of the Group Areas Act and the Population Registration Act and to grant universal citizenship to all South Africans, including homeland residents; and (4) the use of a third party to bring about negotiations to establish power sharing with the black majority.

It urged the president to seek cooperation among all individuals, groups, and nations to end apartheid.

It expressed the sense of the congress that the African National Congress should strongly condemn and take effective actions against the execution by fire, commonly known as "necklacing", of any person.

It expressed the sense of the senate that the US ambassador should request a meeting with Nelson Mandela.

It expressed the sense of the congress that US employers operating in South Africa are obliged both generally to oppose apartheid and specifically to recruit and train black and coloured South Africans for management responsibilities.

When the act was passed by the US Congress on 2 October 1986, it was fully reported in the press. The extent or growing effect of it did not really create material hardship in the short term. The period of time up to 1989 was not long enough for sanctions to become effective. The new act did encourage the ANC to sustain their resistance because of important foreign support.

Church and Society. A new DRC document on racial policy 1986

A DRC confession in 1986 that racial discrimination is a sin was led by Prof. Johan Heyns, moderator.

The 1978 Synod of the Dutch Reformed Mission Church (mainly coloured members) repudiated apartheid. One of the most noteworthy appeals came in 1980 from *Die Ligdraer*, official organ of the Dutch Reformed Mission Church. This journal wrote on 16 August 1980 that through its missionary policy the Dutch Reformed Church was, in fact, the formulator and propagator of a constitutional and economic apartheid policy. It wrote: The Dutch Reformed Church honestly believed that it was the only policy which could serve the highest interests of the whites and the non-whites, and that as a defence against racial conflict, it would be a lasting solution to South African social and political problems.

The fruits of the policy, however, are the quintessence of ambivalence, of good and evil, of opportunities for self-realisation intertwined with circumstances of gross dehumanization, of large-scale material and technical progress coupled with unbelievable deprivations in human values. For this reason the members of the (black and coloured) churches had experienced the apartheid policy, with all the benefits it had brought, as extremely oppressive.

In September 1982 the Synod of the Dutch Reformed Mission Church (mainly coloured members) reconfirmed its 1978 decision that apartheid (separate development) was a sin, that the moral and theological justification thereof was a mockery of the gospel, and that its consistent disobedience to the word of God was a theological heresy. The Synod of the Dutch Reformed Mission Church declared in 1982 that its resolution of 1978 implied that it had no choice but to accuse the Dutch Reformed Church of theological heresy and idolatry in the light of its theologically formulated stance and implementation thereof in practice. [278]The apartheid situation in South Africa and the stance of the Dutch Reformed Church on it, declared the Synod of the Dutch Reformed Mission Church, created a *status confessionis*. This decision of the Synod of the Dutch Reformed Mission Church was in line with a resolution adopted by the World Alliance of Reformed Churches (WARC) earlier the same year when it suspended the membership of the Dutch Reformed Church.[279]

Therefore, wrote *Die Ligdraer*, the Dutch Reformed Mission Church asked the Dutch Reformed Church to turn on its tracks and repudiate the policy of apartheid, and to help bring about the repeal of the Mixed Marriages Act, section 16 of the Immorality Act, and the Group Areas Act.

In the same year in which the Synod of the Dutch Reformed Mission Church declared that the apartheid situation in South Africa and the stance of the Dutch Reformed Church on it crated a *status confessionis*, the World Alliance of Reformed Churches (WARC), of which the Dutch Reformed Church and the Dutch Reformed Mission Church were members at that stage, took a similar decision.

---

278   Handelinge [Proceedings], Synod of the Dutch Reformed Mission Church, 1982, pp 604 and 706

279   Journey

The World Alliance of Reformed Churches (WARC) is the oldest and largest reformed ecumenical body in the world. On the basis of the view that the Dutch Reformed Church – and the Nederduitsch Hervormde Church of Afrika, which was also a member – had attempted to justify apartheid by misusing the gospel and the reformed confession, their membership was suspended. This suspension would remain in force until the two churches proved through their utterances and actions that their disposition had changed.

The General Synod of the Dutch Reformed Church in October 1982 was shaken by the WARC decision, and although the majority of synod delegates requested that the Dutch Reformed Church withdraw completely from the WARC, the two-thirds majority required for such a decision could not be obtained. In July 1997 the Dutch Reformed Church was still a "suspended member" of the WARC.

In 1985, a year before the DRC's document, *Church and Society*, declared racial discrimination a sin, Dr Beyers Naude still despaired about the hope for a change in attitude in the ordinary members of the DRC.

"We are deluding ourselves," Dr Naude is quoted in the *Belydendekring Bulletin* as saying. "Even if a new leadership emerges which is more open and verlig, the rank and file of the white membership has been so successfully indoctrinated with the concept of apartheid that it would take many years before the DRC could make any real contribution to the process of change in our country."[280]

This time round there was a possibility that even Beyers Naude was not picking up the early signs of a change developing in the Afrikaner's apartheid mindset. It was starting to form in the intellectual group in the Broederbond.

In the early eighties, the Lutheran World Federation took the lead with a further step opposing apartheid in a statement on confessional integrity. The Reformed Churches in South Africa and the World Alliance of Reformed Churches followed suit.

The statement by the Lutheran World Federation on confessional integrity added a new theological dimension to the debate about apartheid and its rejection as unchristian. The term status confessionis was soon taken up by the Reformed churches in South Africa, and when the WARC met in Ottawa, Canada, in 1982, it declared that the situation in South Africa "constitutes a status confessionis for our churches, which means that we regard this as an issue on which it is not possible to differ without seriously jeopardizing the integrity of our common confession as Reformed churches"[281]

---

280   *Ecunews*, March 1985
281   Peter Lodberg

The delegates agreed that the situation in South Africa posed a unique challenge to the church, and especially the churches in the Reformed tradition, because over the years the white Afrikaner Reformed churches of South Africa had worked out in considerable detail both the policy itself and the theological and moral justification for the apartheid system. Compared to the LWF, the WARC brought the new insight that apartheid must be qualified theologically and ethically as a pseudo-religious ideology as well as a political policy. The apartheid system depended to a large extent on this moral and theological justification, which had to be challenged for the sake of faith itself.

The issue of apartheid and racism had given the churches an important and independent voice in the international church community. They were challenging the content of many theological statements by their life experience and forced an ecumenical consensus about the issue of apartheid as heresy, a status confessionis, because they were living examples of suppression and exploitation.

The consensus about resisting apartheid as a matter of faith had paved the way for a more coherent understanding of the challenge to ecumenical ecclesiology from the field of justice, peace, and human rights. In line with Dietrich Bonhoeffer, Allan Boesak gave voice to the experience of the present-day Confessing Church in his speech at the WCC's sixth assembly in Vancouver in 1983, when he stated that the issues of justice, racism, hunger, and poverty are largely unresolved issues for the ecumenical movement, because these issues present the churches with painful dilemmas.

The history of apartheid and the ecumenical movement is a history of how it is possible to face the dilemma between ethics and ecclesiology, action and faith by saying that they assume each other. The experience from the South African church struggle has been that theological clarity means clarity in action. The clarity of what should be done with the evil apartheid system has a parallel development of clarity in the theological reflections of the churches in southern Africa.

Especially the Lutheran churches have learned that confession is confessing--an ongoing dynamic process within a broader ecumenical context, because the purpose of the confession is to express the faith of the whole universal church in a particular situation.

Confession as confessing brings the church out of its neutrality, because true confession assumes that the oppressor must be named. In the apartheid system, the oppressor was named by a careful analysis of the deep crisis which finally brought apartheid as a governmental system to its end. It was a long, dangerous and painful process for many people.

With the adoption of the doctrinal document *Church and Society*, the General Synod of 1986 firmly moved away from certain views contained in the *Race People Nation* document of 1974 and also fell into line with the resolutions taken by the Western Cape Synod three years earlier.[282]

Concerning apartheid, the following resolutions were contained in the document:

- In South Africa the idea and policy of separate development, with the ideal of territorial separation, evolved in the course of history. This was seen as a component of the whites' guardianship of the other groups, and had as its purpose the optimum development of all groups.

- Following the reflection that had taken place through the years in church periodicals, conferences, committees, and synods concerning the policy which had become known as apartheid, the conviction had gradually grown that a forced separation and division of peoples could not be considered a biblical imperative. The attempt to justify such an injunction as derived from the Bible had to be recognised as an error and be rejected.

- The Dutch Reformed Church was convinced that the application of apartheid as a political and social system by which human dignity is adversely affected, and whereby one particular group is detrimentally suppressed by another, could not be accepted on Christian-ethical grounds because it contravened the very essence of neighbourly love and righteousness and inevitably the human dignity of all involved.

- The suffering of people for whom the church had concern should, however, not have been attributed solely to the system of apartheid but to a variety of factors such as economic, social, and political realities in which persons of different communities had not been accepted by one another. To the extent that the church and its members were involved in this, it confessed its participation with humility and sorrow.

- The Dutch Reformed Church declared that it was prepared to cooperate in the spirit of Christ to seek a solution which would enable every sector of the South African society to attain the highest possible level of well-being.

Concerning marriage, the following was resolved, *inter alia*:

- The scriptures did not forbid racially mixed marriages. In its pastoral work, however, the church gave due warning that social circumstances, as well as ideological, philosophical, cultural, and socio-economic differences and other factors, could cause serious tensions. Where such marriages did take place, those involved needed to receive pastoral guidance in all aspects of marriage.

The resolutions of the General Synod of 1986 – particularly those which declared the membership of the Dutch Reformed Church open, and that services of worship and other meetings were open to all visitors who desire to listen to the word in fellowship with other believers – caused great commotion.[283] Eight months after the synod, this led to schism when a large number of members left the DRC to establish a new church, the Afrikaans Protestant Church.

The Afrikaans Protestant Church was founded, partly as a consequence of the rejection of the demand by aggrieved members for the repeal of all resolutions contained in Kerk en Samelewing 1986 and for an express injunction that membership of the Dutch Reformed Church be reserved for white Afrikaners and whites who associated themselves with white Afrikaner society.[284]

An important question was in what way the members of the DRC were informed and advised of the implications of Kerk en Samelewing. It was widely reported in the newspapers; the church authorities accepted the newspapers reporting as sufficient information and did not encourage or organise any other method of dissemination. The "platteland" members of the DRC were opposed to the new directive and the church ministers made no effort to have the document discussed. They feared disunity. In the urban areas, many but not all churches did discuss the synod document. Overall, the DRC members as a whole did not express their support or changed convictions about apartheid.

The Nederduitsch Hervormde Kerk could still not reject apartheid on theological grounds at its General Council meeting in September 2007, to the disappointment of its leadership, because a theological rejection of apartheid was necessary before it could quality for membership of the WARC.[285]

---

283 *Kerk en Samelewing 1986*, par 270
284 *Die Kerkbode*, 1 July 1987
285 *Rapport*, 30 September 2007

CHAPTER 6

ENDING IT ALL UNDER PRESIDENT F. W. DE KLERK, 1990–94

Untangling policy and security in the security establishment

When F. W. de Klerk assumed the presidency in August 1989, political expectations and fears arose among South Africans, both black and white, as a result of his efforts towards the "normalization" of political activities within the country. This normalization was accompanied by an escalating spiral of violence—often indiscriminate and motiveless, whether political or criminal. In this ongoing period of political transition and intense violence, the question was what the nature of President de Klerk's relationship with the various South African intelligence services he inherited was.[286]

Was the "old" securocrat network still in place?

Under former president P. W. Botha, the securocrats seconded personnel from the South African security establishment, exercised extensive influence

---

286 Commentary No 15, November 1991 by Dr R. Henderson, a publication of the Analysis and Production Branch of the Canadian Security and Intelligence Service (CSIS)

over state decision-making and policy implementation. The key elements of the securocrat establishment were the State Security Council (SSC) and its implementation instrument, the National Security Management System (NSMS).

The SSC was established by the 1972 Security Intelligence and State Security Act, with responsibility to "advise the government on the formulation of national policy and strategy in relation to the security of the country" and for determining national intelligence priorities. Although the only cabinet-level committee created by statute, it was not referred to as such in the act. Its standing membership was designated to include the prime minister (later state president) as chairman, the four ministers of defence, foreign affairs, justice, and police (now law and order), the senior cabinet member if not already included in the above portfolios, the senior officials for security intelligence, now the National Intelligence Service (NIS), South African Defence Force (SADF), the Ministries of Foreign Affairs and Justice, and South African police (SAP), and other cabinet ministers and department heads who "may from time to time be co-opted" by the chairman.

In response to the country-wide black unrest of 1984-86, the NSMS was developed to provide the SSC with a network of regional security committees with broad "law and order" powers to implement and co-ordinate local political and security policies. Operating from Joint Management Committees (JMCs) headed by the SADF regional commanders, the main objective of the system was to placate local socio-economic grievances in the black townships while suppressing protest movements. In effect, the JMCs managed improvements to local infrastructure and housing, while also coordinating the security crackdowns on anti-apartheid activists.

Repeatedly, the South African government and its security components were described in terms of a so-called division between "hawks", who were seen to include some members of de Klerk's cabinet and the security establishment as a whole; and "doves", who constituted the majority in the cabinet; as well as the key departments of constitutional development, finance, and foreign affairs. Another perspective separated these two groups into securocrat commanders and civilian politicians. What was often missed in these ongoing perspectives was that the so-called securocrat hawks and civilian doves in the South African government tended to share common concerns about what they saw as major threats to South Africa's – primarily white South Africans' – security. Their differences centred on the issue of the "means to be utilized" to ensure this security – destabilization by use of force or negotiation by strength.

In addition to those who supported "reform with security" and those who favoured "force to ensure white security", there was a further sinister "element" within South Africa responsible for some of the repeated indiscriminate acts of violence—whether by direct action, indirect manipulation or financial commission. All of its components appeared to be products of the "security and destabilization" milieu in the Southern African region over the last two decades. Although often referred to in the South African media as "a third force", African National Congress (ANC) president Nelson Mandela acknowledged that the people who carried out the killings "may not be belonging to any particular organization".[287]

Rather, this amorphous "mafia-like network"—including whites and blacks—seemed to be comprised of former securocrat officials, ex-government security personnel, individuals who had financially gained (or lost) as a result of regional upheaval, and a variety of non-governmental units which practiced clandestine activities. These latter units included various black homeland security forces, extremist groupings (white and black), and some private business concerns—including those from former Rhodesia and the Portuguese African colonies—which had benefited from the previous security-dominated policy agenda of the South African government.

Presidential change of command

In his position as head of government, de Klerk's cabinet leadership style was reputed to be by "consensus, persuasion and argument ... consulting closely with his cabinet before taking major decisions".[288] He increased the number of cabinet meetings, including introducing *bosberaads* (brainstorming retreats) in the Transvaal bush with his key ministers.

Even so, de Klerk inherited all his ministers concerned with security affairs, as well as key public service bureaucrats, from the former president's securocrat network. The ministers, all with substantial service under P. W. Botha, included the defence minister, General Magnus Malan (former SADF chief under then defence minister Botha), the law and order minister Adriaan Vlok (responsible for the SAP and former deputy minister of defence and of law and order), Justice Minister Kobie Coetsee (former deputy minister of defence and a longtime special adviser to President Botha on intelligence and security matters, including the 1979 NIS reorganization) and Foreign Affairs Minister R. F. "Pik" Botha.

But de Klerk's early reform proposals suggested he would rely less on the secretive National Security Management System (NSMS) structure and the securocrats who manned it and more on his own political advisers—including Constitutional Development Minister Gerrit Viljoen and Justice

287 *New York Times*, 10 September 1991
288 *The Star*, Johannesburg, 10 February 1990

Minister Coetsee—who called for power-sharing negotiations with moderate black leaders. In an interview given before de Klerk assumed the office of the president, his brother political commentator Wimpie de Klerk, suggested that while being unable totally to exclude the military presence from the South African policy-making, "he [the president-designate] will be more dependent on national intelligence [service], not on military intelligence" upon becoming president.[289]

One of de Klerk's first decisions upon assuming the post of state president following the September 1989 election was to move the Bureau for Information (BI) and the NIS under the Office of the President. This meant that the government agencies for both open government media activities and secret intelligence coordination were to be directly responsible to him. (Under Botha, the NIS had reported to both the president and the SSC.) At this stage, de Klerk had already decided to use the NIS—unlike Botha's use of the SSC—as his principal source of intelligence and his personal instrument for conducting confidential presidential initiatives.

In the fall of 1989, the de Klerk government's essential prelude to beginning its own political reform agenda was to draft Namibia's independence constitution. This called for an elected constituent assembly and specified that the election, in order to be internationally recognized, had to be declared "free and fair" by the United Nations.

Re-asserting cabinet control

The incidence of renegade intelligence activities drove de Klerk finally to definitive action in his dealings with the South African intelligence services. He issued a number of directives intended to impose firm cabinet control over the intelligence services and their ongoing covert operations.

The NSMS implementation structure was dismantled while the SSC was restructured to operate under the newly created Cabinet Committee for Security Affairs (CCSA), one of the four standing cabinet committees. Meeting fortnightly under the chairmanship of the president himself, the CCSA appeared to convene separately from or jointly with the SSC as determined by de Klerk, who chaired both.

The formerly dominant SSC—now operating under the decision-making CCSA in an advisory capacity—included all security affairs ministers and other co-opted ministers as well as all the heads of the relevant departments and security commands. This restructuring restored the cabinet to its constitutional role as the highest decision-making body. Also, as a result, the Office of the President, which had grown under P. W. Botha to accommodate

289 Africa Report, July-august 1989, p36

the increasingly centralized decision-making by his circle of security advisers, was scaled down, with policy-making functions returned to the responsible departments.

Along with the SCC's downgrading, its vast secretariat was "streamlined" from its 100-plus staff of seconded securocrats to only the few needed to coordinate information from the various security services. The restructuring, replaced the SSC's previously accumulated roles of analyzing multiservice intelligence input, generating policy options within the Botha government's "total strategy" and implementing SSC-approved ones through the NSMS committee structure. According to de Klerk, the NSMS structure itself was to be abolished and an inquiry into "mechanisms to fill this gap" instituted.

Turning to **covert operations and special accounts**, de Klerk ordered a full investigation of "covert security force functions" with the declared purpose "to ensure and exercise not only financial control but also cabinet control over such (secret) projects". In addition, "some" secret projects were "immediately cancelled", including a reduction in the anti-sanctions activities funded by the Department of Foreign Affairs.

In a March 1990 special session of the South African parliament, de Klerk publicly announced that he had initiated the "covert functions" investigation, even though it was still ongoing. He went on to point out that a cabinet decision had been taken to restrict all "special secret projects", that covert actions should be limited to the "absolutely essential minimum" and that there would be a review of the legislation controlling the use of secret funds.[290]

A number of **changes in the security legislation** were made, including cancelling the previous power of the minister of finance to suppress information about unauthorized expenditure if he considered it in the national interest, or to exclude specific amounts from the scrutiny of the government auditor general.[291] When the investigation was completed in mid-1990, "numerous covert actions were cancelled in an orderly fashion", though some actions "continued in the broad national interest ... subject to cabinet control and are being carefully and firmly managed", according to President de Klerk.[292]

Furthermore, a "standing instruction" for **a comprehensive re-evaluation of all remaining projects** had been issued "with a view to scaling them down and adapting them to the new circumstances in the country". Even so, secret expenditures could still be requested and used in special projects by a minister if his department did not possess a special account, with the approval of the minister from whose special account the funds were drawn.

290   SAPA, 1 March 1990
291   *The Star*, Johannesburg, 2 August 1991
292   SAPA, 19 and 31 July 1991

Finally, the expenditure records were made available for annual review by the auditor general.

The **government intelligence services**—the NIS, the SAP's security branch, and the SADF's Directorate of Military Intelligence (DMI)—were all, at this time, covertly operating within the country as well as elsewhere on the continent and overseas. This resulted not only in some duplication of their clandestine activities but also in intra-service rivalries.

To regularize their areas of responsibility, de Klerk reportedly imposed functional limits on the three intelligence services as "numerous covert actions were cancelled in an orderly fashion".[293] On 10 January 1990, he addressed 500 senior SAP commanders on the need to concentrate on rising crime rather than on anti-state political activities, although the security branch was to continue its functions of field (internal) intelligence gathering and detection of military underground structures. In April 1991 the security branch was combined with the criminal investigation division into a new Crime Combating and Investigation unit (CCI). But the new CCI has been placed under the command of SAP General Basie Smit, who had commanded the security branch prior to the merger and, according to Department of Law and Order press releases, the security branch organization and command structure have been retained within the CCI.

At the same time, the NIS was to retain its role of national intelligence coordination and assessment for the president and the SSC, but answerable only to the president. It was also to maintain liaison with "friendly" intelligence agencies in Africa and overseas through a combination of information exchanges and, in some cases, provision of training and material assistance—while also expanding its contacts and intelligence gathering.

The emergence of the NIS as *primus inter pares* was unambiguously underlined by the civilian-oriented state president in April 1990, according to a South African academic with strong links with the security establishment.[294] Speaking at the NIS twenty-first anniversary banquet, de Klerk reportedly praised "the NIS's objective reporting" whilst obliquely intimating that the other services had blotted their copybooks by advancing subjective preferences and interests. However, even the NIS has suffered from leaked security information.

In the case of the Directorate of Military Intelligence (DMI), de Klerk has acknowledged that soon after taking office, he was briefed on the internal workings of the SADF, including its clandestine special forces, "the eyes and ears of the SADF". Although this briefing reportedly included covert operations, he has since stated that the smaller subsections of the many

293 SAPA, 1 March 1990
294 Simon Baynham, *Journal of Modern African Studies*, September 1990, p.429

branches of the defence force were not explained in any detail. As such, he claimed to have learned of the existence of the clandestine Civil Co-operation Bureau—accused of having directed government death squads against anti-apartheid activists—for the first time only in January 1990, when General Malan, the defence minister at the time, had informed him.

In turn, General Malan himself claimed to have learned of its existence only during the previous November, apparently at de Klerk's request to the "covert functions" investigation. In terms of ministerial authority, however, Malan would have had to approve the use of any defence special account funding for its 1986 creation and subsequent operations.

While the effect and extent of the restrictions placed on military intelligence remain unclear, it was most likely de Klerk's intention to curb the range of SADF covert activities within the country relative to the security branch and the NIS. On 7 March 1990, he held a further SAP commanders' meeting, with one meeting for senior SADF commanders where he pointed out that the armed forces in the future would concentrate on securing the country's borders while providing internal assistance in controlling unrest areas only "if requested" by the SAP regional commands.

In November 1990, partially to alleviate the increasing demands of "intelligence matters" on the state president, de Klerk appointed Roelf Meyer as deputy minister of information services in the president's office. Meyer was placed in charge of both the government's public information image and "intelligence matters"—the NIS and the SSC. The appointment has been seen as a move by which Meyer would mould the intelligence service into an institution able to supply analysis, interpretation and intelligence "more appropriate to a negotiating president".[295]

The "new" securocrats?

Inherited from the P. W. Botha era, Defence Minister Malan and Law and Order Minister Vlok have been repeatedly denounced by opposition groups and the media as hard-line "hawks" for their confrontational approach and their failure to halt the violence. The ANC in particular had consistently called for their resignations. Despite evidence from recent judicial inquiries into secret government death squads, de Klerk continued to support his ministers publicly, pointing out "that the army and the police are not under investigation as organizations".[296]

His support gave way soon after. With the July 1991 revelations about the government's "Inkathagate" covert funding to Chief Mangesuthu

---

295   South Scan, 16 November 1990, p.325
296   SAPA News Report, 23 February 1990

Buthelezi's Inkatha Freedom Party (IFP) and covert funding to seven anti-SWAPO political parties in the 1989 Namibian elections, Malan and Vlok were demoted from their security-related portfolios. Although they lost their seniority as well as their *ex-officio* membership on both the CCSA and the SSC, they retained their positions as full cabinet members. De Klerk, as chairman of both forums, could co-opt them onto each or both without public notice.

When asked about his cabinet demotion, General Malan replied that "a good man succeeds me and I will help him where I can."[297] This assistance seemed to include advice in cabinet on security matters. His replacement, Roelf Meyer, in addition to his new portfolio as minister of defence, was appointed minister of communications with responsibility for the South African Communications Service. While Meyer appears to have retained responsibility for the government's media efforts, he dropped his responsibility for "intelligence matters" in the president's office to focus on defence per se.

Theo Alant, in addition to his previous post as deputy minister of finance, was appointed deputy minister for the National Intelligence Service. In view of the government revelations concerning the finance ministry's administration of special accounts and secret funding, with which Alant would have been involved, his new joint responsibility suggests he had become the cabinet watchdog over continuing covert operations and their funding. And the new minister of law and order, Hernus Kriel—first appointed to the cabinet as minister of planning and housing by de Klerk following the 1989 election—would deal with crime fighting and the government's image in the urban areas and townships in his present post.

Prospects

President de Klerk continued to be accused of having done "little or nothing to shake off the culture of clandestine operations and secret funds" inherited from the P. W. Botha era.[298]

But just like the ANC with its clandestine Operation Vula to establish safe houses and arms caches within the country—discovered by the security branch in July 1990 but started three years earlier—the de Klerk government with its Inkathagate slush fund scandal found that covert operations begun before the political normalization were difficult to stop or revise. After nearly three decades of active armed struggle between government security services and militant activists, it is almost certain that there were security commanders

---

297   SAPA, 29 July 1991
298   *The Cape Times*, editorial, 22 July 1991

in each case who advised that it was best to let the operations proceed "just in case the negotiations process broke down."

Based on his detailed parliamentary speeches, de Klerk had made substantial changes in the way the intelligence services and clandestine operations were run—albeit within his reformist view of "law and order" (see *Commentary*, No 5, August 1990) and in accordance with his constitutional negotiating strategy. Even so, "grudge leaks" of security information and covert activities had been released to the media, both by conservative elements among the government security services and by political opposition "moles" who had infiltrated government ranks.

They had different reasons for leaking this information. By embarrassing de Klerk and his key ministers, information had been leaked by ANC supporters in the hope of providing the black opposition with negotiating leverage over the government. Alternatively, the leaks by white conservative elements were almost certainly intended to try to derail the negotiations process or, however unlikely, to provoke the government into re-implementing the earlier "armed suppression" approach in line with the traditional view of "law and order."

Informing the police of Nelson Mandela's release

Prior to F. W. de Klerk's public announcement regarding the release of Nelson Mandela from prison it was made known to the securocrats 286[299] who until then, were the mainstay of the government's staunch, relentless, and highly effective social engineering machinery. One of the first levels to which de Klerk's policy regarding Mandela was made known was the weekly meeting of senior officers of the security branch of the South African police, ironically nicknamed the "Sanhedrin". The news was received with shock by everybody, and many were thereafter traumatised because of the uncertainty of the consequences and how it would affect them. The most junior officer in the meeting, a young, decorated colonel responsible for monitoring a broad spectrum of the Tripartite Alliance (ANC, SACTU and SACP), immediately took the floor declaring that this would happen "over my dead body."

---

299 Securocrat : politically influential military or police officer: a senior military, police or intelligence officer with power to influence government policy, often from behind the scenes. Blend of security and bureaucrat

The Rustenburg Conference of Churches, November 1990

The recommendations on changes which were to be proposed to the DRC in respect of Kerk and Samelewing 1986 had already been finalised on 6 November 1989, some considerable time before the date for the signing scheduled for October 1990.

Three years earlier Prof. J. A. Heyns, moderator of the Dutch Reformed Church General Synod, had suggested that a meeting of South African churches be organised to discuss the issues in the *Church and Society* document.

Mr F. W. de Klerk, who became president in August 1989, followed up on this suggestion. In his 1989 Christmas message de Klerk said that he would like to hear what the churches jointly had to say to the government and the country about the situation in South Africa. It soon became obvious that his involvement in convening such a conference would be a problem for some churches. He then stepped back, and a committee of Christian leaders was formed under the chairmanship of Dr Louw Alberts and Pastor Frank Chikane. They succeeded in getting representatives of eighty churches in South Africa to the conference in the Bushveld. The four official delegates of the Dutch Reformed Church were Prof. P. C. Potgieter, moderator of the General Synod of 1990, and Drs P. Rossouw, D. J. Hattingh, and F. M. Gaum. Two Dutch Reformed Church academics, Profs J. A. Heyns and W. D. Jonker, attended the conference as speakers.

On 2 February 1990 the state president, Mr F. W. de Klerk , announced in parliament that several political organisations were being unbanned, including the ANC and the Communist Party, expressed himself in favour of a negotiated settlement of South Africa's constitutional problems, and thereby announced the end of the apartheid era in South Africa.

The revised document, *Church and Society 1990*, reiterated that the church should not prescribe political models to the government, but it would, by virtue of its prophetic function, continue to test every existing and proposed political model against biblical principles and norms.

A fairly comprehensive resolution was adopted by the DRC Synod on apartheid in October 1990 (par. 278–88). It read:

> In the evaluation of apartheid the church is confronted with strong and emotionally-laden differences. While a part of the white population considers it a just way to protect the identity and the best interest of the different population groups in the country, other perceive it as a racist and oppressive system which protects and promotes the interest of

the white minority to the detriment of the majority of the population. Consequently, numerous churches condemn it as unchristian and sinful. Apartheid is condemned by states and political institutions worldwide as a form of racism and a transgression against humanity.

The Dutch Reformed Church realises that the ideal and policy of apartheid took form and shape over a long period in our history. There were also honest and noble intentions by those concerned to achieve the optimal development of all population groups within the framework of their own cultural traditions.

It would also be unreasonable to brand as wrong and bad everything which took place within the political structure of apartheid and to deny the positive developments achieved in various fields.

In principle the right and freedom of peoples to preserve and promote their own cultural and other values are acknowledged as integral to human rights, provided that the rights and freedom of others are not affected thereby, and the biblical demand to love one's neighbour and to accept one's fellow man are not negated.

The Dutch Reformed Church, however, acknowledges that for too long it had adjudged the policy of apartheid on the above named grounds too abstractly and theoretically, and therefore too uncritically. The Dutch Reformed Church had not sufficiently perceived that apartheid as a system had *inter alia* in its struggle against integration also received an ideological and ethnocentric basis. The right and freedom to remain true to one's own cultural heritage was extended to become a political ideology of apartheid as a system for the protection of the white minority's own interests to the detriment of others. Love for one's own often took the shape of racism and was expressed in legal and structural terms.

While the Dutch Reformed Church over the years seriously and persistently sought the will of God and His Word for our society, the church made the error of allowing forced separation and division of peoples in its own circle to be considered a Biblical imperative. The Dutch Reformed Church should have distanced itself much earlier from this view and admits and confesses its neglect.

Gradually it became clear to the Dutch Reformed Church that the policy of apartheid as a political system in practice went much further than the acknowledgement of the right and freedom of all peoples and cultural groups to stay true to their own values. Apartheid began to function in such a way that the largest part of the population of the country experienced it as an oppressive system which through the forced separation of peoples was in reality favouring one group wrongfully above the others. In this way the human dignity of one's fellow man became adversely affected and was in conflict with the principles of love and righteousness.

Any system which in practice functions in this way is unacceptable in the light of Scripture and the Christian conscience and must be rejected as sinful. Any attempt by a church to try to defend such a system biblically and ethically must be seen as a serious fallacy, that is to say it is in conflict with the Bible.

The Dutch Reformed Church wants to state clearly that it condemns all forms of discrimination and the suppression of peoples and wholeheartedly desires that all will be free to share in the privileges of the fatherland and will receive reasonable and equal opportunities to acquire prosperity and riches.

The church has, above all, compassion for the poverty and suffering of large numbers of people in our country and declares that it is prepared to co-operate in an ecclesiastical way in attempts to relieve the present need and to make it possible for all people in our country to have a better future.

The church, however, is convinced that a satisfactory political solution is necessary for the social problems which exist at present, and therefore urges all political leaders to co-operate in a responsible way to find a political dispensation which will ensure freedom, justice and a decent existence for all.

The Conference of Churches at Rustenburg took place in November 1990. In some respects it was an event comparable to the Cottesloe Conference thirty years before.

At the end of his speech, Prof. Jonker, of the theological seminary at Stellenbosch, declared, "I confess before you and before God not just my own sin and guilt, and my personal responsibility for the political, social, economic, and structural injustices under which you and our entire country are still suffering, but I also venture to do so vicariously on behalf of the Dutch Reformed Church, of which I am a member, and for the Afrikaners. I am at liberty to do so because at its last General Synod the Dutch Reformed Church declared apartheid a sin and acknowledged guilt for its own omission, in that it did not long ago warn against apartheid and distance the church from it." [translation]

After Jonker's speech, Archbishop Desmond Tutu of the Anglican Church said, of his own accord, that he accepted the confession of guilt and had no doubts about its sincerity.

Potgieter, leader of the Dutch Reformed Church delegation, told the conference the following day, "The delegation of the Dutch Reformed Church wishes to state unequivocally that we fully associate ourselves with

Prof. Jonker's statement on the position of this church. In fact, he was conveying the decisions of our General Synod in Bloemfontein. We would like to see the synod's decisions as the basis for reconciliation with all people and all churches.

"The question of restitution after confession has also been raised. The minutes of our synod show clearly that we have already begun a process of restitution, both in our relationship with our own family of Dutch Reformed Churches and in our relationship with South African society as a whole."

After Potgieter's declaration Tutu went to the podium, as he had the previous day, and said that he had been subjected to a great deal of criticism for accepting Jonker's confession of guilt. He had been asked what authority he had to do that. Some church figures also felt that the guilt of the Dutch Reformed Church could not be forgiven so easily, he said. But he had no doubts: if guilt was confessed, the Lord would forgive – and Christians should forgive one another similarly. "Up to seventy times seven", said the Lord Jesus.

Reaction in Dutch Reformed Church ranks to the "Rustenburg confession"

The Rustenburg conference caused great disquiet in ecclesiastical ranks, just like Cottesloe three decades earlier, and this led to a special meeting of the General Synodal Commission. The GSC criticised both Jonker and the Dutch Reformed Church delegation to the Rustenburg conference because in their statements they "had not referred to the full context of the synod's decisions" and explained, "This could have caused confusion amongst members."

In its statement after the meeting the GSC reiterated the resolution on apartheid by the General Synod and said, "The General Synod came to the conclusion that in the light of the scriptures and Christian conscience, apartheid – and this would also apply to any other system which functioned similarly in practice – was unacceptable and, being sinful, should be rejected. The GSC wished to point out that the General Synod was judging apartheid within a qualified context and rejected apartheid thus defined as sinful."[300]

As a result of the prominent media coverage given to the Rustenburg Conference of Churches and what followed, these events became, in the public mind, the time and place of the Dutch Reformed Church's confession of guilt for apartheid, rather than the General Synod a few months earlier, where it actually happened officially. In a certain sense the Dutch Reformed Church's "journey with apartheid" ended with the "arrival at Rustenburg."

---

300 *Die Kerkbode*, 14 December 1990

A leading article in *Die Kerkbode* of 16 November 1990 described the confession of guilt as follows: "For the Dutch Reformed Church the confession of guilt at the General Synod of 1990, and its communication to the Rustenburg Conference of Churches, was a moment of liberation. Now everyone who needs to know does know: the official Dutch Reformed Church acknowledges that apartheid is a sin and confesses that its part in enforcing and upholding apartheid was wrong".

The article continued: "Confessing one's guilt is never easy: not to God, nor to one's husband or wife or child, nor to another people or another church. But, as long as it is done in the name of Christ, one will always receive forgiveness from God and, fortunately, often from other people as well – and even from other churches. This happened last week at Rustenburg in a moving, unforgettable way. The fact that Archbishop Desmond Tutu – often regarded, on account of his highly controversial statements, as an arch-opponent of the Dutch Reformed Church – played a part made it all the more remarkable.

It concluded: "The Dutch Reformed Church knows that confession of guilt inevitably leads to restitution – the putting right of the wrong that was done. The church already began to attend to that with some of its resolutions at the General Synod of 1990. This will continue in future. Meanwhile, we shall also continue to thank the Lord for the many good and right things done by the Dutch Reformed Church in the past, things which truly served to honour and glorify His Name."[301]

On 13 October 1994 the president of the Republic of South Africa, Mr N. R. Mandela, visited and addressed the General Synod of the Dutch Reformed Church. He said, amongst other things: "Apartheid was a scorched-earth policy against the majority of people in our country. Apartheid was fundamentally wrong and sinful. I do not say these things in order to rub salt into the wounds, because I am aware of the long struggle in the Dutch Reformed Church concerning apartheid and the profound inner struggle which many members have gone through. *Church and Society* was an important milestone, but it was not the beginning for the long road which has brought you to this synod, neither can it be the end, because the quest for enlightenment and truth always continues ... With the Dutch Reformed Church's acknowledgement that apartheid was wrong, a special prophetic task now rests on your shoulders. Having searched your own hearts, you must now join hands with all the rest of us to ensure that the Reconstruction and Development Programme succeeds"[302]

---

301 Journey
302 *Handelinge* [Proceedings] of the General Synod 1994, p.536 (Journey, p.28)

Mandela referred to "the constructive role which the leadership of the Dutch Reformed Church played during the turbulent period leading up to the election of 27 April 1994." "Your readiness to caution some of your own members against racism and reckless war talk was an important contribution to the miracle of South Africa's peaceful transition to democracy. You are an integral part of South Africa's peaceful transition to democracy. You are an integral part of South Africa's unique testimony in a world in which so much violence and intolerance still prevails," he said.[303]

Group rights, the idea that persuaded whites but which was rejected by the ANC

After nothing came of visits by Minister Coetzee to Mandela in prison, Mandela wrote a memorandum to P. W. Botha in March 1988. In his memorandum Mandela suggested negotiations on two political issues: the demand for majority rule in a unitary state and the concern of white South Africa over this demand, as well as the insistence of whites on structural guarantees that majority rule will not mean domination of the white minority by blacks.

Botha set up a secret working group under Minister Kobie Coetsee to host discussions with Mandela. The first of many meetings took place in May 1988 outside Pollsmoor prison. One area of discussion was the issue of majority rule. Botha's delegates felt that if there was majority rule, the rights of minorities would be trampled. How would the ANC protect the rights of the white minority, they wanted to know. Mandela said that there was no organisation in the history of South Africa to compare with the ANC in terms of trying to unite all the people and races of South Africa. He referred them to the preamble of the Freedom Charter: "South Africa belongs to all who live in it, black and white," and told them that whites were Africans as well, and that in any future dispensation the majority would need the minority. "We do not want to drive you into the sea," he said.[304]

These discussions were followed by a visit arranged for Mandela to meet P. W. Botha at his official residence. A little more than a month after Botha met Mandela in Tuynhuys, his official residence in Cape Town, he resigned as state president in August 1989. The next day de Klerk was sworn in as acting president and affirmed his commitment to change and reform. De Klerk was inaugurated as state president on 20 September 1989.

---

303 Journey, p.39
304 Mandela, p.527

A development of great significance, which must have put pressure on de Klerk to accelerate his announcement on 2 February 1990 to start negotiations, was a successful meeting that took place in Switzerland on 12 September 1989, eight days before de Klerk's inauguration as state president. The meeting was between an ANC delegation led by Thabo Mbeki and Jacob Zuma and senior officials of the National Intelligence Service. According to de Klerk, it was the first official and direct contact between the South African government and the ANC and was arranged in terms of a decision of the State Security Council without his knowledge.[305] As the first meeting, it was of historical importance since it had ended the decades-long period of antagonism and non-contact.

In the interim, before Mandela's meeting with de Klerk, Mandela continued to meet the secret negotiations committee started by P. W. Botha. He wrote to de Klerk about how impressed he was by the emphasis he placed on reconciliation in his inaugural speech, but added that the first step to reconciliation was the complete dismantling of apartheid and all measures to enforce it. A meeting was arranged for Mandela to meet de Klerk in Tuynhuys on 13 December 1989.

One of the issues Mandela emphasised during his interview with de Klerk was the National Party's five-year plan, which contained the concept of group rights. The idea of group rights was that no racial or ethnic group could take precedence over any other. Although it defined group rights as a way of protecting the freedom of minorities in a new South Africa, in fact he believed that the proposal was a means of preserving white domination. Mandela told Mr de Klerk that group rights was unacceptable to the ANC.[306]

"An oppressive system cannot be reformed," Mandela said. "It must be entirely cast aside." He mentioned a recent editorial which had appeared in *Die Burger*, the mouthpiece of the National Party in the Cape, implying that the group rights concept was conceived as an attempt to bring back apartheid through the back door. Mandela added that the ANC had not struggled against apartheid for seventy-five years only to yield to a disguised form of it, and that if it was de Klerk's intention to preserve apartheid through the Trojan horse of group rights, then he did not truly believe in ending apartheid.[307]

De Klerk replied that his aim was no different from Mandela's. Mandela's memo to P. W. Botha said the ANC and the government should work together to deal with white fears of black domination, and the idea of group rights was how the NP government proposed to deal with it. Mandela responded that the idea of group rights did more to increase black fears than allay white

---

305 De Klerk, p.174
306 Mandela, p.544
307 Ibid

ones. Then, according to Mandela, de Klerk said, "We will have to change it, then."[308]

De Klerk's biography does not contain the last sentence about change away from group rights that Mandela reported in his version of their talks.

The ANC's insistence on equal rights that would give blacks a majority without conditions and de Klerk's advocacy of group rights to protect the white minority was the heart of the issue. Mandela said this idea of group rights meant retention of apartheid. Logically group rights could only be guaranteed if race classification and group areas legislation were retained, which was at the core of apartheid.

De Klerk deserves credit for accepting the responsibility to immediately introduce far reaching changes. After his election as state president he immediately took decisive steps to change the status quo. It is almost as if he had been preparing himself for it beforehand and carefully, as is his leadership style, assessed the extent to which the National Party would go along with his new direction that required drastic and immediate measures.

In De Klerk's speech on 2 February 1990 in parliament, he announced that Mandela would be released, the ANC, SACP, the PAC and others unbanned, the release of further groups of ANC prisoners, and the lifting of the state of emergency regulations affecting the media and education. Talks with the ANC about negotiations would follow.

A few weeks later, F. Van Zyl Slabbert, previous opposition leader, asked de Klerk in Tuynhuys why he had made the announcements in his speech. One of two reasons he responded, was that he had made a spiritual leap in terms of his acceptance that apartheid was morally indefensible and secondly the opportunities created by the fall of the Berlin Wall and the collapse of communism.[309] Reference has already been made to de Klerk's reason for rejecting apartheid and the indication of a connection between the date of his new conviction and the resolution and confession of the DRC in 1986 that apartheid is a sin.

The key part of de Klerk's strategy was to lead the NP with a concept that embodied the idea of change to black rule that would protect white minority rights. He used the concept of group rights that would allow black majority rule and safeguard white interests.

The tempo of change depended exclusively on the degree to which de Klerk accepted the need for change; his strategy and tactics to lead the NP to accept drastic change called for considerable political skill for which de Klerk was well schooled; to take risks in the process and to maintain unity in the NP ranks in the process of change. The main risk was that the reform minded

---

308   Mandela, p.545
309   Van Zyl Slabbert, p.35

supporters in the NP and the electorate would remain a majority. Another risk was that violence by black and white could destroy the peaceful process.

The difficulty was that the attitude of white supremacy that had been formed for generations over 150 years had to be changed in a very short time without disunity that would divide the party. De Klerk's tactic was not to change the attitude of the Afrikaners in the NP but to persuade them with promises of protection of group rights. He knew Mandela and the ANC would not accept this tactic. After all, Mandela had told him so in his first interview at Tuynhuys in Cape Town, in addition to all similar statements Mandela made that de Klerk read in his briefings.

The ongoing violence and difficult economic circumstances favoured the opposition in parliament, the Conservative Party. Their propaganda exploited every agreement and progress made with reform as concessions and deviations made under pressure by the NP government to meet its 1989 election promises. In a by-election in Virginia in the Orange Free State at the end of 1991, the Conservative Party won with a majority of more than 2000 votes. This large swing in a former NP held constituency indicated a victory for the Conservative Party in a general election among white voters. De Klerk's mandate of 1989 was slipping away, which meant he had to advance the contemplated referendum date.

Another by-election followed in Potchefstroom in the Western Transvaal on 19 February 1992. The NP propaganda did not shy away from the consequences of one-man, one-vote in a united South Africa. The results gave the Conservative Party a majority of 2140 against a 2000 majority for the NP in the previous election. It was interpreted as a no-vote for the NP's constitutional reform proposals, also country wide. Consequently de Klerk announced a referendum to take place on 17 March 1992. De Klerk took a calculated risk for the cause he believed in and in the possibility that the majority of voters could be persuaded to vote in favour of reforms and negotiations at that time. For this decision he deserves credit.

During the weeks preceding the referendum, de Klerk campaigned vigorously for a "yes" vote throughout the country. He addressed meeting after meeting during which he reassured voters that the NP would ensure that their basic interests would be protected in the negotiations which lay ahead. He stressed that the NP had already reached consensus in the negotiations on a number of key aspects relating to the future constitution – including a multiparty democracy, a bicameral parliament, a charter of fundamental rights, the division of powers between the branches of government, an independent judiciary, proportional representation, a strong basis for regional government, the maintenance of language and cultural rights, and community-based education for those who wanted it.[310]

While making it clear that consensus still had to be reached on a number of minimum requirements, de Klerk committed himself and the government not to accept any agreements that did not offer reasonable provision for the prevention from domination and the effective protection of minorities, the protection of property, career security for the public service, a market-oriented economy with free enterprise and fiscal responsibility, constitutionally protected devolution of power to regional and local governments, and a form of power sharing.[311]

Some of the messages of the NP in their street posters were: "Negotiations yes, majority government – never" and "white schools".

The NP won the support of the white electorate in the referendum. Sixty nine percent of the white voters voted yes to the question whether the voters supported the continuation of the reform process aimed at a new constitution through negotiations. According to de Klerk, the NP received the unambiguous mandate needed to continue with the negotiation process.[312]

With this vote, although the voters did not realise it at the time, they signed their abdication papers. Hereafter de Klerk and his cabinet took all the decisions in the negotiations and approved the draft constitution on their behalf that did not incorporate the referendum promises of group rights, minority rights, power sharing, and consensus.

On 26 November 1992, de Klerk announced a timetable for completion of the constitutional process. A multilateral negotiating forum would be assembled before end of March 1993. Agreement on a transitional constitution was envisaged before the end of May, the date of enactment before the end of September 1993, and the first elections under the transitional constitution to be held by March/April 1994.

The dates at which progress was made in the second part of 1993 showed the speed towards majority rule without conditions.

In July 1993, the majority of parties announced that the first democratic elections would be held on 27 April 1994.

On 23 September, parliament adopted the Transitional Executive Council Act which made provision for the establishment of a multiparty Transitional Executive Council which would monitor the government during the run-up to the election to ensure that none of its actions favoured or harmed any of the political parties.[313]

---

310   De Klerk, p.233
311   Ibid
312   De Klerk, p.234
313   De Klerk, p.281

On 16 November 1993, de Klerk and his cabinet worked through the draft constitution and decided to try to negotiate unsatisfactory elements before 18 November.

The draft constitution was adopted by the plenary of the multiparty negotiations forum on 18 November 1993.

On 22 December 1993, the interim constitution was adopted by parliament.[314] De Klerk himself admits that heated debates and vicious recriminations followed on whether he and the NP delivered in the negotiations on the undertakings they gave during the referendum and said he thought they had.[315]

There is room for disagreement with de Klerk on this statement. The reports on the negotiations indicate the opposite to de Klerk's claim. Not one of the primary conditions of de Klerk's cabinet for the new constitution or his referendum promises were agreed to by the ANC. All the major issues that were held up to the voters as conditions for the new constitution were rejected, such as power sharing, group rights, protection of minority rights against black domination, consensus form of government, devolution of power with a federal structure. This is indeed a dismal record for the NP negotiating team, and the question is, how did it happen?

A good account is given by Jan Heunis, one of the State legal advisors at the negotiations of how the NP negotiators fared in his book, *The Inner Circle* (Jonathan Ball Publishers, Johannesburg). He wrote that Roelf Meyer, the government negotiator, accepted the principle of majority government at a meeting of the negotiation committee, and when he reported it to de Klerk, the president remarked that he had given the country away (Heunis p. 147). Heunis had responded with shock because Meyer had had no mandate to accept the principle of majority government.[316]

The president's reported remark that Meyer had given the country away does not ring true. He personally knew firsthand that the ANC had had a simple demand of equal rights which would give the blacks majority rule, without any strings attached, and that the ANC opposed the NP's conditions of minority rights, group rights, consensus government, and no black domination of minorities. A few years earlier in 1986, Mandela gave the Commonwealth Prominent Persons Group the assurance that the ANC demand was contained in the Freedom Charter : equal rights. It is certain that de Klerk would have studied this report. He also studied the reports of the Coetzee working group on their secret discussions with Mandela, particularly where Mandela reaffirmed the ANC position on equal rights as expressed

---

314   De Klerk, p.290
315   De Klerk, p.233
316   Ibid

in the Freedom Charter. Other aspects de Klerk quoted to Mandela in their first meeting in Tuynhuys, from Mandela's memorandum to P. W. Botha, was that the issue of black domination as perceived by whites needed to be reconciled in negotiations for black majority rule. To de Klerk personally Mandela stressed at their meeting that group rights would not be accepted by the ANC since it meant the retention of apartheid. Mandela pointed out to de Klerk that even *Die Burger* agreed with this view.

This meant that de Klerk's referendum campaign with the message of group rights, power sharing, and consensus was an unattainable ideal and not practical politics since the possibility of its acceptance by the ANC was zero. The white voters voted in favour of negotiations to secure such an idealistic myth. De Klerk could well have believed he would persuade the majority of voters to support him and approve negotiations and reform with this message. But it is an altogether different question whether he believed he would persuade the ANC and Mandela to approve of the NP conditions.

At the negotiation table the NP was a single party representing 69 percent of the white voters, which included the Democratic Party supporters. Opposite the NP was the ANC representing the total black population of nearly 30 million people and backed by Africa and the whole of the international community. Added to this strong position the ANC was free to call off negotiations and exert pressure through boycotts, which the NP could not do.

In their hearts the government knew that there was no possibility of a negotiated constitutional settlement that would hold out any hope of it retaining power. That the power would go to the ANC was a foregone conclusion. Consequently much of the NP preparation for the multi-party talks concerned intricate power-sharing and consensus-seeking models and the protection of minorities, particularly through vetoes and significant provincial powers.[317] It turned out to be a futile exercise.

At times these power-sharing models became so artificial and intricate that Heunis said he did not even bother to try and understand them. The ANC would never have accepted them.[318] He added that de Klerk, and certainly Roelf Meyer, must have known that many of the non-negotiables solemnly identified by the cabinet would not survive for long. "Meyer sometimes did not even bother to state the government's non-negotiable positions in respect of certain issues once he had gauged the ANC's likely reaction."[319]

---

317   Heunis, p.155
318   Ibid
319   Ibid

Heunis wrote that it was not his responsibility as the government's law advisor to promote acceptance of its constitutional blueprints, but he could not remember a single occasion when the government or the NP delegates seriously insisted on an issue to the point of actually arguing about it.[320]

Frequently, having sensed that something would be unpalatable to the ANC delegation, Heunis wrote, the government delegation would not even get to the point of stating the government's or the National Party's position, often in respect of matters that had been termed non-negotiable by the cabinet. Non-negotiables became eminently negotiable in a matter of minutes. After an hour's talks with Cyril Ramaphosa, Pik Botha phoned de Klerk to get the go-ahead for a concession to the effect that the TBVC states would be re-incorporated into South Africa before the election. Previously, the government's non-negotiable position was that the TBVC states should be allowed to decide for themselves whether or not to rejoin South Africa, and that they would not be obliged to do so before the election.[321]

Heunis said he was convinced that de Klerk knew that nothing would come of the sometimes almost ludicrous formulae to protect minority participation in all spheres of government and many of the other non-negotiable positions in respect of certain key issues. Ultimately he was prepared to compromise with the ANC on the basis of his own and that of his closest allies' inclusion in government at very senior level.[322]

De Klerk knew that the die was cast and that there was no turning back. Even the most short-sighted of his cabinet colleagues realised that.

This poor performance of the NP government negotiators begs an explanation. The negotiators, as representatives of the Afrikaner Nationalists, were demotivated after having to face up to the reality and the truth of South African politics in the form of the ANC representing the disenfranchised black majority. It was the end of the road of white political supremacy and exclusivity which had started with the constitution of the Union of South Africa in 1910. The provisions in the constitution, which excluded universal voting rights for blacks, was opposed by the ANC, who asked for representation at its founding in 1912, which was changed to demands of everything for everybody (black and white) in the Freedom Charter of 1955. Throughout all these years the NP steadfastly refused even considering talks with the ANC. Now there was no escape from capitulation.

---

320 Ibid, p.156
321 Ibid p. 157
322 Ibid

The NP negotiators had to receive approval from the ANC for the impossible conditions set by the cabinet – all the strings to tie down a black majority to white demands for special protective rights in a power sharing cloak that hid away the perpetuation of a fearful white minority's apartheid world view. This is the same policy that was declared unjust, unchristian, unrighteous, and as sinful racial discrimination by the DRC and eighty South African Churches at the 1990 conference in Rustenburg. This resolution of the Conferences of Churches did not instantly remove the delusional belief of the Afrikaner in apartheid as a righteous system or his fear of a black majority. The NP negotiators came to represent the Afrikaner Nationalist at the negotiations after the referendum vote of approval to realise the conditions of the cabinet, which were impossible and which was the carrot leading the NP supporters up the garden path of deception that the ANC would not attain the position of a parliamentary representation in which the black majority would share equal rights with the white minority.

The NP cabinet and the Afrikaner Nationalists may have deluded themselves, but not their negotiators, who did not have the confidence and conviction of belief in the moral justification of the NP conditions at the point in time when the whole apartheid edifice was all but collapsed in the face of economic sanctions, threatening violence and mass action leading to an ungovernable situation.

De Klerk had manoeuvred himself into a difficult position with the deceptive way he persuaded the voters that the negotiators would achieve group rights, protection of minority rights, and power sharing. This deception was a short cut to avoid convincing the conservative-inclined voters that black majority rule was inevitable and not something to be afraid of. But the consequences of this deception were that he had to stick to his standpoint and statements.

When de Klerk was asked by F. van Zyl Slabbert in a TV interview on the KykNET channel in 2004 when he and/or the NP had accepted the principal of majority government, he responded that it was approved as party policy at a NP congress in February 1986. In fact it was in August 1986 that the Federal Congress of the NP had approved a new policy of one person, one vote, with protection of minorities against domination. Black majority rule was not approved. Immediately after the program three previous cabinet ministers phoned Van Zyl Slabbert independently to assure him de Klerk had been lying. They were Pik Botha, former minister of foreign affairs, Barend du Plessis, former minister of finance, and Roelf Meyer, former minister of constitutional development and chief negotiator of the NP.[323]

During a panel discussion with Van Zyl Slabbert the following week, these three former cabinet ministers disputed de Klerk's claim that he consulted the party (NP), caucus and cabinet about his speech in February 1990. They also described the difficulties they experienced, particularly Roelf Meyer, to get hold of de Klerk during critical stages of the negotiation process.[324]

---

323   Van Zyl Slabbert, p.34
324   Ibid, p.35

CHAPTER 7

THE TRUTH AND RECONCILIATION COMMISSION

Proceedings and evidence

The establishment of the TRC, its proceedings, and the recalcitrant behaviour of P. W. Botha was foreshadowed by a letter written in January 1986 by Anton Rupert, a leading Afrikaner business man, responding to comments by Botha that it was better to be poor than to yield. Rupert wrote, "I am appealing to you personally. Reaffirm your rejection of apartheid. It is crucifying us; it is destroying our language; it is degrading a once heroic nation into the lepers of the world. Remove the burden of the curse of a transgression against mankind from the backs of our children and grandchildren .... Should you fail in this God-given task, then one day we shall surely end up with a Nuremberg."[325]

The negotiations at the World Trade Centre in Kempton Park concluded with the draft constitution that included a guideline on how to deal with the country's past. The final clause of the draft constitution stated that the adoption of the constitution laid the foundation for the people of South Africa to transcend the divisions and strife of the past, which had generated gross violations of human rights, the transgression of humanitarian principles in violent conflicts, and a legacy of hatred, fear, guilt, and revenge.

---

325   Krog, p.266

At their trial in the Chikane case in August 2007 where former minister Vlok and General Van der Merwe had been found guilty and given suspended sentences, Vlok said "he felt deeply wronged by, and even embittered towards, those ... people in positions of power then [1996] (P. W. Botha) and now (de Klerk), who have not ensured that the unambiguous stipulation of the interim constitution of 1993 was complied with".[326]

"This stipulation," said Vlok, "was clearly as follows: 'To advance reconciliation and reconstruction, amnesty *shall be granted* [Vlok's emphasis] in respect of acts, omissions, and offences associated with political objectives committed in the course of the conflicts of the past.'"

De Klerk's explanation was that the best the NP negotiation team could do was to reach agreement on the inclusion of a paragraph at the end of the interim constitution that stipulated that amnesty shall be granted in respect of acts, omissions and offences associated with political objectives and committed in the course of the conflicts of the past.[327]

According to de Klerk, amnesty was to be dealt with in a spirit of reconciliation, on the basis that there was a need for understanding but not for vengeance, a need for reparation but not for retaliation, a need for *ubuntu* (traditional African humanism) but not for victimization. This wording – although guaranteeing that amnesty would be granted for politically motivated acts – provided, according to de Klerk, little or no indication of how the process would be managed in practice by the new government after the election.[328]

The Truth Commission Bill drafted by the Justice Portfolio Committee of parliament became law in 1995: the Promotion of National Unity and Reconciliation Act, 1995, (Act No. 34 of 1995). The ANC delayed the clarification of this question until after the election, when it could enforce its will through its majority in parliament. By that time, during the committee stage of the bill, all that the National Party could do was to fight a rearguard action and reach agreement on the best deal that was then possible. The manner in which the NP dealt with the question of amnesty was probably their greatest failure during the negotiating process.[329] The act established a Truth and Reconciliation Commission consisting of three committees: Human Rights Violations Committee, Amnesty Committee, and the Reparation and Rehabilitation Committee. It also determined a cut-off date and provided for mechanisms, criteria, and procedures, including tribunals, if any, through which such amnesty would be dealt with at any time after the law had been passed.

326   *The Sunday Independent*, 19 August 2007
327   De Klerk, p.288
328   Ibid
329   De Klerk, p.289

The commission had to investigate the period between 1960 and 1990 and received more than 7000 applications for amnesty from perpetrators. Amnesty would be granted only if the TRC was, in terms of the legislation, convinced that those who applied for amnesty had made a full disclosure, amongst other factors.

One of the first submissions at the public hearings of the Justice Portfolio Committee on the draft legislation establishing a Truth Commission was from Mary Burton, chairperson of the Black Sash organisation. She concluded her submission in the same way the meetings of the Black Sash closed, by reading the names of people who died in police custody. She read the names of 120 people, including that of the first victim, Looksmart Ngudle, and of Steve Bantu Biko.

The Bones of Memory, written by Gcina Mhlope was read by her at the Truth and Reconciliation Commission in 1997. Mhlope is a well-known South African freedom fighter, activist, actor, storyteller, poet, and playwright.

Where do they come from,
Tell me, tell me, where do they come from.
Tales so brave, tales so strong,
Tell me, where do they come from.
Tales so brave, tales so strong.

These tales are from the bones of memory,
of memory, of memory, of memory,
from the bones of memory,
from the bones of memory,
from the bones of memory.

Some are so funny, so crazy, unbelievable,
Some are so funny, so crazy, unbelievable.
They come from the bones of memory.
Watch my eyes, hear my voice, I tell you true.
These tales are from the bones of memory.[330]

Reconciliation was in reality an issue between the Afrikaners and the ANC. It is therefore important to note the stand taken by the two major representatives of the Afrikaners, namely the NP and the DRC, towards the TRC.

A few months after the election politicians and *dominees* and reporters were invited to a workshop in Stellenbosch on the possibility of a Truth

330 *The Star*, 7 June 2007

Commission, but they snubbed the invitation by the Afrikaans author Antjie Krog. *Die Burger*, which could have reached Afrikaans-speakers in the Cape, refused to cover the event. Later, Antjie Krog reported on the drafting of the legislation for the commission, that the NP politicians had only one strategy and that was to try and score political points by accusing the ANC of one-sidedness. Petty grandstanding suited them better than actually explaining to their voters what it was all about, she wrote.

The NP was represented at the hearings of the TRC by President de Klerk only. The chairmen of the four provincial congresses of the NP were not involved. The documented response that he submitted was prepared under his supervision with the assistance of cabinet ministers and members of parliament with a judicial background. He represented the NP, which included the cabinet, the parliamentary caucus, the party with its provincial congresses, and all the Nationalist supporters.

The NP did not encourage its members, supporters, and the public in general (i.e., the citizens of the apartheid state) to participate in the proceedings of the TRC.

The idea of reconciliation did not mean that only one person would represent a government, party or part of the electorate. The NP did not show any support or sympathy for the cause of the TRC. Neither did it encourage citizens to support the TRC, to attend the hearings, or read the reported evidence in order to become knowledgeable about the truth. The truth was regarded as an embarrassment. The party had been conditioned over so many decades not to think for itself, not to be critical in a constructive sense but rather to believe everything the leaders put forward as the truth. Intolerance was king. It did not bode well for the person who dared to have critical views. This approach was a legacy handed down by Verwoerd, Vorster, and P. W. Botha.

One of the dilemmas was the conditioning of the party since 1910 that apartheid was the only political solution, and that voting rights would not be granted to black people in a common parliament. White supremacy was not negotiable; it would be sustained.

The turn around in 1990 by de Klerk to immediately opt for negotiations with the ANC as against the die-hard attitude to consider piece meal concessions was a sudden event.

The reforms that P. W. Botha was formulating for black participation before the end of his reign were based on a system of partly indirect participation by blacks, entrenchment of minority rights (whites, coloureds, Indians), and the continuation of the independent black territories, if they so wished.

Indirectly, this policy concept still maintained the idea of separate groups. The constitutional negotiations eventually ended in an agreement for a constitution of a democratic unitary state with equal universal rights.

The white voters accepted the negotiated settlement and supported the new constitution with black majority voting rights, which was contrary to their historical ideals. The unresolved issue in the new nation of a unitary state was confronting the truth of the injustices of the past and the atrocities that took place during the oppression of resistance.

There cannot be doubt that the announcement by de Klerk of a new dispensation to be negotiated in 1990 was an issue that was subconsciously expected by many Nationalists for at least fifteen years. But he did not try to persuade the NP to reject apartheid. He persuaded them to support negotiations and reform by accepting that the NP would attain a constitution with group rights, protecting the white minority.

After the (TRC) hearings, de Klerk wrote lofty words in his autobiography about acknowledgement of deeds of the past under apartheid, but before the fact he did not write to his followers and supporters to testify before the TRC about it: "We need to acknowledge the deep injustices of apartheid; but we must also acknowledge the historical dilemma in which Afrikaners, as a separate nation with their own right to independence, found themselves. We need to acknowledge the suffering caused by apartheid, and particularly by forced removals, the pass laws and the so-called Immorality Act, but at the same time we must acknowledge the undeniable progress that many black South Africans made during this period and the many sincere efforts that former governments made to improve their circumstances. We need to acknowledge the atrocities committed in the name of former governments, but we must also acknowledge the brutalities committed in the name of the revolution."[331]

Most of the important former political leaders appeared before the TRC. P. W. Botha refused to appear before the commission. He said he did not perform in circuses and would not allow himself to be threatened. The Truth Commission in his opinion was tearing Afrikaners apart, and he was not asking for amnesty. He said he had never authorised murders and would not apologise for the fight against a Marxist revolutionary onslaught.

When P. W. Botha refused to address the Truth and Reconciliation Commission, many leaders in the Afrikaans community followed his example. P. W. Botha had told minister Adriaan Vlok to decide for himself whether to testify before the Truth and Reconciliation Commission but that he (P. W. Botha) would not do so.

---

331   De Klerk, p.383

P. W. Botha also refused a personal request by F. W. de Klerk, who visited him at his home in the wilderness, to cooperate with him in drafting the NP's submission to the TRC.

The Marxist onslaught Botha referred to would probably have been a combination of communism and black resistance. But communism had been on the decline and fell in Eastern Europe in 1989, and the South African black majority was demanding democratic rights.

Considering the "total onslaught" strategy of P. W. Botha, managed by defence minister Magnus Malan, and the operations of the secret SADF organisation, the Civil Cooperation Bureau (CCB), the TRC had caught Botha in a quandary. De Klerk revealed that his former minister of justice (law and order) Vlok, said that President P. W. Botha had given instructions in 1988 for the bombings of buildings used by government opponents, including the headquarters of the South African Council of Churches and the Congress of South African Trade Unions (Cosatu).[332]

In the Chikane trial in August 2007, Vlok and Van der Merwe told the court in their argument they had "presumed" that the order to kill certain anti-apartheid activists – such as Chikane – "in exceptional circumstances" had come from the president, the late P. W. Botha.

Though they conceded that they had not received confirmation of this presumption, they said it demonstrated that political leaders and other people in positions of authority had been largely protected from post-1994 prosecution, whereas the "foot soldiers" had "paid the price."

The late General Kat Liebenberg, then chief of the army, chaired a meeting in 1987 at which, on the instruction of a higher authority, it was said that drastic steps had to be taken to curtail the activities of certain political activists. The law had to be utilised in every way to disrupt and frustrate the activists. Should this not succeed, but only in extreme cases, consideration could be given to eliminate such activists.

Early in January 1990 Malan told de Klerk that he had just then discovered the nature of the operations of the CCB, started as an underground structure of the defence force in the mid-eighties. He said the CCB had been using totally unacceptable methods and strategies against the ANC and other revolutionary organisations. He remarked that these things have to happen in war and armed struggle. The problem was that Malan, de Klerk, P. W. Botha, and the SADF, jointly with the security forces, had beforehand not decided on their stance vis-à-vis the TRC. P. W. Botha had now to face the music before the TRC on his own. By this time he had become old and weak. His hard headedness showed only rejection of the TRC processes and did not allow for remorse or apology. It can also be explained as P. W. Botha's attitude

---

332   De Klerk, p.210

of resentment. He was at this stage resentful toward his old party, F. W. de Klerk, the TRC, and the ANC. In his case, considering his quoted references to his belief in God and his prayers to God, his resentment towards the TRC and the fact that acknowledgement of the wrongs of apartheid and an apology was required, could be described as religious pride. For that matter, many of his followers mirrored his attitude.

Since the hearings the whites, unfortunately, had to live with the consequences of P. W. Botha's recalcitrance.

The NP did not publically express their regret at P. W. Botha's position and attitude. His refusal to appear before the TRC had become a symbol of the Afrikaner's negative attitude towards the commission. Botha represented the unrepentant white political leaders of the previous era who were enjoying financial and political privileges as if nothing in their lives had changed.

De Klerk's stand in his submission to the TRC on behalf of the NP in the process designed to confront the past so as to clear a path to the future was a cue to those that he led. Many of them rejected the TRC or ignored it and went on with their lives.

In an article in *Rapport* (26 August 2007) Hendrik Wyngaard wrote that most Afrikaners were from the outset opposed to the negotiated settlement of the TRC. It was derided as a confessing commission, an absurdity with Tutu, the devil, as chairman.

The negative view of the Afrikaner towards the TRC was not only formed by the NP leadership under de Klerk but to a great extend strengthened by the role and influence of the Afrikaans Press, who supported the NP leadership and strongly opposed the work of the TRC.

In an article in a supplement to *Beeld*, *By*, on the role of the Afrikaans press in support of apartheid (9 February 2008), a writer and media researcher, Arrie de Beer, questioned the assertion by a former editor of Volksblad, Hennie van Deventer, that the Afrikaans Press did play a formidable role in the breaking down of apartheid. De Beer, together with Max du Preez, editor of Vrye Weekblad, were the only members from the Afrikaans press and academic journalism that had accepted invitations from the TRC to testify at the media sittings of the commission. They testified at a time when the Afrikaans press establishment rejected the commission's invitations to testify.

Arrie de Beer refers to comments by Herman Wassernaar, media researcher and former journalist at *Die Burger*, how the Afrikaans press demonized the TRC as a commission of lies and confession, and also how it denounced the 130 journalists as traitors who had signed the TRC – declaration.

In the opinion of a columnist, their (NP and security forces) temerity knew no bounds. "These were apartheid heroes who for decades had committed crimes against the majority in this country and knew – as they killed and maimed men, women and children – that they were protected by their political masters. Nothing at the time would happen to them."[333]

After ignoring three subpoenas of the TRC, Botha was summoned on a criminal charge laid by the attorney general of the Western Cape to appear in the court in George before a black magistrate. The case was postponed, and Botha never appeared again. To a journalist looking Botha in the eye when he left court it was a defining moment. Her impression after all the efforts to persuade him to testify before the TRC was that he was dumb and a fool, and concluded, "We have been governed by this stupidity for decades."[334]

The response of the DRC

In May 1997, the General Synodal Commission of the DRC received a letter from the TRC, also directed to other churches and faith groups, requesting a submission concerning its investigations.

The General Synodal Commission had the historical account of the Dutch Reformed Church concerning people and race relations in South Africa written as it had developed since 1962, the date of the establishment of the General Synod. This document was made available to all interested parties.

The document *The story of the DR Church's Journey with Apartheid*, a testimony and a confession written by Dr Fritz Gaum, was approved by the executive committee and published in August 1997 by the Hugenot Publishers, Wellington. Copies were made available to the TRC at their request.

The Western Cape Synod of the DRC decided in October 1997 to make its own submission to the TRC, which in many instances corresponded with the Journey with apartheid document.

In October 1997, a further invitation was received from the TRC that the DRC participate in a public profession event, held on 19 November 1997 in East London.

The General Synodal Commission decided that its chairman, Rev. Freek Swanepoel, should represent the DRC and address the meeting.

The General Synodal Commission of the DRC ordered the production of an English extract from the Afrikaans document. The document is outlined in twenty-six theses.

The insight which the Dutch Reformed Church gained that the church may not prescribe political models to the government, but it will, by virtue of its prophetic function, continue to test every existing and proposed political model against biblical principles and norms was the result of years of grappling

---

333   Jojial Rantao, *The Star*, 29 June 2007
334   Krog p.271

with this issue, and came after the Dutch Reformed Church had travelled a long road with the apartheid albatross around its neck.[335] (Thesis No1)

It was precisely the zeal with which the Dutch Reformed Church wanted the scriptures to pronounce on all the relationships and circumstances of life that led it to seek scriptural endorsement for one specific political model as being the one true, divinely ordained model for this country. At a stage there was broad consensus in Dutch Reformed Church circles that separate development, with neighbourly love and justly applied, was a biblical imperative for the regulation of our society.(Thesis No 2)

Unfortunately, however, the policy of apartheid was allowed to degenerate into an ideology which had to be put into practice at all costs, even against the will of most people in the country. People became pawns in a game of chess, and their innate human dignity was not fully recognised. Even after it became obvious that the ideal of independent states for the different peoples was unattainable, the discrimination and injustice of forced removals were allowed to continue.(Thesis No 4)

While in a sense the Dutch Reformed Church took the lead in establishing the apartheid concept, it was the National Party that later adopted it as a political policy. Because the members of one were in many cases also members of the other, there was an interaction between church and party/government. This is understandable, but the result was that the church did not always maintain the desirable critical distance in relation to the government.(Thesis No 6)

The concept of separate states for separate peoples did not appear out of thin air. It exists elsewhere in the world (Europe) and also in our own region, with Lesotho and Swaziland being the most obvious examples, and a social arrangement of this kind is clearly not wrong or bad as such. The problem comes when such an arrangement is forced on people and even advocated by the church as a biblical imperative. (Thesis No 7)

Also in relation to the ecclesiastical dispensation, it is not wrong if the word of God is brought to people in their own language and cultural context, or if the church, precisely by virtue of its "universality", chooses to take on the colour of its surroundings. But the unity of the church cannot be subordinated to its diversity. If, in this regard, the church's diversity is virtually the only part of it which is visible, and visible unity steadily disappears into the background, the world will be less and less inclined to believe the church's message. (Thesis No 8)

It was on account of its profound and justifiable identification with the destiny of the people whom it served in the first instance—the Afrikaners—that the Dutch Reformed Church often tended to put the interests of its

---

335   *Kerk en Samelewing 1990*, par. 275

people above those of other people. The church was concerned for the survival of the Afrikaners and did not always pay the same attention to the desperate circumstances daily endured by other people. (Thesis No 9)

The church must acknowledge to its members, old and young, that the guidance given by ecclesiastical assemblies in respect of societal matters over the past decades was sometimes sadly lacking. For that we are deeply and sincerely sorry. (Thesis No 10)

It must be said that there were also cases in which sound guidance from the church was unfortunately not followed by all members and assemblies. (Thesis No 12)

The Dutch Reformed Church had always treated the word of God most seriously, and had consistently striven to proclaim and apply its pristine essence. However, the church did not always hear the word of the Lord correctly. That must be confessed. (Thesis No 13)

Christ provides us with the outstanding example of a servant who thought not of Himself, but of others. If, in the past, the Dutch Reformed Church was tempted to think of itself as a great and "powerful" church, the situation has clearly now changed to such an extent that the church has to see itself differently. The servant model now fits best—and that, after all, is what Christ expects of His church. (Thesis No 14)

The Dutch Reformed Church's heart goes out to those in our country who suffered in past decades because of the system which prevailed. The church sometimes raised its voice in protest and sometimes in compassion, but often too softly. For that we apologise. (Thesis No 15)

The Dutch Reformed Church has to acknowledge that there were numerous occasions when its prophetic voice should have spoken more clearly to the then government, many of whom were members of that church. On occasion the scriptural guidance which the church gave to the government fell short. It is also true that the church unfortunately sometimes allowed itself to be led by political leaders. (Thesis No 17)

In various ways, for purposes of the church's pastoral ministry to members, the Dutch Reformed Church, with other churches, became involved in the struggle/war of the 1970s and 1980s. In its actions the Dutch Reformed Church showed that it regarded this as a just struggle, particularly because at the time the atheistic ideology of Communism displayed a great thirst for expansion, with South Africa as one of its targets. The church did not regard the war as an attempt to maintain an unjust system in South Africa. (Thesis No 21)

Ministers of the Dutch Reformed Church who were chaplains general of the defence force and the police force at that time have testified that they were not aware or informed of covert actions against which they should have protested. With hindsight, it is clear that the Dutch Reformed Church should have made more urgent and penetrating enquiries about the various activities of the security forces. (Thesis No 22)

Similarly, the Dutch Reformed Church should have made more serious enquiries about what was happening and what was permitted in South Africa under the blanket of the various states of emergency. (Thesis No 23)

It is with shock and revulsion that we now take note of alleged unchristian deeds committed by some members of the security forces. Such deeds cannot be condoned, even taking into account the circumstances prevailing at the time. If these allegations prove to be true, profound abhorrence must be expressed. (Thesis No 24)

The Dutch Reformed Church has completed its journey with apartheid. It has cast off the albatross from around its neck, once and for all. We thank the Lord for a fresh opportunity, together with other Christians in South Africa, to go into the future, to help build up the church of the Lord, to help make this country a good home for all those who call it their fatherland, and to seek the will of the Lord in South Africa. (Thesis No 26) (Archives and Management MIS of the DRC of Transvaal).

A question mark could be put behind the statements of three of these theses concerning conflict, security and violence.

Thesis No 21. "The church did not regard the war as an attempt to maintain an unjust system in South Africa." It probably refers to the war in Angola and also the attacks by the armed forces on targets – Transkei and neighbouring states such as Lesotho and Botswana.

Thesis No 22. "That the DRC should have made more urgent and penetrating inquiries about the various activities of the security forces."

Thesis No 24. "If these allegations ('alleged unchristian deeds committed by some members of the security forces') proved to be true, profound abhorrence must be expressed." The records of the TRC contain ample proof of the atrocities; also those that lead to prosecutions and sentences. A good read of the English press should have sufficed. There is still time for an expression of abhorrence since reports have been published that proved many of the allegations to be factual and true.

It is strange that the DRC did not react positively by directly submitting its response to the TRC, an official government commission instituted by legislation in terms of the constitution, on request to do so. This attitude raises the question of the sincerity of its relationship with the TRC. It did not submit a formal submission, but made available copies of its document, *The Story of the DRC's Journey with Apartheid*, and gave a copy to the TRC at its request.

Final report – October 1998

The report of the Truth and Reconciliation Commission consists of five volumes, each with a particular focus, with the bulk of the findings in the final volume. In the chairperson's foreword (Volume 1, Chapter 1) Archbishop Tutu made an urgent appeal for tolerance and reconciliation. He concluded:

"Having looked the beast of the past in the eye, having asked and received forgiveness and having made amends, let us shut the door on the past – not in order to forget it but in order not to allow it to imprison us. Let us move into the glorious future of a new kind of society where people count, not because of biological irrelevancies or other extraneous attributes, but because they are persons of infinite worth created in the image of God...." (paragraph 91).

The roots of the conflict that emerged during the mandate period 1960 to 1990 is set out in the **Historical Context** (Volume 1, Chapter 2, paragraph 1), although the origins of the South African conflict began much earlier than 1960. The commission's brief was to report only a small part of the much larger story of human rights abuse in South Africa. Thus:

"The importation of slaves to the Cape and the brutal treatment they endured .... The many wars of dispossession and colonial conquest dating from the first war against the Khoisan in 1659 ... The systematic hunting and elimination of indigenous nomadic peoples ... The Difaquane or Mfecane where thousands died (killed by Zulu impis) ... The South African war of 1899 – 1902 during which British forces herded Boer women and children into concentration camps in which some 20,000 (26,000) died ... The genocidal war ... directed by the German colonial administration in South West Africa at the Herero people, which took them to the brink of extinction." (paragraph 7)

The chapter described how the South African parliament transformed the laissez-faire pattern of pre-1948 legislation into a systematic pattern of legalized racial discrimination and constructed and armed an internal security apparatus with legal power to crush opposition. The chapter concluded:

"To many, notably those in the leadership in the government and security forces in the 1980s, the conclusion that the state sanctioned murder may and probably will be an unpalatable assertion. It is also probably not what the Commission expected to find when it started work two years ago. It is, however, a 'truth' to which it has been drawn by the evidence" (paragraph 80).

The victims of gross violations of human rights is explored in **The Mandate** (Volume 1, Chapter 4, paragraph 51).

"... It can never be forgotten that the system itself was evil, inhumane and degrading for the many millions who became its second and third class citizens. Amongst its many crimes, perhaps the greatest was its power to humiliate, to denigrate and to remove the self-confidence, self-esteem and dignity of its millions of victims ..."

The development of international legal opinion in respect of the declaration of apartheid as a crime against humanity is traced in paragraph 1 of **The Appendix to Chapter 2** :

"... the Commission ... affirms its judgement that apartheid, as a system of enforced racial discrimination and separation, was a crime against humanity ... At the same time, the Commission acknowledges that there are those who sincerely believed differently and those, too, who were blinded by their fear of a Criminal 'total onslaught.'" (paragraph 1)

The conceptual framework within which the commission operated is discussed in **Concepts and Principles** (Volume 1, Chapter 5, paragraph 1).

In it the promotion of national unity and reconciliation is discussed, including reconciliation as a goal and a process and the different levels at which reconciliation takes place – namely, coming to terms with painful truth, reconciliation between victims and perpetrators, reconciliation at a community level, and reconciliation and redistribution. Thus:

"Given the magnitude of this exercise, the Commission's quest for truth should be viewed as a contribution to a much longer-term goal and vision. Its purpose in attempting to uncover the past had nothing to do with vengeance; it had to do, rather, with helping victims to become more visible and more valuable citizens through the public recognition and official acknowledgement of their experiences ... In addition, by bringing the darker side of the past to the fore, those responsible for violations of human rights could also be held accountable for their actions. In the process, they were given the opportunity to acknowledge their responsibility to contribute to the creation of a new South African society." (paragraphs 27-28)

In the section on the relationship between truth and reconciliation, the report stressed that: "The road to reconciliation requires more than forgiveness and respectful remembrance. It is, in this respect, worth remembering the difficult history of reconciliation between Afrikaners and white English-speaking South Africans after the devastating Anglo-Boer/South African War ... Despite coexistence and participation with English-speaking South Africans in the political system that followed the war, it took many decades to rebuild relationships and redistribute resources ... Reconciliation requires not only individual justice, but also social justice." (paragraph 52)

Details of the Commission's investigation into the records of the former state and of the process whereby so many crucial state records were destroyed, particularly in early 1990s when the destruction of documents was undertaken on a massive scale, is described in *The Destruction of Records* (Volume 1, Chapter 8, paragraph 1). The chapter records that the NIA (National Intelligence Agency) was still destroying records as late as 1996, some two and a half years after the first democratic elections. The commission found that:

"The mass destruction of records ... has had a severe impact on South Africa's social memory. Swathes of official documentary memory, particularly around the inner workings of the apartheid state's security apparatus, have been obliterated ... Ultimately, of course, all South Africans have suffered the consequences – all are victims of the apartheid state's attempted imposition of a selective amnesia" (paragraphs 104 and 106).

An overview of insurgency and counter-insurgency strategies is given in the first chapter of Volume 2. It traces their development from internal repression and the emergence of armed opposition movements (1960–64); the regionalization of conflict (1965–73); the collapse of the buffer and the re-emergence of internal opposition (1974–8); 'total strategy', regional destabilisation and resistance (1979–84); the war comes home (1985–9) and the transitional phase (1990–4).

The State inside South Africa (1960–90) (Volume 2, Chapter 3, paragraph 1) traces the different forms of violations conducted by the state inside South Africa. These include bannings and banishment; judicial executions, public order policing, the use of auxiliary forces, torture, and deaths in custody. The various methods of torture discussed are, amongst others, beating, the imaginary chair, electric shock, and the incidence of sexual torture.

The Liberation Movements from 1960–90 (Volume 2, Chapter Four, paragraph 1) describes the commission's investigation into the ANC, the PAC, the Azanian National Liberation Army and the Mass Democratic Movement.

In reviewing the activities of the African National Congress (ANC) and the Pan Africanist Congress (PAC), the commission endorsed the position in international law that the policy of apartheid was a crime against humanity, and that both the ANC and PAC were internationally recognised liberation movements conducting legitimate struggles against the former South African government and its policy of apartheid.

The institutional hearing on **The Faith Community** (Volume 4, Chapter 3, paragraph 1) explores the role of faith communities in South Africa and the role they played during the mandate period. It describes the various faith communities, and explores their role as "agents of oppression", stating that:

"Contrary to their own deepest principles, many faith communities mirrored apartheid society, giving the lie to their profession to a loyalty that transcended social divisions." (paragraph 29)

Reconciliation (Volume 5, Chapter 9, paragraph 1) reports on the experience of reconciliation, chiefly through the stories of people who approached the commission, both victims and perpetrators. It discusses the concepts of forgiveness and the value of acknowledgements and apologies and looks at the issues of reconciliation between victim and perpetrator, reconciliation without forgiveness and restitution or reparation. It also gives some examples of initiatives, in the faith, health and business sectors.

The institutional hearing on **The Media** (Volume 4, Chapter 6, paragraph 1) explores the role of the different media organisations. It describes the various attempts by the state to control the media.

Findings on the media included, inter alia, the following:

"The management of the mainstream English language media often adopted a policy of appeasement towards the state, ensuring that a large measure of self-censorship occurred .... The role of the Newspaper Press Union – not least concerning security matters – reflects willingness by the mainstream media not to deal with matters that exposed the activities of the security forces" (paragraph 113).

"The Afrikaans media (at least until the last few months of P. W. Botha's tenure as state president) chose to provide direct support for apartheid and the activities of the security forces" (paragraph 115).

"The employment practices of the newspaper industry, with few exceptions, reflected the racial and gender discrimination that characterised South African society" (paragraph 116).

"The SABC willingly cooperated with the security forces of the former state in the conscious employment of and/or cooperation with SAP and SADF spies, making it a direct servant of the government of the day" (paragraph 117).

"With the notable exception of certain individuals, the mainstream newspapers and the SABC failed to report adequately on gross human rights violations. In so doing, they helped sustain and prolong the existence of apartheid" (paragraph 120).

Boraine, a former president of the Methodist Church of Southern Africa and a member of parliament who opposed apartheid, wrote that it was necessary to subject the Truth and Reconciliation Commission to "critical scrutiny" as part of "the search for the elusive peace which always seems to be beyond our grasp." The Truth and Reconciliation Commission succeeded in quickly establishing some painful truths. Its success in promoting reconciliation between the races is questionable. The hearings, though, provided catharsis to many victims, furnished survivors with important insights into the plight of loved ones who had disappeared, and led to many poignant expressions of regret and forgiveness.[336]

Boraine declared the Truth and Reconciliation Commission to have been a miraculous success and advocated it as a model for other places, such as Kosovo. The establishment of the commission eased a peaceful transfer of power from the white minority to the black majority, and its members made a heroic effort in giving South Africa its best chance for reconciliation.[337] Disappointingly absent, however, was any meaningful acceptance of responsibility by white government officials. President P. W. Botha, who led South Africa during the decades of the most violent oppression of blacks, refused to cooperate with the commission. Botha's successor, F. W. de Klerk, as well as his colleagues, qualified their expressions of regret by insisting that they had not known about the atrocities committed by their government's police and security forces.[338]

There is also continuing controversy among blacks as to whether they ought to forgive their oppressors and move on. The vast majority of South African whites who refused to acknowledge the wrongs of apartheid still have a chance to reach a peaceful relationship with the governing black majority by simply showing remorse for the wrongs of the apartheid era.

In early in 2008 the Australian government apologized to the indigenous people for past injustices, including the forced removal of mixed-race children from their families. It was delivered by the newly elected prime minister, Mr Rudd, in the Australian parliament and broadcasted countrywide.

A columnist in *The Sunday Independent*, Vuyo Jack, commented that the biggest impact of the apology was acceptance of accountability by Rudd. There was no pointing of fingers or shifting of responsibility to anyone in the past or the present. This was quite a brave thing to do and a lesson everyone in South Africa can learn from.

"Being accountable is necessary for both blacks and whites. It is the refusal to be accountable that contributes to many of the problems in the transformation process," Jack wrote.

"Some white people pay lip service to economic transformation, forgetting that many of their foundations and their continued well-being have their roots in the economic injustices of the past, in one way or the other.

"It is not suggested that white people flagellate themselves and feel forever guilty about the past, but there is a need to acknowledge that the past had a part in getting them where they are. This would enable us to close the

---

336   Mark L Wolf, The New York Times Company, 27 May 2001
337   Ibid
338   Ibid

chapter on the past and focus attention on what needs to be done presently to accelerate progress.

"On the other side there is lack of accountability by black people. The entitlement mentality is a tool that allows people to evade the responsibility of doing something for themselves and getting their hands dirty through participating in the economy."

The greatest lesson South Africans can learn from the Australian apology is the importance of being accountable, ultimately to themselves, which, while not an easy feat, is a very worthwhile one," Jack wrote in the *Sunday Independent*, 17 February 2008.

CHAPTER 8

BLACK AND WHITE ISSUES UNDER THE ANC GOVERNMENT

The question of political murder

In the opinion of Mr Alex Boraine, deputy chairman of the Truth and Reconciliation Commission as stated in his book, *A Country Unmasked: Inside South Africa's Truth and Reconciliation Commission*,[339] the work of the commission gave South Africa its best chance for reconciliation. Unfortunately, polls at that time indicated that the vast majority of South African whites continued to refuse to acknowledge the atrocities perpetrated on their behalf or to accept responsibility for such actions.[340]

The Israeli commission which inquired into the massacre in Beirut in 1982 elevated the principle or doctrine of indirect responsibility to international cognizance. Thomas Aquinas first described this principle as "the sin of omission," but it was a principle readily applied in the days of the Old Testament prophets. Today it goes by the name of negligence: by doing nothing to stop a wrongful act, even if one could do so, one must share in the blame. Such a person is not necessarily stupid, incompetent, or careless. It could be that his knowledge, power and experience *demanded* beyond reasonable doubt that he should have acted differently. As *Time* magazine wrote in an essay on *The Laws of the Mind*, the words, "you should have

339   Oxford University Press, New York, 2001
340   Ibid

193

known," in certain circumstances become a way of elegantly telling someone that he is a liar, a liar more to himself than to others, but a liar nonetheless. The Israeli government of Mr Menachim Begin was accused by its own commission of indifference, conspicuous lack of concern, and nonfulfilment of duty, citing indirect responsibility for the massacre of 1982 in Beirut as an example.[341]

General Johan van der Merwe, a previous commissioner of the SA police, said in an interview with a Sunday paper that SAP attacks on ANC activists started to develop for the worst after President P. W. Botha told the SAP general staff many times, "But people, can you not make a plan?" [342]

Van der Merwe said the security police believed if they had had to make plans, those plans would have been outside the ordinary legal means, as the president knew all the legal instruments had already been applied. It was about such plans that General van der Merwe and his former minister of justice, Adriaan Vlok, appeared in court on 17 August 2007 as accused in the case of poisoning Pastor Frank Chikane.

"The message was, we are fighting with our backs to the wall. Use every means at your disposal. The means serve the ends. It did not matter which means. A very big mistake was to mix the police and army cultures because it created a total unholy alliance". [343]

Van der Merwe said the poor policemen who only carried out orders as foot soldiers were now exposed targets for prosecution. They had operated in a climate of terror, and it is true to say that they could have gained the impression that it was expected of them to operate and take actions outside the law. "In some orders and documents words such as eliminate were used which to the ordinary policemen meant only one thing: kill," General van der Merwe explained. The old State Security Council or cabinet never issued orders for the use of unlawful violence, only P. W. Botha did that in his personal capacity, he said. [344]

But as far as state security was concerned, the state president could not issue orders in his personal capacity. According to the general, it had to have been in his official capacity as head of state. These orders issued by P. W. Botha could be one of the explanations for his refusal to testify before the TRC. The general's statement that state President P. W. Botha had given orders for political murder is the only source to pinpoint political accountability. It does explain the astonishing absence of NP governmental leadership not having negotiated a settlement with the ANC and the NP governments failure to inform voters of the government's true intentions with the total

341 *Jerusalem Post*, August 2007
342 *Rapport*, 29 June 2007
343 Ibid
344 Ibid

onslaught policy. Secrecy was used to hide unlawful deeds. Exceeding the limits of lawful actions and orders for criminal deeds should have persuaded right minded political leaders to opt for negotiations.

The question remains as to why no one ever queried these violent acts. The general said that Leon Wessels (deputy minister) openly declared they (members of Botha's cabinet) did not want to know. They looked the other way. All these instances passed them by. [345]

Van der Merwe said that the former government left the police shockingly in the lurch because of political opportunism or short sightedness. The police became the scapegoats of circumstances." The SAP did what they did for their nation and fatherland. Those who are guilty of excesses did not do it for personal gain or glory, they put their careers on the line. The SAP was supported by the church, Van der Merwe said. [346]

He expressed the opinion that the political leaders of the other parties in the conflict should also come under the scrutiny of the prosecution. Among them are the 122 ANC members who did not receive amnesty and some of the PAC leaders. He said all the members in the ANC National Executive Committee and in particular those who served in the Political Military Council are full square accountable for the ANC atrocities. [347]

By comparison the fifty to sixty cases in which at the most two hundred died is a drop in the ocean compared to the thousands of ANC victims, such as those involved in the necklacing murders, the violence in 1991 and 1992, and the power struggle between the ANC and Inkatha, which the ANC unsuccessfully tried to pin on a third force, Van der Merwe explained. The outstanding issue of missing persons from the ANC camp should be addressed to the ANC, who should be asked what happened to those in their punishment camps who disappeared. Many South Africans remain concerned about persons who lost loved ones and do not know what happened to them, whether on the side of the SAP or ANC.

In return for pleading guilty to attempting to murder the Rev. Frank Chikane, now the director-general of the presidency but then an anti-apartheid activist, by having poison put on his clothes in April 1989, Vlok and Van der Merwe each received a sentence of ten years in jail, suspended for ten years.

---

345 Ibid
346 Ibid
347 Ibid

Affirmative action, black economic empowerment and racial nativism

While South Africa went through the truth and reconciliation process, the issue of compensation always hung in the background. Some people view black economic empowerment (BEE) policy as part of the compensation for the economic injustices of the past. Others viewed it as a growth strategy meant to increase the division of the economic pie so that all South Africans could have an adequate share. Broad-based BEE encompassed both being redistributive in one respect, especially through the ownership element, and also being growth orientated through the preferential procurement and enterprise development components, is Vuyo Jack's opinion.[348]

The aspect of redressing past inequalities through affirmative action and black economic empowerment are provided for in section 9 of the constitution. Nobody is arguing with the constitution. It is the subjective preferences and politicized manner in which affirmative action and BEE is applied that is discriminatory and cause dissatisfaction. Many interpretations and decisions are political influences and discriminatory instead of being fair.

Albie Sachs, a judge on the Constitutional Court, gave an exposition on BEE in a chapter on "The Constitutional Principles Underpinning BEE" in a collection of essays in *Visions of Black Economic Empowerment*. In an edited extract from Sachs's essay in *Business Report* (17 August 2007) Sachs wrote that section 9 of the constitution presents a choice between the need to take affirmative action to remedy social inequalities [section 9 (2)] and the duty of the state not to discriminate unfairly against anyone on the grounds of race [section 9 (3)]. It is a debate that directly concerns BEE.

In the dialogue between its clauses, the constitution presents a holistic view of equality in the South African context. However, Sachs wrote he believed there is no paradox here at all. Sections 9 (2) and 9 (3) are the flip sides of the same coin. While the main focus of section 9 (2) is on the group advanced and the mechanism used, the primary focus of section 9 (3) is on the group discriminated against. The necessary reconciliation between the different interests of those positively and negatively affected by affirmative action should be done in a manner that takes account of both: the severe degree of structural inequality with which we still live, and the constitutional goal of achieving an egalitarian society based on nonsexism and nonracism.

In this context, according to Sachs, redress is not an option; it is an imperative. Without major transformation, one cannot heal the divisions of

---

348 *Sunday Independent*, 17 February 2008

the past and establish a society based on democratic values, social justice and fundamental human rights. At the same time, it is important to ensure that the process of achieving equity is conducted in such a way that the baby of nonracialism is not thrown out with the bathwater of remedial action."

The overall effect of section 9 (2), is to anchor the equality provision around the need to dismantle the structures of disadvantages left behind by centuries of racial domination, and millennia of partriarchal subordination. In this respect, it gives clear constitutional authorization for proactive measures to be taken to protect or advance persons disadvantaged because of factors that have operated and continue to operate to disadvantage people.

"The whole trust of section 9 (2) is to ensure that equality is looked at from a contextual and substantive point of view, and not a purely formal one. "The substantive approach requires that the test for constitutionality is not whether the measure concerned treats all affected in an identical fashion. Rather, it focuses on whether it serves to advance or retard the equal enjoyment in practice of the rights and freedoms promised by the constitution, but which have not yet been achieved.

"It means that where disadvantage was imposed because of race, then race may be taken into account in dealing with such disadvantage. It accordingly makes it clear that properly designed race-conscious and gender-conscious measures are not automatically suspect and unfair," Sachs concluded.[349]

General Constant Viljoen, leader of the Freedom Front, was the only political leader who in his submission and testimony to the TRC requested that a special reconciliation commission be set up in the future to deal with the hardening of attitudes he experienced daily.[350] This is a remarkable statement. President de Klerk made a similar observation as regards the hardening of attitudes among the ANC.

In his speech as vice president at the adoption of the new constitution in 1996, Mr Mbeki set out a picture of inclusion of the new ruling black majority together with the other groups, including the whites. Commenting on this statement, Patrick Laurence wrote that in reality relations between black and white after 1996 had not improved but to some extent had deteriorated, because process of polarization had been taking place between blacks and whites since Mr Mbeki's speech.[351]

Laurence described a hardening of attitude within the ruling ANC elite that favoured only blacks and excluded whites. This actually is a reversal of the old discrimination of the ruling white minority against blacks. It is in

---

349 Krog, p.131
350 Ibid
351 Patrick Laurence, contributing editor and independent political analyst, in an article in *The Star*, 29 May 2007

contrast to the acclaimed nonracial policy and attitude proclaimed by the ANC government.

Laurence wrote that the contradiction between nonracialism and racial preferencing in favour of blacks is manifest in the speeches of President Thabo Mbeki, though in general his speeches reflect far less concern with reconciliation than those of his predecessor, President Nelson Mandela.

Mbeki's most vigorous endorsement of nonracialism is contained in his "I–am–an–African" speech, delivered on 8 May 1996 to mark the formal adoption of the constitution crafted by the first South African parliament that was elected by adult South Africans of all races, cultures, and creeds. Mbeki uses the label African in an inclusive sense, thereby extending it far beyond the indigenous people that inhabited the subcontinent before the arrival of migrants from Europe and indentured labourers from Asia. According to Laurence, his inclusive definition at that momentous moment in South Africa's history conveys to readers a picture of Africans covering a vast range of cultures and languages and varying in colour. Since then, says Laurence, Mbeki and the ANC generally have used the appellation African in a narrow, exclusive sense that refers to indigenous blacks only.

"ANC lexicography increasingly differentiates between blacks and whites, with blacks being defined broadly as Africans, coloured, and Indians and deemed to be historically disadvantaged and worthy of preferential treatment.

"While transformation, also known as racial preferencing, is designed to compensate blacks generally for past historical injustices, its primary purpose is to liberate Africans, particularly from the bondage of past oppression.

"Seen from the perspective of ANC transformative doctrinal justification, whites appear to be cast into the role of alien interlopers whose main historical role was to exploit blacks for their own enrichment. No allowance is made for those who opposed apartheid – unless they joined the ANC to do so – or for those who are too young to have played a political role in the past.

"Consequently, many young skilled and educated whites migrate, either literally or metaphorically, by withdrawal into enclosed or gated communities instead of contributing positively to the new South Africa and, crucially, to accelerate economic growth and be involved in job creation.

"The ANC's narrow definition of the collective noun African is, sadly, reminiscent of Afrikaner Nationalists who used to speak of *ware Suid Afrikaners* or true South Africans, meaning supporters of the National Party.

"While increasingly disqualifying their white compatriots from identifying themselves as Africans, the ANC describes the people of North Africa as Africans, although, like the people of Europe, they are Caucasians, anthropologically speaking. Many North Africans are, moreover, as light-skinned as the descendants of the settlers in South Africa.

"Perhaps it is time that the ANC re-examined and revitalised its commitment to nonracialism and, in the process give serious thought to the need to set a time-frame to its policy of black economic empowerment, particularly as all too often the beneficiaries appear to be the newly advantaged black capitalists.

"Perhaps, too, it is time for Mbeki to re-read his I–am–an–African speech and to ponder the advantages of broadening the definition of African to include whites who are committed to Africa in general and South Africa in particular."[352]

A letter writer in The Star (6 June 2007) says that there is a contradiction between commitment to nonracialism and a policy of racial preferencing, but the ANC's policies of black economic empowerment and affirmative action are based on the concept of fair discrimination. Equity and fairness demand that blacks be compensated for historical injustices.

According to the writer, the objectives of the relevant legislation show that it was not the intention for every single institution to reflect the racial composition of the population, but this is how it is being interpreted by some in positions through which they have the power to influence appointments or the procurement of goods and services. The writer sensed a growing anger in people who relished the idea of a future without discrimination and who are now beginning to feel excluded because of race.[353]

Rapprochement should however, start with the whites and not as Laurence indicates with the ANC government. It is the majority of whites who refrained from participating in the Truth and Reconciliation Commission's investigations that should eradicate the legacies of the past by admitting that apartheid was wrong.

Nationalist grandstanding by the Africans had come to typify our political culture, and this cultural dynamic goes under the ruse of racial nativism, argues Xolela Mangcu, executive chairman of the Platform for Public Deliberation, in his book *To the Brink, The State of Democracy in South Africa*. In an edited abstract in *The Star* from his book he stated that racial nativism is the idea that the true custodians of African culture are the natives. The natives are often defined as black Africans because they are indigenous to the country, and within that group the true natives are those who participated in the resistance struggle. And even among those who participated in the liberation, the truest natives are those who are on the side of the government.

---

352   *The Star*, 29 May 2007
353   *The Star*, 6 June 2007

By dint of their authenticity, these natives have the right to silence white interlopers or black sell-outs (*The Star*, 13 February 2008).

Racial nativism goes against the long traditions of racial syncretism that have always characterised South African political and intellectual history. In this syncretic approach, natives are all the people born in the country, irrespective of their struggle history or where they stand in relation to government. In a democratic society no group of people has greater authenticity or licence than another. Instead, the defining ethos of a syncretic approach to national belonging is captured by the Freedom Charter's opening line: "South Africa belongs to all who live in it, black and white."

To reduce this theory to its most simple form, Mangcu's argument is that the current, particularly political trend of condemning anyone who is not black and who is not on the side of the government (what can be called racial nativism) is a negative and destructive one that has developed in the past eight years.

Mangcu says the journalist Jonny Steinberg attributes this nativism to a sense of siege in the Mbeki government. He argues that Mbeki's controversial response to HIV/AIDS is an example of a leadership that feels its authority and sovereignty being usurped by foreign forces in cahoots with local civil society organisations: "What Mbeki coaxed to the surface of South Africa's political culture was an anxious man's nationalism and a paranoid's nativism."

By its very nature, racial nativism is exclusionary and inevitably leads to political intolerance, which has manifested through the racial labelling of political critics as traitors on the side of the non-native population, Mangcu writes.

Instead of trying to exert hegemonic influence over society, the ANC should learn more how to lead a complex, differentiated, and pluralistic society with constantly shifting alliances, interests, and identities, states Mangcu. He concludes that nativist siege mentality should give way to a new ethos of building bridges with all of the sectors of society.

Negative comments on the question whether the ANC was fit to govern and criticisms of its failures after thirteen years of government

Questioning the ability of the black man to govern goes back a long way, argues Ronald Suresh Roberts in president Mbeki's biography, *Fit to Govern, The Native Intelligence of Thabo Mbeki*, the authorised biography of South Africa's president.

The opinions of the Afrikaner about apartheid are well known and recorded, but there is another side to the coin. That is the belief and pronouncements of British intellectuals on the question whether the ANC was necessarily fit to govern. Some of the statements on this subject reported in president Mbeki's authorised biography are the following:

But now, in what William Kentridge brilliantly terms the post–anti-apartheid era, with native governance firmly in place, the question apparently arose, was the ANC necessarily fit to govern?

It is one thing to raise the rights and wrongs of particular policies and or alleged misdeeds, but what was being raised was the colonial and wholesale question of fitness to govern.

This was an ironic twist. In its anti-apartheid days, the *Mail & Guardian* was predictably reviled by Western neo-colonials such as the Oxford don, R. W. Johnson, who in 1990 called it 'the main mouthpiece of white pro-ANC liberalism' which simply 'cannot bear to believe that the next government is likely to be just as authoritarian and corrupt as the old one'.

In a letter to the London *Independent on Sunday*, Mbeki, who at the time was the ANC's secretary for International Affairs, wrote that he found Johnson's reporting 'very distressing' from someone 'who is viewed as an "authority" on South Africa.'

It was not just that Johnson had his facts wrong, but rather that he was commenting upon 'facts' that were not available even in principle, even possibly, because they lay in the future.

"It cannot be acceptable journalistic practice," Mbeki continued, "to seek to discredit the ANC by accusing it of misdeeds which Mr Johnson, for some reason, presumes the ANC will, in future, be guilty of. Fitness to govern was already on trial even before a single vote had been cast. It was demonstrably not fact, but rather stereotype and historical prejudice, that was at stake in this 'debate'.

And once the ANC entered government, the 'fitness' discourse, which had previously been a figment of such minds as Johnson's, invaded the previously anti-apartheid space of the *Mail and Guardian*.

The ideologically loaded notion of native 'fitness', previously taken as obvious by the anti-apartheid forces, had become a consensual agenda, uniting Harber and Johnson alike, across the political spectrum of whiteness.

The paragraphs he had contributed were of the 'on the one hand, on the other hand' sort," David Beresford explained about his role in the 1996 *Mail & Guardian* article, still apparently not grasping – even as he looked back in 2006 – the offensiveness of casual debate over the very question of wholesale native "fitness" for governance that had inspired centuries of colonialism and apartheid.

Johnson explained in the pages of the ordinarily progressive *London Prospect* magazine in November 1996 that he had come back to South African to help out because "The new government is, in many ways, naïve and incompetent." And his August 1991 *New Statesman* article had a decidedly spooky headline: "Fit to Govern? The ANC faces psychological trauma in its quest for power".

Johnson explained: "One can, all too easily, imagine an interim government in which the ANC ministers keep missing cabinet meetings through forgetfulness, oversleeping, or because they let someone else borrow their car."

The ANC lacked "the habits of mind necessary to govern", Johnson continued to assert in 2004.

"The prevailing tradition, at the missionary run school, Lovedale, which Mbeki attended, posed both obstacle and opportunity. In a pamphlet entitled *On Native Education: South Africa* Lovedale's Dr James Stewart wrote: 'the mind of the African is empty".

"This was the tradition set out in the 1841 *Glasgow Missionary Society Autumn Quarterly Intelligence*, according to which Africans should be enabled to 'drink at the English fountains of literature, science, and practical godliness'".

"Stewart addressed the Lovedale Literary Society with a talk called 'The Experiment of Native Education,' cautioning his native audience that while it might yet rise, it should not believe that it was prematurely the equal of the white: 'What single thing have you done as a race which the world will preserve, that you sit down contentedly and say we are as good as our white neighbour? Who first utilised steam and perfected the steam engine? Was he born on the banks of the Kei or the Clyde? Was his name James Watt or Umpunga Wamanzi?'

"The Enlightenment tradition was famously unenlightened in its disparagement of black intellect. This is often – and ironically – traced to the great Scottish philosopher, David Hume. Even as he advanced Enlightenment thinking by leaps and bounds, Hume at the same time consigned blacks into a space outside the light he was igniting: 'I am apt to suspect the negroes, and in general all other species of men (for there are four or five different kinds) to be naturally inferior to the whites. There never was a civilized nation of any other complexion than white, nor even any individual eminent either in action or speculation.[354]'

---

354 Ronald Suresh Roberts, *Fit to Govern, Mbeki's biography*

According to his biographer, throughout his two presidential terms president Thabo Mbeki has proved critics wrong. But does this statement measure up to the truth considering the failures of Mbeki's ANC government after thirteen years of ANC rule?

In a commentary article, Rhoda Kadalie, executive director of the Impumelelo Innovations Award Trust wrote in *The Star* (7 February 2008) that the Eskom fiasco, the acknowledgement by the National Electricity Commission that it is unable to supply the country with its electricity power needs for a further six years, epitomized what South Africa has become under an ANC government. A veritable mess-up. Eskom also acknowledged that it did not prepare for the country's growing needs, despite recommendations as to the necessity to plan and implement new capacity many years ago, and together with the government had chosen to ignore it. A national disaster of such epic proportions demands a change of government, wrote Kadalie.

"The ANC, very clearly, is incapable of governing the country. Under its command virtually every state institution has collapsed, the rule of law is under question, organs of the security apparatus are in conflict with each other; and the nation is deeply demoralized." This would include among others, health, education, the road accident fund, justice, local government, and the supply of clean water.

"Having been warned eight years ago about an impending energy crisis, should they fail to adopt certain measures, the government focused elsewhere. Engaged in political mongering here and abroad, ANC leaders became detached from the people they were supposed to serve. Sidetracked by temporary ideologies of transformation, black economic empowerment, the African renaissance, linked to the perks of office, Eskom became a casualty of this modus operandi.

"Transformation rather than delivery became its driving force. Rewarding themselves richly for achieving racial targets instead of delivery. Eskom bosses replaced most of their qualified and experienced staff with inexperienced and inappropriately qualified black people.
And the result is load-shedding, the euphemism for power failures.

"It is widely known that South Africa is worst on the continent in mathematics, science, and technology. All the more reason to retain our highly trained scientists, technicians, and engineers, regardless of their colour, especially if we want to grow the economy.

"Eskom is a failure because the people who run it are not suitably qualified. Worse, they have been protected by a president and ministers, equally guilty of a gross dereliction of duty. It is high time we realised that those in power have become our greatest liabilities.

"Merely saying sorry (Mbeki and his cabinet's response) is not enough. Those to whom we entrust the money to run the economy should be fired when they fail to do so, especially when they pay themselves exorbitant salaries. In any civilized democracy, the public would have demanded their resignation, but South Africans unfortunately have become politically lethargic.

"The middle classes despair or emigrate, and the poor engage in violent protests. But these very disaffected poor will vote again and again the very people who exploit them back into office. They are, according to a recent *Time* magazine article commenting on the voters in Africa, and Kenya in particular, to some extent complicit in the undermining of democracy. When given an opportunity to vote out one corrupt leader, they often elect another, hoping he will be more generous with his ill-gotten gains".

Having criticised Eskom and Mbeki's ANC government, Rhoda Kadalie comments further on Mbeki's abuse of political power and the corruption caused by the notion of entitlement.

She wrote, "thrown into this quagmire was Mbeki's ever-readiness to use state institutions to fight age-old party vendettas against political competitors who dared stick out their necks. And so the National Prosecution Authority, the Scorpions, the SAPS, Ministry of Intelligence were all spying on one another, backstabbing one another, undermining one another, while the country was running itself.

"This notion of struggle (to overthrow the apartheid regime) breeds an entitlement that lays claim to the economy, fuelling the culture of patronage and corruption, the extent of which makes the apartheid government look like a tea party. More seriously, this entitlement also lays claim to the abuse of state institutions for party purposes – the police, the judiciary, parliament, the NPA, the Scorpions – anything to assist it to further its own ends."

She wrote that the internal fights are indelibly etched into the minds of strugglers whose fight ultimately is over control of the economy. In her opinion government intervention to guide a developmental state is what we should be wary about.

Kadalie wrote that land redistribution, the regulation of foreign ownership of land, the creation of an institutionalized centre for government-wide economic planning," broad-based economic empowerment, and employment equity are some of the resolutions that will need constant scrutiny.

Rhoda Kadalie then answers her own question, what's to be done? "South Africans need to wake up. More than ever, we need a reinvigoration of civil society organisations, women's groups, human rights organisations, and opposition parties which will unite and hold government accountable.

We should jettison those self-servicing civic organisations that suck up to government and placate it when it is so obviously out of touch and corrupt."

A third testimony of Mbeki's racial nationalism and also his failures comes from the leader of the Democratic Alliance, Hellen Zille, in her weekly letter, *SA Today*, in April 2008. She wrote, Mbeki's capacity for denial is his greatest failing, and will define his legacy. It is an even greater failing than the other hallmark of his presidency, the growth of racial nationalism.

She expanded on Mbeki's denials of failures with reference to its lowest ebb in April 2008 with the image of Thabo Mbeki and Robert Mugabe, holding hands alongside the headline "What crisis?" It destroyed whatever credibility he still held at chief proponent of an African Renaissance.

He did it again soon thereafter when asked about the seventy-seven-ton shipload of Chinese weapons destined for Zimbabwe, he replied, "What weapons? I think you should ask the Chinese." His responses typify the denialism of his presidency. It echoes his infamous denial of the AIDS pandemic.

While many regard crime as the biggest crisis of all, Mbeki said, "Nobody can prove the majority of the country's citizens think crime is spinning out of control." Similarly, in 2006 when challenged about our electricity generation capacity, he responded "There is no crisis …whatever needs to be done is being done."

She concluded that Mbeki will be remembered as Mugabe's junior partner in the brutal oppression of the people of Zimbabwe. (*The Citizen*, 19 April 2008) The fears of many white South Africans are that Zimbabwe's experience of bad government will be repeated in South Africa.

CHAPTER 9

UNFINISHED RECONCILIATION

In the political arena, the TRC provided an outlet for everyone to examine the dark deeds of the past. This worked to a certain extent, but there are still some gaping holes, wrote Vuyo Jack in his political column. (*The Sunday Independent Business Report*, 9 March 2008). The TRC was an event, but, Jack added, what we need now is a practical process that will help us to deal with the past in our daily lives.

It's not too late for white South Africans to apologise for the wrongs committed during the apartheid era, even fourteen years after it came to an end. That's according to South African Human Rights Commission chairperson Jody Kollapen, who said that the apology by the Australian government to the aboriginal people in 2008 would have been equally welcome in South Africa.[355]

"One would have hoped that that kind of apology – where there was no excuse in terms of saying they didn't know or that it was just a bunch of loose cannons – would have been offered (in SA) at the appropriate time. Even if it didn't happen then, it is never too late," he said at a conference at the University of the Western Cape, Cape Town. He added that there should be some discussion around it, and it should not be only former leaders and former presidents who should tender the apology, as South Africa was not moving towards healing and reconciliation in the right way, and that there were still gaps left behind by the Truth and Reconciliation Commission. The hurt was not addressed because everyone was so in awe of the miraculous transition. Kollapen added there were certain fundamental faults in the TRC's

355   *The Star*, 28 February 2008

work, as it did not create sufficient space for the ordinary South African to reflect. There needed to be a serious conversation about the past, and people needed to be given space to ask themselves what their role was.

The Afrikaners' change of mindset and responsibility

Good relations with black South Africans could be established if the majority of voters who withheld making statements to the TRC in 1998 concerning their acknowledgement of the wrongs of apartheid, did so now. It would change their attitude towards whites and in turn would change the attitude of the ruling ANC from the lower ranks upwards. The end result would be a new relationship between the ANC elite and the whites as pictured by Mbeki in his 1996 speech.

Cooperation between black and white and ANC and Afrikaner would then become natural and the discriminatory elements in the application of the empowerment policies and affirmative action would fall away.

From polls taken by an Afrikaans newspaper in 2006 to establish readers' opinions on whether they would support or reject minister Adriaan Vlok's gesture of washing the feet of Frank Chikane, director in the president's office, who was a victim of a security police assault under Vlok as minister, 76 percent rejected his act of contrition. Eight years earlier 85 percent of readers of the same paper rejected Adriaan Vlok's 1997 acknowledgement to the TRC that apartheid was wrong as well as the measures to suppress opponents.

The people rejecting Vlok's confession to the TRC were themselves rejecting such declaration of a change in beliefs. This is the crux of the reconciliation between erstwhile white minority rulers and the new black majority rulers.

A contradiction lies in the support the whites gave to a new constitution providing for black majority rule and their obstinate refusal to declare their acknowledgement to the TRC that apartheid was wrong. If only 10 percent changed their opinion concerning Vlok's contrite actions in a period of almost ten years, it shows a very small opinion shift.

The reality is that the people who believed in apartheid had actually made this belief part of their world and life view. This world and life view was part of the Afrikaners' system of beliefs in which they also totally identified themselves with the policy of apartheid, with their allegiance as citizens to South Africa and with their belief that it was God's will. In 1986, the General Synod of the Dutch Reformed Church declared racial discrimination and apartheid to be a sin. This declaration destroyed apartheid's sinful justifications.

In the new constitution the Afrikaners lost their governing role as a minority, their concept of supremacy, and their identification as Afrikaner Nationalists with the state. Now the Afrikaner Nationalist is left with citizenship as a minority in a rainbow nation of a majority of black and non-white voters.

Bringing about peace and reconciliation is hardly possible by actions of the previous government leaders. That would be a top down instead of a bottom up process. It has to be genuine reconciliation between people and individuals and should include the Nationalists' disclaiming of apartheid and accepting their responsibility for the perpetration of violent acts against individuals.

With the wisdom of hindsight it would have been better if de Klerk had not on his own represented the government and the NP at the TRC. Many groups on the side of the apartheid government were involved in the system of discrimination and oppression. The state president, the cabinet, the parliamentary caucus, the provincial congresses of the NP, the security forces, police and military, government departments, and the NP supporters. These representatives should have come together to jointly and individually confess their involvement, responsibility, and accountability. It could have, although confidential, without identification of the perpetrators, disclosed information and the truth about unknown and dreadful deeds. No one could then have denied not knowing anything. The situation changed with the dissolution of the NP.

We should be sensitive when it comes to national reconciliation, said Dave Steward, spokesperson for F. W. de Klerk. After the Vlok and Van der Merwe trial in August 2007, the public debate in the run-up to the trial was at best emotional and at worst ugly, he said: "It has reopened a lot of old wounds and showed the extent to which the past is still unresolved in this country."[356] It highlighted the degree to which the Afrikaners actually failed to reach some kind of definitive agreement about the past. Once again, it cast light on the failings of the TRC to "produce a history with which we could all agree, primarily because it was composed of commissioners from the struggle side." And he recalled the words of de Klerk a few weeks previously "when he said that any prosecutions would have to be made with great sensitivity and circumspection and in an even-handed manner, taking into full account the negotiation on amnesty and the provisions of the constitution."[357]

For a balanced point of view, it is valuable to consider a truthful and insightful observation of an Irish priest who made South Africa his home: an

---

356   *The Sunday Independent*, 19 August 2007
357   Ibid

anger is spreading throughout the country among blacks and whites against each other.

"I used to love living in the hospice in Leratong near Pretoria," explained Creagh. "It was such a very special place. I loved what I did, I loved the people I worked with."[358]   But the events of 28 February 2007, when nine hooded men came knocking on his door late at night, changed all that. They beat him badly, stripped him, and planted three bullets in his body before making off with a cell phone, a broken CD player, a DVD player, and an empty safe. They left him helpless and fighting for his life. Three hours passed before he received medical attention, but he pulled through, and he described his comeback as nothing short of miraculous.

Creagh set up the Leratong hospice in 1998. He felt he had a role to play. He became the first person in Africa to be injected with a vaccine intended to prevent people from contracting HIV. Although free from the virus, he volunteered to be injected with the drug, which had been tested only on animals.

Considering Creagh's observation, one has to admit if the whites in a society in transformation do not take the lead in establishing improved relations with the blacks, the goodwill that does exist and is the predominant relationship should not be taken for granted nor neglected, as negative traits could grow. As with reconciliation, the Christian's answer remains prayer and good works.

Concerning the relationships between Africans and so-called non-Africans in South Africa, an important comment was made by Bobby Godsell, chairman of the Anglo American Gold Mining Company, that in South African politics one should remember that 75 percent of the people in the country are Africans, and if the remaining 25 percent is not involved in its future, the country is doomed.[359]

Dr Theuns Eloff, vice-chancellor of the University of the North West, said in a lecture to the FAK at Potchefstroom, that the Afrikaner is part of this 25 percent non-Africans that Godsell referred to. According to him the new type of Afrikaner that is needed in the country must be active in the process of seeking solutions, reconciliation, better governance, better performances in all fields, and he should be allowed to do it. He added that the new Afrikaners should not be grouped together with the rest of the Afrikaners as racists, and that further debate on the grouping of the new Afrikaners is necessary, elsewise everyone's opportunity in the future of the new South Africa is lost.[360]

---

358   *The Star*, 28 September 2007
359   *The Star*, 29 September 2007
360   Die Vrye Afrikaan, FAK, 2007

CHAPTER 10

A CHRISTIAN PERSPECTIVE

The Afrikaners' first step in finding an intimate place in the new state in relation to the other groups is reconciliation. Acknowledgement of the wrongs of apartheid and the measures of oppression would bring about this reconciliation. If the Afrikaners, from a Christian perspective, publicly declare their acknowledgement of apartheid's wrongs they would have confessed their guilt as Christians, and thereby cleared their guilty conscience. This perspective would enlighten them to the commands of scripture to love their neighbours and become part of the unity of all believers. "But you are a chosen generation, a royal priesthood, a holy nation, His own special people … who once were not a people but are now the people of God, who had not obtained mercy but now have obtained mercy" (1 Peter 2:9–10).

The Christian believer is in this world but not part of this world. Understanding of this concept brings comprehension of a dual citizenship. The believer is a citizen of his state but also a subject of God's Kingdom. The acceptance of God's command in the Bible to follow Christ in truth and in life goes against the old striving to realise an apartheid system under the misguided belief that it was in accordance with the scripture and therefore God's will. The Christian Afrikaner now has the freedom to be part of a new society and to truthfully fulfil God's calling to be obedient to his word. It gives the Christian believer joy, being a citizen in the new South Africa, being in God's will, and a subject of His Kingdom together with black Christians, filled with love for others and liberated from fear.

A shift in allegiance has to take place. The Christian Afrikaner needs to switch his erstwhile allegiance to the ungodly apartheid state to the new state of the "rainbow nation" and the Kingdom of God. In the rainbow nation's state, nondiscrimination is proclaimed as a policy, but its practice and application may sometimes be questionable. In God's Kingdom nondiscrimination is an absolute.

A world and life view represents a set of assumptions or propositions of the world and man's place in it. A worldview is the sum total of man's beliefs, and every worldview – be it secularism, humanism, atheism – is based on faith. Faith as basis of the Christian world view is an understanding of everything in relationship to God. The Afrikaner, though, extended this Christian world and life view to include his belief that God called him to establish an exclusive area for himself as white man in South Africa. This then is the foundation of the Afrikaners' apartheid ideology, which became the dominant part of his world view. But it could not last forever, nor a thousand years as Hitler thought the Nazi regime would last.

Ultimately apartheid was found to be based on a false foundation and unchristian. Referring to apartheid President F. W. de Klerk said that it was all wrong.[361] In Russia, Alexander Solzenitshen, the Nobel Prize author, wrote in *Cancer Ward* that the whole system of communism was wrong. Both systems collapsed.

Comparing the two statements of de Klerk and Solzenitshen in the context of the Christian's belief in the Bible that proclaims that God raises up governments and puts them down, the communist ideology and the regime in Russia rejected God and practiced unchristian and anti-Christian policies. Christians believe the downfall of the communist power was God's will. God determines the course of world events. He gives wisdom to the wise and knowledge to those who have understanding (Daniel 2:21).

The apartheid system in South Africa was upheld by a white Christian regime. Many Christian Afrikaners realised that Almighty God brought the apartheid system to a fall. He is the force behind history (His story) and behind the forces of history. Factors such as fear, economics, external pressures, or the forces of nationalism and democracy were not the dominant forces that ended apartheid.

The Afrikaner's acceptance of the transition of power to the black majority, which miraculously happened in a peaceful way, is his unexpressed recognition of God's will. They were also grateful that it happened in such a peaceful way, realising that it could have been a bloody revolution but for God's amazing grace.

---

361 *The Star*, 24 May 2007

The contradiction in the Afrikaner's support of apartheid as God's will and his acceptance of black majority rule, also as God's will, is founded in this growing conviction that the premise was wrong. The statement of confession by the Dutch Reformed Church in 1986 declaring discrimination and apartheid a sin finally clarified the issue. But the majority of Afrikaners, however, have not yet confirmed their change of mindset.

The Afrikaners represent the biggest factor in the unfinished business of reconciliation. It is realistic to expect that a percentage of these Afrikaners will not change their mindset. But they would be a minority, although most of them call themselves Christians.

Originally, the white Christians of South Africa did not bring their national dispensation under the lordship of Jesus Christ, and so a false god was involved to rule over white politics, according to Alan Hirsch . The result was a sinful and ungodly crushing of non-whites. Any sphere not brought under the domain of Jesus becomes autonomous and susceptible to the rule of other gods.[362]

What happened in South Africa was that to a large extent, white European Christianity actually sanctioned the racial prejudice and legitimized the oppressive power structures of the white people of South Africa in the name of a doctrine called Christian paternalism. This idea of paternalism developed socially and politically, and it resulted in the policy of apartheid.[363]

This was syncretism and not just political expedience as the vast majority of whites in South Africa lived under a very religious Calvinist code. Theologians gave apartheid its original legitimacy and sustaining authority. God, under the syncretistic influence of the apartheid theologians, became a racist god who justified the suppression of the "inferior" black people. Apartheid was simply the refusal to live under the claims of love and justice that were part of what is meant to worship the one true God. How could one worship the God of justice by acting unjustly? The biblical answer is, one cannot. In this case, acting in love and justice toward black people was perceived as a threat to the ongoing identity and viability of the Afrikaner people, and they therefore took race and politics out of the equation of the lordship of Jesus in the name of racial survival and dominance. They co-opted God to their racist agenda. Paradoxically, the rest of the culture was devoutly Christian, but the god over politics and social life was a different god to the God in the church.

---

362 Hirsch, p.97
363 Ibid

To change his mindset the Christian Afrikaner must on this issue become converted. It would involve the direct engagement of the central confession that "Jesus is Lord".[364] This, in many cases, may take time.

This necessity to reject the apartheid ideology is well illustrated by the attitude of the Nederduitsch Hervormde Church, who in the year 2007, twelve years after the establishment of the new democratic constitution of South Africa, are still struggling to come to terms with the past and the evil of apartheid. At the meeting of the general council of the Hervormde Church in September 2007 in Pretoria, they refused to adopt a resolution that disapproved of apartheid on theological grounds.[365] The World Alliance of Reformed Churches (WARC) had suspended the membership of the Hervormde Church in 1982 because the Church supported apartheid. A positive response was seen as an opportunity as never before to become part of the international church community, but it was spurned.

The clause in the constitution of the ZAR of 1858 that declared that the citizens were not prepared to allow any equality of non-whites with the white burgers in the church or the state could well still be resonating in the minds of many of these church members.

God says in his word: If my people who are called by my name will humble themselves, and pray and seek my face, and turn from their wicked ways, then I will hear from heaven, and will forgive their sin and heal their land.[366]

---

364 *Rapport*, 30 September 2007
365 Ibid
366 2 Chronicles 7:14

CHAPTER 11

AFRIKANERS AND AFRICANS IN SOUTH AFRICA – A LOOK INTO THEIR FUTURE

After a century of injustice during which the Afrikaners and their government effectively kept their African countrymen from obtaining voting rights in parliament, negotiations between the two parties miraculously brought about a new democratic constitution in 1994 with universal suffrage.

The final report in 1998 of the Truth and Reconciliation Commission under chairman Desmond Tutu left many issues unresolved, although it did achieve goodwill and clarified many difficult problems stemming from violence and political murder on both sides.

The ANC government, particularly under President Mbeki, rushed to implement their policy of transformation, which is the other side of the coin called revolution. They radically and speedily replaced white with black, took over all governmental, municipal, semi-government offices and positions from top to bottom and filled all vacancies, old and new positions, with blacks, regardless of suitable qualifications and experience, and even those with questionable backgrounds.

Government tender procedures follow the same policy with preference given to applications by blacks regardless of merit. Many big contracts such as housing projects for blacks never delivered. Affirmative action and black economic empowerment, sometimes referred to as racial nativism, did not bring about unmitigated success.

After fourteen years of democratic rule under the ANC government, South Africa is experiencing its own set of uncertainties amidst worldwide dangers of climate change, economic downturns, and scarcity of natural resources. These uncertainties are increasing levels of crime that have taken on the form of mini-wars with fifty murders daily; the constantly high rate of seven hundred deaths per day due to HIV/AIDS; the occurrences of power failures; service delivery is decreasing, corruption and abuse of power are increasing, the systems of education and justice are weakening, businesses are closing, people on farms, in cities, and in townships are being murdered, the number of hijackings and transit robberies is rising; resulting in a feeling that the pillars of society are falling apart. [367]

In the opinion of Bantu Holomisa, MP and leader of the United Democratic Movement (UDM), a small opposition party, the current confusion has undermined investor confidence as well as the South African currency. According to Holomisa, the consequences are social instability and an abundance of corruption and misrule.[368]

The steady slide in business confidence that the South African Chamber of Commerce and Industry has recorded for the two years since 2006 is set to continue. The chamber reported that the business confidence index in June 2008 slipped to 92.6 points, its lowest since October 2003. A poll of shoppers by the University of Stellenbosch Bureau of Economic Research, BER, during the second quarter of 2008 registered the biggest drop in consumer confidence in twenty-four years. The BER's purchasing managers' index for June 2008 showed a 5.3-point drop in confidence. Factories have been laying off workers since February, and the survey indicates more job losses are on the way. [369]

A debate on political realignment initiated by the leader of the Democratic Alliance, Helen Zille, received positive response, and Holomisa is of the opinion that the South African history is demanding a willingness from all South Africans to fight the resurgence of racial hostilities and conflicts, and in recognition of this historical legacy of society his party is committed to the vision of a new South Africa. [370]

The possible realignment of political parties could well be the focus for an emerging political formation, which will articulate the concerns and aspirations of the vast number of marginalized people of all colours and races in South Africa. According to Holomisa, the emergence of this major

367   *Die Kerkblad*, June 2008
368   *The Sunday Times*, 6 July 2008
369   Ibid.
370   Ibid.

political grouping that represents the interests of the marginalized will remove the confusion created by the ruling ambivalent tripartite alliance (ANC, Cosatu, and SACP). There is a definite need to encourage these debates about realigning the political landscape in the country. Holomisa visualises a paradigm shift that focuses on a process that will lead to the establishment of an alternative government. [371]

The first target should to be reduce the ANC majority in parliament of more than 66 percent, which gives them the power to amend the constitution.

Basic to the relationships between Africans and so-called non-Africans in South Africa is the numerical division of the population into 75 percent Africans and 25 percent non-Africans, of which whites form the majority. A great improvement in race relations could come about at this time of uncertainty and marginalization caused by ANC radicals when the Afrikaners finally confess the wrong of apartheid and express their apologies.

To do this they will have to humble themselves. The Christian Afrikaners are ready to follow new leadership. They believed apartheid was scripturally justified, saw themselves as superior, and therefore knew what was right and wrong. They thought they had all the right answers. This world and life view has changed with hindsight and with the loss of their independence.

The future thus holds exciting opportunities of reconciliation and political realignment, but depends partly on the Afrikaners confessing their wrongdoing. Mutual respect would create harmony among the races and would even accommodate differences in political views.

---

371   Ibid

LIST OF ABBREVIATIONS

ANC	African National Congress
BCM	Black Consciousness Movement
BEE	Black Economic Empowerment
BER	Bureau of Economic Research of the University of Stellenbosch
CAAA	Comprehensive Anti-Apartheid Act
CCB	Civil Co-operation Bureau
CCSA	Cabinet Committee for Security Affairs
CI	Christian Institute
CIA	Central Intelligence Agency
CSIS	Canadian Security and Intelligence Service
DMI	Directorate of Military Intelligence
DRC	Dutch Reformed Church
FAK	Federasie van Afrikaanse Kultuurverenigings
GSC	General Synodal Commission
HPC	Health Professions Council
IFP	Inkatha Freedom Party
JMC	Joint Management Committees
LWF	Lutheran World Federation
MDF	Mass Democratic Front
MDM	Mass Democratic Movement
MIS	Management Information Service
MK	Umkhonto we Sizwe
MP	Member of Parliament
NG	Nederduits Gereformeerde Kerk
NIA	National Intelligence Agency
NIS	National Intelligence Service
NP	National Party
NSMS	National Security Management System
PAC	Pan African Congress
RSA	Republic of South Africa
RSC	Regional Services Council
SABC	South African Broadcasting Corporation
SACP	South African Communist Party
SADF	South African Defence Force
SAMDC	South African Medical and Dental Council

SAP	South African Police
SAPA	South African Press Association
SASO	South African Students' Organisation
SETA	Sector Education and Training Authority
SSC	State Security Council
SWA	South West Africa
SWAPO	South West Africa Peoples Organisation
TBVC	Transkei/Bophuthatswana/Venda/Ciskei
TRC	Truth and Reconciliation Commission
UDF	Untied Democratic Front
UDM	United Democratic Movement
UK	United Kingdom
UN	United Nations
UNISA	University of South Africa
USA	United States of America
WARC	World Alliance of Reformed Churches
WCC	World Council of Churches
ZAR	Zuid Afrikaansche Republiek

BIBLIOGRAPHY

Archives: Report of the Native Laws and Customs Commission, Cape Colony, (Report of the Native Commission for the years 1925-1926) G4/1883

Bierman, H. H. H. (Ed); The case for South Africa, as put forth in the public statements of Eric H. Louw, Foreign Minister of South Africa, MacFadden Books, MacFadden-Bartell Corp. New York, 1963

Bizos, George; Odyssey to Freedom, Random House, Cape Town, 2007

Botha, H. J.; Die Administrasie van Universiteitsonderwys vir Swart bevolkingsgroepe in Suid Afrika. Unpublished thesis, May 1988.

Botha, W. A.; Agtergrond tot die onafhanklikwording van die Transkei, 1976: Beleid ten opsigte van grond en politieke regte vir swartes sedert 1877, Unpublished Thesis, November 1989.

Botha, W. A.; Die Parlementêre Verkiesing van 1948. 'n Onleding van die faktore wat die verkiesing beinvloed het. Unpublished Dissertation, June 1967.

Botha, W. A.; Die Bewind van Genl Louis Botha 1910–1919, Joernaal vir Eietydse Geskiedenis, University of the Orange Free State.

City of Johannesburg. Fact File on Melville Koppies

D'Oliveira, John; Vorster – The man, Ernest Stanton (Publishers) (Pty) Ltd, Johannesburg, 1977.

De Klerk, F. W.; The Last Trek – A new beginning The Autobiography, Macmillan, Thornton, 1998.

De Locale Wetten der Zuid-Afrikaansche Republiek 1849-1885, published by J. F. Celliers, Pretoria, 1887

Dunan, M. (Ed.); Larousse Encyclopedia of Modern History from 1500 to the present day, Hamlyn, London, revised edition 1981, Second impression 1984

Ecunews, South African Council of Churches, Johannesburg, March 1985

Eloff, Dr Theuns, Die Vrye Afrikaan, FAK, 2007

ETDP.SETA, Education Training Development Practices, SETA, Study notes on Social issues, Johannesburg 2003

Foreign Policy Study Foundation, Inc., South Africa : Time Running Out, The Report of the Study Commission on US Policy towards Southern Africa, University of California Press, Los Angeles, 1981.

General Synodal Commission of the Dutch Reformed Church; The story of the Dutch Reformed Church's Journey with Apartheid 1960–1994, a testimony and a confession

Gilliomee, Herman; The Afrikaners, Biography of a people, Tafelberg, Publishers Ltd, Cape Town, 2003.

Hansard. Debates of the House of Assembly. (Including the first years reported in the Cape Times.

Heunis, Jan; The Inner Circle. Reflections of the last days of white rule, Jonathan Ball Publishers, Johannesburg, 2007.

Hirsch, Alan; The Forgotten Ways, Brazos Press, Grand Rapids, Michigan 2006

Krog, Antjie; Country of my skull, Random House, Johannesburg, 1998.

Krüger, D. W.; The Age of the Generals: A Short Political History of the Union of South Africa, 1910–1948, Dagbreek Book Store, Johannesburg, 1958.

Kruger, H. B.; Die Politieke Aspekte van generaal J. B. M. Hertzog se Naturellebeleid vanaf Unifikasie tot aan die einde van sy Parlementêre Loopbaan, unpublished thesis, Unisa, 1976

Lodberg, Peter; Apartheid as a church-dividing ethical issue. The Ecumenical Review, Vol. 48, Issue 2, World Council of Churches, 1996

Mandela, Nelson; Long walk to freedom, The autobiography, Macdonald Purnell, Randburg, 1994.

Paton, Alan; Hofmeyr, Oxford University Press, Cape Town, 1964.

Pelzer, A. N. (Ed); Verwoerd aan die Woord, Speeches 1948–1966, Afrikaanse Pers-Boekhandel, Johannesburg, 1966.

Plaatje, Sol T; Native Life in Southern Africa, Picador Africa 2007, Johannesburg

Republic of Transkei ; Debates of the National Assembly, 1976

Rhoodie, Eschel; P. W. Botha The last betrayal, SA Politics, Melville, 1989.

Roberts, R. S.; Mbeki's biography, Fit to Govern, The Native Intelligence of Thabo Mbeki, the authorised biography of South Africa's president

Scholtz, G. D.; Die Ondertekening van die Sandrivier – Konvensie Herdenk (1852–1952) FAK, Johannesburg, 1951

Slabbert, F. van Zyl; The other side of History: An anecdotal reflection on political transition in South Africa, Johnathan Ball Publishers, Johannesburg, 2005

Storm, J. M. G.; Die Konvensie van Sandrivier as afsluiting van die Groot Trek, Hervormde Teologiese Studies, Jaargang 45, Aflewering 3, September 1989.

Thompson, L. M.; The unification of South Africa 1902-1910, Oxford University Press, London, 1960

Truth and Reconciliation Commission, Report, Volume 1-5, October 1998

UG 30-1953, Union of South Africa, Report of the Department of Native Affairs for the years 1950-1951

United States Congress: Summary of the Comprehensive Anti-Apartheid Act, 2 October 1986

University of Pretoria, Merensky Library. M. D. C. De Wet Nel Collection, Native affairs, Band No. 1-3, Algemene Beginsels en Konstitusionele Ontwikkelingsplan vir die toekenning van Verteenwoordigende Regering aan Bantoevolkseenhede op Tuisland grondslag in die Republiek van Suid Afrika en Suidwes-Afrika, 1961

Van Schoor, M C E: Die Nasionale Vrouemonument, Oorlogsmuseum van die Boererepubliek, Bloemfontein 1993

Van Zyl Slabbert, Frederick; Duskant die geskiedenis. 'n Persoonlike terugblik op die politieke oorgang in Suid Afrika. Tafelberg Uitgewers, Kaapstad, 2006.

NEWSPAPERS

Business Report	New York Times
By	Pro Veritate
Daily Dispatch	Rand Daily Mail
De Zuid-Afrikaan	Rapport
Die Beeld	SA Today
Die Burger	
Die Kerkblad	The Cape Times
Die Kerkbode	The Citizen
Foreign Affairs	The Star
Jerusalem Post	The Sunday Independent

London Daily Telegraph   The Sunday Times

London Economist   The Times

London Observer   This Day

London Times   Volksblad

Mail and Guardian

Index